What's Wrong with Lookism?

NEW TOPICS IN APPLIED PHILOSOPHY

Series editor
Kasper Lippert-Rasmussen

This series presents works of original research on practical issues that are not yet well covered by philosophy. The aim is not only to present work that meets high philosophical standards while being informed by a good understanding of relevant empirical matters, but also to open up new areas for philosophical exploration. The series will demonstrate the value and interest of practical issues for philosophy and vice versa.

PUBLISHED IN THE SERIES

The Politics of Social Cohesion
Immigration, Community, and Justice
Nils Holtug

Not in Their Name
Are Citizens Culpable for Their States' Actions?
Holly Lawford-Smith

The Inheritance of Wealth
Justice, Equality, and the Right to Bequeath
Daniel Halliday

Sharing Territories
Overlapping Self-Determination and Resource Rights
Cara Nine

Exploitation as Domination
What Makes Capitalism Unjust
Nicholas Vrousalis

Spying through a Glass Darkly
The Ethics of Espionage and Counter-Intelligence
Cécile Fabre

What's Wrong with Lookism?

Personal Appearance, Discrimination, and Disadvantage

ANDREW MASON

Great Clarendon Street, Oxford, OX2 6DP,
United Kingdom

Oxford University Press is a department of the University of Oxford.
It furthers the University's objective of excellence in research, scholarship,
and education by publishing worldwide. Oxford is a registered trade mark of
Oxford University Press in the UK and in certain other countries

© Andrew Mason 2023

The moral rights of the author have been asserted

All rights reserved. No part of this publication may be reproduced, stored in
a retrieval system, or transmitted, in any form or by any means, without the
prior permission in writing of Oxford University Press, or as expressly permitted
by law, by licence or under terms agreed with the appropriate reprographics
rights organization. Enquiries concerning reproduction outside the scope of the
above should be sent to the Rights Department, Oxford University Press, at the
address above

You must not circulate this work in any other form
and you must impose this same condition on any acquirer

Published in the United States of America by Oxford University Press
198 Madison Avenue, New York, NY 10016, United States of America

British Library Cataloguing in Publication Data
Data available

Library of Congress Control Number: 2023935137

ISBN 978–0–19–285979–2

DOI: 10.1093/oso/9780192859792.001.0001

Printed and bound by
CPI Group (UK) Ltd, Croydon, CR0 4YY

Links to third party websites are provided by Oxford in good faith and
for information only. Oxford disclaims any responsibility for the materials
contained in any third party website referenced in this work.

Contents

Acknowledgements	vii
1. Introduction	1

I. WHAT MAKES DISCRIMINATION WRONG?

2. Non-contingent Wrongness	33
3. Contingent Wrongness	50

II. CONTEXTS OF APPEARANCE DISCRIMINATION

4. Appearance, Race, and Employment	73
5. Appearance as a Reaction Qualification	104
6. Appearance and Personal Relationships	129
7. Everyday Lookism	159

III. RESPONDING TO APPEARANCE DISCRIMINATION

8. Prevention	181
9. Compensation and Beyond	200
Bibliography	223
Index	233

Acknowledgements

I first became interested in the issue of appearance discrimination about fifteen years ago, partly as a result of a conversation with a colleague whilst I was working at the University of Southampton. Her partner was a tree surgeon. He was offered employment by a company in the New Forest on condition that he cut off his dreadlocks, which he wasn't willing to do. The requirement that he do so before taking up the job, which was imposed on grounds of appearance rather than any concerns about health and safety, struck me as unfair and got me thinking about the morally problematic character of many of the ways in which appearance discrimination impacts upon our lives, and how it intersects with other forms of discrimination.

This book is the culmination of these reflections. It has benefitted considerably from the help given to me by a number of people. I am immensely grateful to Matthew Clayton, Søren Flinch Midtgaard, Francesca Minerva, Tom Parr, and two anonymous referees for OUP, each of whom gave me detailed written comments on an early draft. Matthew, Francesca, and Tom, together with Catalina Carpan, Ida Lübben, and Nici Mulkeen, were also members of a reading group which discussed that draft in virtual meetings during the pandemic. In a kind and generous way, they helped me to see a range of problems with my arguments in it. The book would have been much worse without their input.

Søren organized a workshop on a second draft of the manuscript, at the Centre for the Experimental-Philosophical Study of Discrimination (CEPDISC) at Aarhus University in October 2021. This was my first trip away after the pandemic. Not only was it very enjoyable to be part of an in-person event again, I also learnt a lot from the criticisms and suggestions offered by the participants, especially Simone Sommer Degn, Renaud-Philippe Garner, Nils Holtug, Kasper Lippert-Rasmussen, Lauritz Munch, Astrid Fly Oredsson, Viki Møller Lyngby Pedersen, and Søren himself, who commented on individual chapters. I returned to CEPDISC for a month in May 2022 whilst writing the final draft. I am grateful to Søren again, and to Kasper, for facilitating my stay in such a friendly and stimulating environment.

There are also a number of friends, colleagues, family members, and acquaintances who have given me feedback on individual chapters or papers on which those chapters are based, or have provided me with help when I sought it. I would like to express my warmest thanks to the following people: Chris Armstrong, Rima Basu, Richard Bellamy, Rossella De Bernardi, Paul Billingham, Kim Brownlee, Cheshire Calhoun, Simon Caney, Clare Chambers, Raf Geenens, Bob Goodin, Deborah Hellman, Eszter Kollar, Lauren Lyons, Matt Mason, Sam Mason, Véronique Munoz-Dardé, Merten Reglitz, Becca Rothfeld, Ben Sachs, Mike Saward, Gina Schouten, Helder De Schutter, Shlomi Segall, Rob Simpson, Adam Slavny, Tom Sorell, Hillel Steiner, Adam Swift, Lynn Thomas, Annamari Vitikainen, Bouke de Vries, Albert Weale, Katy Wells, and Heather Widdows.

Individual chapters, or the papers or ideas on which they are based, were presented at a number of workshops and seminars. Some of the central ideas of the book were aired at the Legal and Political Theory Working Group seminar series at the European University Institute, and later at the Philosophy Department seminar at the University of Otago. I also enjoyed extended stays at both places, the former courtesy of a Fernand Braudel Fellowship. I am grateful to Rainer Bauböck and Richard Bellamy for taking care of me at the EUI, and Andrew Moore for facilitating my stay at Otago. I would also especially like to thank Lisa Ellis, Michael LeBuffe, James Maclaurin, and David Tombs for their support whilst I was in Dunedin.

My paper 'Appearance, Discrimination, and Reaction Qualifications', which was published in the *Journal of Political Philosophy* and in a somewhat revised form provides the basis of Chapter 5, was presented at different stages of development at various workshops and colloquia. I would like to thank participants in these at Goethe University Frankfurt, the University of Manchester, Nuffield College, Oxford, and the University of Warwick for their constructive criticisms. The final version of the paper was written whilst I was a visiting fellow at the Justitia Amplificata Centre for Advanced Studies at Goethe University. I would like to thank Rainer Forst for inviting me to spend time at the Centre, and the fellows and staff at the Forschungskolleg Humanwissenschaften for making my period of residence there so enjoyable and productive.

The paper 'What's Wrong with Everyday Lookism?', which forms the basis of Chapter 7, and which was published by *Politics, Philosophy and Economics*, was presented under a different title at a number of places: the summer school on 'The Morality of Discrimination' held at the Central European University in Budapest; the CEPPA seminar at the University of St Andrews; the Law, Politics, and Philosophy Colloquium at University College London; and the RIPPLE seminar at KU Leuven. My spell as a visiting fellow at RIPPLE was cut short by the emerging pandemic and the lockdown introduced to combat it, but I am very grateful to the members of that research group, especially Eszter Kollar and Helder De Schutter, for making me so welcome.

I would not have been able to complete the book were it not for a Leverhulme Research Project Grant (RPG-2018-316). I would like to thank the Trust for this award, and Roger Crisp and Sue Mendus for the encouragement and support they gave to me in relation to my research plans. Francesca Minerva was also part of this Leverhulme funded project, providing me with much valued research assistance during the early stages of it. I would like to thank her for permission to re-use (in Chapter 8) material from our co-authored article, 'Should the Equality Act 2010 Be Extended to Prohibit Appearance Discrimination?', which was published in *Political Studies*. When Francesca moved to the University of Milan, Rossella De Bernardi took over her role and offered a fresh perspective on some of the issues I have discussed in the book. Joost Pietschmann also provided additional research assistance in the first year of the project. Finally, I am grateful to Peter Momtchiloff, the editor in charge of the book at OUP, and Tara Werger, the title manager, for guiding it so expertly through the publication process.

1
Introduction

You never just get called a bitch, it's always 'fat bitch'.... When it comes to being plus-size, it's always that descriptor that's thrown in there to remind you of who you are, what's your place, and why you're not equal. And that sucks.[1]

My old boss was against body modifications because of her religious beliefs. I was constantly harassed about my piercings and tattoos. I had hours cut after getting my tattoos, even though they aren't visible. I have both feet done as well, but always wear socks and shoes. I work in childcare and was told that even out in public I had to keep appearances up, so to keep covered, because I might see the children I looked after outside hours.[2]

I am West African, and I work at a consultancy firm in London. I am always being made to feel that my natural hair gives the impression that I am unprofessional.... A few years ago I had my hair styled in cornrows and I was asked quite blatantly by my boss how long it would be before my hair was back to 'normal'. I was taken aback. I could not believe what I was hearing. Although shocked, I did change my hairstyle—I did not want my hair to be the cause of problems for me at work.[3]

The reality is, as a short man you can expect eight out of 10 women to immediately dismiss you as a potential sexual partner at first sight. The chances are, the remaining two out of 10 will only give you a couple of minutes to make your case before making excuses.[4]

---

[1] From *The Guardian*, at https://www.theguardian.com/lifeandstyle/2019/may/12/insults-projectiles-well-intentioned-fat-shaming-the-perils-of-being-a-plus-size-runner. Accessed 2 July 2022.
[2] From BBC News, at https://www.bbc.co.uk/news/magazine-29211526. Accessed 2 July 2022.
[3] From BBC News, at https://www.bbc.co.uk/news/uk-36279845. Accessed 2 July 2022.
[4] From BBC News, at https://www.bbc.co.uk/news/stories/49567527. Accessed 2 July 2022.

2 WHAT'S WRONG WITH LOOKISM?

> Living with a facial disfigurement, in a busy city like London, means I am rarely invisible. Even something as simple as a train journey can turn into a gauntlet of stares, pointing and whispers.[5]

People are treated differently as a result of their appearance. Those regarded as overweight are regularly disadvantaged by their body shape or size when they apply for jobs; it is often harder for them to find romantic partners; and they are vulnerable to harassment and bullying in various settings, such as at school or on social media.[6] The treatment they receive may be rooted in appearance norms that apply demanding aesthetic standards to body shape and size, or have its origins in prejudices that express moral criticism by associating higher weight with a lack of self-discipline. People with prominent tattoos are often treated less favourably in employment decisions and in their everyday encounters as a result of conventional attitudes that are sometimes laced with moral judgements concerning the sanctity of the natural body, or influenced by prejudices that link extensive tattoos with aggression or mental health problems. Afro-textured hairstyles are frequently regarded as unsuitable for the workplace, motivating restrictive appearance codes that disproportionately affect members of racial groups whose hair is naturally suited to being worn in these ways. Short men are commonly regarded as less attractive; they are disadvantaged not only when it comes to dating but also in terms of their career prospects. They are treated less favourably not merely because they are found lacking when judged against appearance norms concerning ideal height, but also because they are the victims of prejudices linking shortness in height to inferiority complexes that supposedly make them over-sensitive and prone to aggression. Those with facial differences, sometimes as a result of physical disabilities, may experience greater difficulty in obtaining employment and finding romantic partners, and they may suffer unwanted attention or bullying in various contexts.

Considerable importance is attached to our appearance—too much, we might reasonably think. But when does *lookism*, by which I mean treating

---

[5] From BBC News, at https://www.bbc.co.uk/news/blogs-ouch-33623011. Accessed 2 July 2022.
[6] I use the expressions 'people regarded as overweight' and 'people with a heavier weight' to pick out victims of 'fat-shaming'. Although the term 'fat' is in the process of being reclaimed by the fat acceptance movement, it still carries negative connotations. See A. Meadows and D. Sigrún, 'What's in a Word? On Weight Stigma and Terminology', *Frontiers in Psychology* 7 (2016), https://doi.org/10.3389/fpsyg.2016.01527.

someone differently on the basis of their appearance in a way that either advantages or disadvantages them, constitute *wrongful* discrimination?[7] This issue matters for at least two reasons that are foreshadowed in the examples with which I began.

First, the advantages experienced as a result of being regarded as attractive are considerable and are enjoyed in a wide variety of contexts.[8] Consider some of the evidence. According to Daniel Hamermesh's analysis of data from the US, below average-looking women earn 4% less than average-looking women, whereas above average-looking women earn 8% more than those who are average-looking; below average-looking men earn 13% less than average-looking men, whereas above average-looking men earn 4% more than average-looking men. In other words, the overall 'beauty premium' for good-looking women is 12%, whereas for men it is 17%.[9] Extensive research on the impact of appearance on success in elections for political office suggests that voters are strongly influenced by the attractiveness of candidates (and also by whether they think they look competent, which correlates to some extent with perceiving them as attractive). This is so especially in the case of male candidates, and especially when voters are less familiar with the candidates' policy preferences, their track records, and the party for which they are standing.[10] In schools, facial attractiveness

---

[7] In framing the question in this way, I am adopting a non-moralized account of both lookism and discrimination, that is, an account which does not automatically imply that either lookism or discrimination is wrongful. For further elucidation of the notion of discrimination I am employing, see Section 2.1.

[8] When I refer to unattractiveness or attractiveness in this book, I mean the possession of an attractive or unattractive appearance.

[9] See D. S. Hamermesh, *Beauty Pays: Why Attractive People Are More Successful* (Princeton, NJ: Princeton University Press, 2011), 45–6. It is worth noting, however, that the evidence that Hamermesh cites concerns facial beauty in particular and much of it is collected on the basis of inter-subjective ratings of photographs of faces, either on a scale of 0–5 or on a scale of 0–10. This raises questions about what features and qualities influence our judgements about a person's visual attractiveness. As Hamermesh acknowledges, overall judgements about it may be based on other features of their appearance, such as their shape and height.

[10] See M. Efran and E. W. J. Patterson, 'Voters Vote Beautiful: The Effect of Physical Appearance on a National Election', *Canadian Journal of Behavioural Science/Revue Canadienne des Sciences du Comportement* 6 (1974): 352–6; A. King and A. Leigh, 'Beautiful Politicians', *Kyklos* 62 (2009): 579–93; N. Berggren, H. Jordahl, and P. Poutvaara, 'The Looks of a Winner: Beauty and Electoral Success', *Journal of Public Economics* 94 (2010): 8–15; S. Banducci, J. Karp, M. Thrasher, and C. Rallings, 'Ballot Photographs as Cues in Low-Information Elections', *Political Psychology* 29 (2008): 903–17; A. Todorov, A. Mandisodza, A. Goren, and C. Hall, 'Inferences of Competence from Faces Predict Election Outcomes', *Science* 308 (2005): 1623–6; D. Stockemer and R. Praino, 'Blinded by Beauty? Physical Attractiveness and Candidate Selection in the U.S. House of Representatives', *Social Science Quarterly* 96 (2015): 430–43; R. Praino, D. Stockemer, and J. Ratis, 'Looking Good or Looking Competent? Physical Appearance and Electoral Success in the 2008 Congressional Elections', *American Politics*

influences the expectations of teachers, and their assessment of their students, with respect to both academic performance and social skills.[11] In the sphere of personal relationships, appearance matters a lot when people are choosing potential romantic partners, although there is some evidence to suggest that it matters more to men than to women, and that it matters less to both sexes when relationships have become established.[12] With respect to crime, people regarded as unattractive are more likely to be convicted of an offence than those regarded as attractive, and when convicted they are more likely to receive harsher punishments.[13] Going beyond the scope of this book, appearance discrimination is not limited in its impact to human beings: people are often more willing to donate to wildlife conservation projects that benefit species that are charismatic partly in virtue of their visual appeal, and organizations as a result tend to use these species as flagships in their marketing campaigns.[14]

Research 42 (2014): 1096–117; W. Hart, V. Ottati, and N. Krumdick, 'Physical Attractiveness and Candidate Evaluation: A Model of Correction', *Political Psychology* 32 (2011): 181–203.

[11] Some studies suggest that this influence weakens over time as teachers get to know their students better, and others that it is not only the expectations of teachers that influence the performance of attractive students but also the expectations of their parents. See J. Dusek and G. Joseph, 'The Bases of Teacher Expectancies: A Meta-Analysis', *Journal of Educational Psychology* 75 (1983): 327–46; V. Ritts, M. Patterson, and M. Tubbs, 'Expectations, Impressions, and Judgments of Physically Attractive Students: A Review', *Review of Educational Research* 62 (1992): 413–26; J. Langlois, L. Kalakanis, A. Rubenstein, A. Larson, M. Hallam, and M. Smoot, 'Maxims or Myths of Beauty? A Meta-Analytic and Theoretical Review', *Psychological Bulletin* 126 (2000): 390–423.

[12] A. Feingold, 'Matching for Attractiveness in Romantic Partners and Same-Sex Friends: A Meta-Analysis and Theoretical Critique', *Psychological Bulletin* 104 (1988): 226–35; J. Sangrador and C. Yela, '"What Is Beautiful Is Loved": Physical Attractiveness in Loving Relationships', *Social Behavior and Personality: An International Journal* 28 (2000): 207–18; S. Sprecher, Q. Sullivan, and E. Hatfield, 'Mate Selection Preferences: Gender Differences Examined in a National Sample', *Journal of Personality and Social Psychology* 66 (1994): 1074–80; L. Lee, G. Loewenstein, D. Ariely, J. Hong, and J. Young, 'If I'm Not Hot, Are You Hot or Not? Physical-Attractiveness Evaluations and Dating Preferences as a Function of One's Own Attractiveness', *Psychological Science* 19 (2008): 669–77; P. Eastwick, L. Luchies, E. Finkel, and L. Hunt, 'The Predictive Validity of Ideal Partner Preferences: A Review and Meta-Analysis', *Psychological Bulletin* 140 (2014): 623–65.

[13] N. Mocan and E. Tekin, 'Ugly Criminals', *Review of Economics and Statistics* 92 (2010): 15–30; B. W. Darby and D. Jeffers, 'The Effects of Defendant and Juror Attractiveness on Simulated Courtroom Trial Decisions', *Social Behavior and Personality* 16 (1988): 39–50; J. Stewart, 'Appearance and Punishment: The Attraction-Leniency Effect in the Courtroom', *Journal of Social Psychology* 125 (1985): 373–8; J. Stewart, 'Defendant's Attractiveness as a Factor in the Outcome of Criminal Trials: An Observational Study', *Journal of Applied Social Psychology* 10 (1980): 348–61.

[14] B. Clucas, K. McHugh, and T. Caro, 'Flagship Species on Covers of US Conservation and Nature Magazines', *Biodiversity and Conservation* 17 (2008): 1517–28; R. Smith, D. Veríssimo, N. Isaac, K. Jones, 'Identifying Cinderella Species: Uncovering Mammals with Conservation Flagship Appeal', *Conservation Letters* 5 (2012): 205–12; J. Lorimer, 'Nonhuman Charisma', *Environment and Planning D: Society and Space* 25 (2007): 911–35.

Second, appearance discrimination is of moral interest not only in its own right but also in terms of its connection to other forms of discrimination. Appearance norms, that is, norms concerning how we should look, often place greater burdens on disadvantaged groups. Some of these norms are harder for Black or mixed-race people to comply with, such as norms that favour straight hair over tight curls; some adversely affect people with particular disabilities, such as norms that value symmetrical bodies; some are gender-specific, such as norms governing breast size and shape, or more demanding for women than they are for men, such as norms governing body shape and size; some are more demanding for older people, such as norms that prize firm, wrinkle-free, unblemished skin; and norms governing how we should dress are often more burdensome for the economically deprived because the clothes required to comply with them are expensive. As a result, discrimination on the basis of appearance, when it rewards people who conform to these norms, may involve, or interact with the effects of, wrongful discrimination on the basis of features other than appearance, in a way that aggravates existing injustices.[15]

Here, for clarity, we need to distinguish between direct and indirect discrimination. According to the notion that I shall be employing, A discriminates against P *directly* if and only if A treats P less favourably than Q *because* P has some property C that Q lacks (or A mistakenly believes P has that property). A man who endorses and complies with an appearance norm that adversely affects members of a disadvantaged group need not be engaged in direct discrimination against them. But even when he is not directly discriminating against them, he is *indirectly* discriminating against them in so far as the norm with which he is complying on average adversely affects members of that group more than it does members of other groups. Understood in these ways, however, there is no automatic valid inference from the occurrence of either direct or indirect discrimination to the conclusion that it is wrongful. Before exploring what makes appearance discrimination of either kind wrongful, we would benefit from a clearer picture of what appearance discrimination is, how we identify it, and how and why it occurs.

---

[15] This is an illustration of the broader phenomenon of 'intersectionality', a term coined by Kimberlé Crenshaw: see K. Crenshaw, 'Demarginalizing the Intersection of Race and Sex: A Black Feminist Critique of Antidiscrimination Doctrine, Feminist Theory and Antiracist Politics', *University of Chicago Legal Forum* 1 (1989): 139–67. For a helpful overview of the origins of the concept, and the way it has been deployed, see A. Carastathis, 'The Concept of Intersectionality in Feminist Theory', *Philosophy Compass* 9 (2014): 304–14.

1.1 What Is Appearance Discrimination, How Do We Identify It, and How and Why Does It Occur?

By a person's appearance, I mean the way (or ways) in which the attributes of his or her body, and how it is adorned or modified, are (or would be) perceived visually under standard conditions by those who possess normal visual capacities together with any relevant cultural knowledge. Possession of relevant cultural knowledge may be necessary in order to perceive visually some bodily features, modifications, or adornments in a way that involves an appreciation of their social significance. At one level of description, a tattoo is merely an ink marking on a person's skin but understanding its meaning may involve specific cultural knowledge.

There is a degree of arbitrariness in defining appearance in this way. I am, in effect, equating appearance with *visual* appearance, and excluding from the realm of appearance other attributes we possess that impinge upon the senses of others, for example, our accents, the register of our voices, and the way we smell. Giving 'appearance' this restricted meaning has some warrant in ordinary usage, but I would not want to deny that many of the same questions that I am raising about discrimination on the basis of (visual) appearance could also be raised about discrimination on the basis of these other attributes.

A person's appearance includes attributes that they are born with (for example, a cleft lip), attributes that they have because of what has happened to them (for example, scarring that occurs a result of an accident), and attributes that are wholly or partly a product of their choices (for example, clothing, tattoos, piercings, and hairstyles), including features that are a result of habitual behaviour that they could change (for example, whether they shave parts of their body). Appearance is therefore a broad category. For some purposes, nothing is lost by lumping together these diverse attributes. For other purposes, we may want to separate out particular attributes, or groups of attributes, and consider them separately. For example, as a result of bullying and body shaming, those who are regarded as overweight may constitute a socially salient group, that is, a group the perceived membership of which is 'important to the structure of social interactions across a wide range of social contexts'.[16] Whether people judged to be attractive, or deemed to be unattractive or ugly, constitute socially salient groups is

---

[16] K. Lippert-Rasmussen, *Born Free and Equal? A Philosophical Inquiry into the Nature of Discrimination* (Oxford: Oxford University Press, 2014), 30.

harder to determine given that attractiveness and unattractiveness take many different forms.

Not all discrimination on the basis of physical attributes constitutes direct discrimination on the basis of appearance. A person's weight is a physical attribute, but if those who weigh more than a hundred kilogrammes are rejected for a job solely because it involves walking on delicate roof structures that would be unable to withstand heavier weights, then they are not being directly discriminated against *on the basis of their appearance*. Weight discrimination counts as a form of direct appearance discrimination only when those engaged in it are ultimately responding to their visual perception of the shape and size of bodies rather than to measurements that are provided by a weighing scale. So too, if applicants for a job as cabin crew are rejected by an airline when they are less than five feet tall because they would be unable to place items in the overhead lockers, then they are not being directly discriminated against on the basis of their appearance. Having a minimum height requirement for a job when people below that height are unable to operate a particular piece of equipment which that job involves may constitute indirect discrimination on the basis of appearance, since it has a worse impact on people who look short, but it does not constitute direct appearance discrimination. An act of discrimination counts as direct appearance discrimination only when it is ultimately rooted in the visual experience of a person's body or how it is adorned, rather than, say, in some objective assessment of its physical attributes which is indifferent to that experience.

Identifying genuine cases of direct appearance discrimination can be difficult for other reasons. What may initially seem to be appearance discrimination can turn out to be merely a disguised form of some other kind of direct discrimination, because a person's appearance is being treated as evidence for, or as indicative of, the possession of a further characteristic that forms the real basis of the discrimination. Those who dress in 'women's clothes' are generally assumed to be women, unless they possess other visual features that mark them out as men or as non-binary. Men who paint their nails or wear flamboyant clothes are often assumed to be gay. (Indeed, those who want to pass as straight in order to avoid discrimination or harassment will generally adopt the styles of dress and adornment that are associated with heterosexuals.) Women who wear headscarves are frequently assumed to be Muslims, especially if they have darker skin. Since appearance characteristics are often treated as indicative of belonging to a socially salient group, discrimination that responds to visual features may in reality be discrimination on some other basis: for instance, a woman who is told that she cannot be employed in a role because she wears a headscarf may be a victim of Islamophobia rather than appearance discrimination.

How do we tell whether a person's appearance is being treated as indicative of membership of some group that forms the real basis of the discrimination they experience? Suppose that a Black man is rejected for a job by a selector and is told that it is because of his dreadlocks not because of his race. How can we determine whether that is true? We might think that if we want to reach a judgement about whether he is genuinely suffering direct discrimination on grounds of appearance, rather than on grounds of race, we need to answer the following counterfactual question: if he had been white, would he have been rejected because of his dreadlocks, or at least, would his dreadlocks have counted against his appointment? If the answer to this question is 'no', then he has been directly discriminated against, at least in part, on grounds of race, whereas if the answer is 'yes', then he has been directly discriminated against, at least in part, on grounds of his appearance.

A counterfactual test of this kind seems inadequate, however. Suppose that the selector we are considering is racially prejudiced and thinks that dreadlocks are messy or unkempt because of his or her racial bias. In that case we might justifiably conclude that the Black candidate has been discriminated against on the basis of his race even though the selector would also have rejected a white candidate if he had had dreadlocks. It seems that we need two counterfactual tests: we need to ask whether the candidate would have been rejected because of his dreadlocks had he been white, and then we need to ask whether, if he would have been rejected because of his dreadlocks had he been white, it is nevertheless the case that the explanation for his rejection would refer to the selector's racial bias against Black and mixed-race people. In practice, perhaps the vast majority of such cases involve racial bias of this kind: when selectors dislike dreadlocks or regard them as messy, and reject candidates who have them even if the candidates are white, then the selectors do so because they associate dreadlocks with Black or mixed-raced people and are biased against such people.

It is possible in principle, however, for a selector's decision to reject a Black candidate because of his dreadlocks to pass these two counterfactual tests. If it were to do so, we might justifiably conclude that the Black candidate has not been directly discriminated against on grounds of race, but solely on grounds of appearance. If we reached that conclusion, we would not need to deny that it is highly likely that an appearance norm that regards dreadlocks as unkempt has its origins, at least in part, in racial prejudice and has gained widespread acceptance over time as a result of racial prejudice.[17] We would merely be holding that in discriminating against the candidate on the basis of his dreadlocks, *the selector* has not been influenced by the candidate's race, and that in so far as the selector endorses this appearance norm, doing so is not the result of any bias he or she has against Black or mixed-race people.

Genuine direct appearance discrimination may be a form of indirect discrimination in relation to some other characteristic, including race, when those who engage in it are not biased against people who possess that characteristic but it has a worse effect on them. The Black candidate who is rejected by a selector because he has dreadlocks, in a way that does not involve any racial bias on the part of the selector, has nevertheless been indirectly discriminated against on grounds of race because, on average, treating the absence of dreadlocks as a qualification for a job has a worse effect on Black and mixed-race people among whom this hairstyle is more common. Indeed, employers' appearance codes that prohibit dreadlocks or hair braids on the grounds that these are messy constitute a form of indirect racial discrimination in virtue of the adverse effect of these codes on members of racial groups who have afro-textured hair that is naturally suited to such hairstyles (although, again, this does not settle the question of whether indirect discrimination of this kind is wrongful). When employers are resistant to changing an appearance code despite being aware of its adverse impact on members of some racial group, we may begin to wonder whether they are practising not indirect but direct racial discrimination, because it might begin to seem that their commitment to this code reflects a racial bias and is simply a means of excluding members of that group. We should leave open the possibility, however, that their resistance to change does not involve any racial bias and merely reflects an aesthetic judgement about appearance, albeit one that is a product of internalizing a norm that may have taken hold in a society because of racial prejudice.

[17] It is implausible to deny that appearance norms that prize straight flowing hair and light skin, and that frown upon afro-textured hair in its natural state and dark skin, have their origins, at least in part, in racial prejudice. See, for example, P. Taylor, *Black Is Beautiful: A Philosophy of Black Aesthetics* (Malden, MA: Wiley-Blackwell, 2016), ch. 4, especially 11–113. But in the absence of evidence to the contrary, we should not rule out the possibility that the widespread acceptance of such norms today may have a different explanation; for example, it might be due in part to the experience of living in partially segregated communities, which reduces the frequency of encounters between members of different racial groups and may lead to the adoption of biased appearance norms even in the absence of racial prejudice.

Direct appearance discrimination may arise in different ways. Firstly, like other forms of direct discrimination, it may stem from widespread *prejudices or stereotypical associations*, for example, the association of good looks with greater competence, or the prejudice that those who are overweight lack self-discipline or are self-indulgent. These prejudices or associations, and the effects they have on behaviour, may be explicit, that is, a person may be aware of them and be aware of the fact that they are influencing his or her behaviour, or they and their effects may be implicit, that is, a person may be unaware of them or unaware of the fact that they are influencing his or her behaviour.

Secondly, direct appearance discrimination may stem from *non-rational responses*, that is, responses for which the agent has no motivating belief or reason, not even an unjustified one. For example, people may simply be disposed to react more favourably to those they find good-looking without making any assumptions about the skills or character traits good-looking people possess, and when they discriminate as a result of possessing these dispositions, they may be unaware that their behaviour is being influenced in this way. (Throughout this book, when I refer to biases without any further specification, I mean to allow that they may be rooted either in prejudices or in non-rational responses.)

Thirdly, direct appearance discrimination may stem from *judgements concerning the aesthetic value* of particular appearance features that influence our treatment of people who possess them, for example, the judgement that 'plus size' bodies are ugly or that scarred faces are unsightly. These judgements may be shaped by appearance norms that have been internalized as a result of learning how people's looks are assessed by others whose opinion matters to us, such as members of our family, our peers, and those we admire. It might be thought that ultimately aesthetic judgements are non-rational because no reasons can be given for them, but even if that is so, when they motivate an action, they provide aesthetic reasons for it, so the responses to which they lead do not count as non-rational in my terms.

Fourthly, direct appearance discrimination may stem from *moral judgements* that express approval or disapproval of someone's appearance, with these judgements influencing our treatment of him or her. For example, our behaviour towards others may be influenced by the moral judgement that scruffiness is a moral flaw because we have a duty to make the best of our appearance. So too, our behaviour towards others may be influenced by the belief that we have a duty to modify, or not to modify, our bodies in certain ways, for example, that we have a duty not to undergo cosmetic surgery because that involves placing excessive weight on our appearance or being too easily influenced by conventional beauty norms, or by the belief that we have a duty to respect our bodies that is violated when we intentionally scar them or decorate them with tattoos.

In relation to each of these sources of appearance discrimination, there may be deeper levels of explanation for how and why it occurs. For example, at one level our aesthetic judgements concerning appearance features and their impact on our behaviour might be explained by reference to the appearance norms we have internalized and our belief that it is permissible to let these norms influence our treatment of others. At a deeper level, the explanation for why we find someone's looks aesthetically appealing, and the explanation for why we treat them differently as a result of their looks—and indeed, for why particular appearance norms are adopted in a society—might appeal to hard-wired responses that owe their existence to the evolutionary advantages that the genes underlying them have conferred over many generations. Sometimes, at least, a full and complete explanation of why we find a person's looks aesthetically appealing, and treat them differently as a result, may need to appeal to some combination of both hard-wired responses and the internalization of appearance norms that reflect those responses.[18]

In many cases, however, the correct explanation of why an appearance norm has emerged and been internalized may not make any reference to evolutionary theories. Some of these norms may have their origins in unjust practices, for example, the way in which the characteristic features of a particular racial group are more closely aligned with the prevailing appearance norms than those of other racial groups might be explained in terms of the oppression of these other groups and how it has been sustained, for example, the norms favouring light skin tone, straight hair, or narrow noses that disadvantage many Black people. The emergence of some appearance norms, and the looks they prize, such as the bold eyebrows that semi-permanent makeup artists are trained to provide, or the large lips that can be created by injectable fillers, might be explained by technological developments and the interests of the beauty industry. By and large, I will remain silent on these issues concerning the deeper origins of appearance norms, except when they affect the normative assessment of the forms of appearance

---

[18] See D. Rhode, *The Beauty Bias. The Injustice of Appearance in Life and Law* (Oxford: Oxford University Press, 2010), ch. 3; F. Minerva, 'The Invisible Discrimination before Our Eyes: A Bioethical Analysis', *Bioethics* 31 (2017): 180–9.

discrimination to which they give rise, or the feasibility of certain kinds of regulatory responses to them.

1.2 Moral Concerns

This book focuses on three contexts in which appearance discrimination occurs: employment, personal relationships, and ordinary practices of commenting (whether negatively or positively) on aspects of people's appearance, in everyday face to face interactions and on social media, which I shall refer to as 'everyday lookism'. I have selected these contexts because, in my view, the appearance discrimination that takes place in them raises particularly vividly the moral concerns that we ought to have about it. What more do we need to know in order to judge whether it is wrongful in these contexts?

Let me consider briefly two rather different approaches to this question, the first of which I shall call the libertarian approach, and the second of which I shall refer to as the utilitarian approach. My primary purpose in considering them is to situate my approach in relation to them, and to draw attention to some challenges they face in order to motivate my own inquiry. I do not aim to refute them, however. In so far as I present a persuasive argument against them in this book, it consists in providing an appealing alternative to both.

According to what I am calling the libertarian approach, it is morally permissible for us to engage in appearance discrimination, whether in the context of employment, personal relationships, or the practice of everyday lookism. Employers (or selectors acting on their behalf) are within their moral rights to select employees on any basis whatsoever, including their own aesthetic preferences, their own prejudices, or indeed the aesthetic preferences or prejudices of their customers and clients. Of course, employers have efficiency reasons for not selecting on the basis of their own aesthetic whims, for example, when employers reject those with beards, piercings, or unconventional hair colours because they do not like their looks, they may appoint less well-qualified candidates who are less good at their jobs; but they also have efficiency reasons to take into account the preferences of their customers and clients to interact with employees who possess particular appearance characteristics because this may increase profits.

The libertarian approach also maintains that, beyond the sphere of employment, when we make choices about with whom to enter friendships and romantic partnerships, we are entitled to do so for whatever reason we want: we may prefer the appearance of people with light skin tone rather than dark skin tone, of people who are tall rather than short, and of people with symmetrical rather than unsymmetrical faces, and we are entitled to act on the basis of these preferences in deciding what friendships to form and what romantic partnerships to enter into.

The libertarian approach I have described is an outlier, however. It would seem to imply that employers have a right to engage in racial discrimination and that they act permissibly in doing so. It is not obvious that it could consistently deny that right whilst maintaining that there is a right to engage in appearance discrimination of all kinds, for some forms of appearance discrimination seem relevantly similar to racial discrimination.[19] We have no more control over aspects of our appearance such as our height than our racial identity; some appearance features over which we have limited control, such as the shape of our bodies, are stigmatized in much the same ways as particular racial identities; and appearance discrimination may limit the opportunities of its victims just as racial discrimination does. Indeed, in Section 4.1, I shall argue that some of what is ordinarily regarded as racial discrimination may *be* appearance discrimination. As a result, the libertarian approach to appearance discrimination that I have described seems to be committed to the conclusion that not only is there a right to engage in appearance discrimination, but also a right to engage in racial discrimination and other forms of discrimination that are normally thought to be impermissible. This is not a *reductio ad absurdum* of the libertarian approach, but it highlights the distance between this approach and conventional moral wisdom. Although the libertarian approach might seem to offer an attractive vision of maximum freedom from moral constraints in relation to how we treat others on the basis of their appearance, it does so at the expense of being forced to deny the existence of more familiar moral rights against discrimination.

As a contrast with the libertarian approach, consider a utilitarian approach which maintains that appearance discrimination is morally

---

[19] Of course, some might think that denying a moral right to engage in appearance discrimination is absurd, and regard this as providing an argument for a right to engage in racial discrimination on the grounds that there can't be one without the other. Robert Post does not develop such an argument, but he does address 'the nagging suspicion that laws prohibiting discrimination based on appearance [are]...somehow a reductio ad absurdum of the basic logic of American antidiscrimination law' (R. Post, *Predjudicial Appearances. The Logic of American Antidiscrimination Law* (Durham, NC: Duke University Press, 2000), 10.)

permissible when it maximizes preference satisfaction or well-being, but morally impermissible when it does not do so. This approach can regard appearance discrimination in the sphere of employment as morally objectionable when, even though it benefits both the employer and applicants for jobs with favoured appearances, it sets back the interests of a much larger group of people, consisting of applicants with unfavoured appearances, and customers and clients who have to deal with less well-qualified appointees. In a discussion that resonates with this approach, Hamermesh leans towards the view that appearance discrimination is morally justified or morally permissible only when it is socially productive and not when it is merely privately productive. We might think that distinguishing between appearance discrimination that is socially productive and that which is only privately productive offers an indirect method for determining when appearance discrimination is likely to maximize overall well-being and when it is not. But what does it mean to say that appearance discrimination is socially productive, as opposed to merely 'privately productive'?

The distinction between what is socially productive and what is privately productive is hard to draw. It is not entirely clear how Hamermesh intends it to be understood, but the basis of it seems to be this: selecting on the basis of a trait is socially productive if and only if doing so benefits others in addition to the employer and those appointed, for example, if it benefits customers or clients by contributing to making an inherently better product or service, or it benefits other members of the wider society, for example, by leading to increased output in a way that has a trickle-down effect.[20] In contrast, it is merely privately productive if it benefits only the employer or the employee, for example, by satisfying the employer's preference for employees with a particular trait, and providing the employee with a job and a salary. Of course, selection on the basis of a trait may be both privately productive and socially productive. For example, it may be the case that selecting the more intelligent candidates from an applicant pool benefits not only the employer (through greater or better productivity and as a consequence higher profits) and the employee (by providing him or her with gainful employment) but also customers or clients, as a result of supplying a more ingenious product that better meets their needs, or a better devised or executed service; and it may be the case that 'this extra production benefits society, in the form of technological advances, more efficient organizations, and even better economic research'.[21]

[20] See Hamermesh, *Beauty Pays*, 109, 121.   [21] Hamermesh, *Beauty Pays*, 109.

In determining whether or not appearance discrimination is socially productive or whether it is merely privately productive, Hamermesh regards it as crucial whether a good or service is inherently better as a result of being created by, or provided by, someone with a particular type of looks. He maintains that unless a product or service is made inherently better by being produced by, or provided by, good-looking individuals, discriminating in favour of them provides 'no gain to society; and by channeling ugly people into certain roles, society is less efficient economically than it would be if people worked in jobs that used their skills most efficiently, independent of their looks'.[22] As he concedes, however, it is hard to draw the distinction between goods or services that are inherently better as a result of being created by, or provided by, those with a particular type of looks. Suppose, for example, that many customers want a certain sort of experience when they go shopping or dine out, namely, the experience of being served by visually attractive store assistants or waiters. Is that enough for it to be the case that the experience of being served by attractive store assistances and waiters is inherently better for those that want it?

In judging whether the occupant of a job has provided an inherently better experience, we might be tempted to appeal to the 'essential activity or purpose' of that job, for which particular looks are either relevant or irrelevant. But how are we to identify the essential activity or purpose of a job? Can we identify it, perhaps, by considering the essential purpose or activity of the enterprise of which it is a part? We might want to say that the essential purpose of a restaurant is to provide high-quality food served in an efficient and congenial manner, so that the skill of a waiter is the same regardless of his or her appearance, and that the service a waiter provides cannot be made inherently better in virtue of his or her attractive appearance. So too we might want to say that the essential purpose of a store, no matter how high class, is to supply goods to its customers and help them to choose what to buy, so that sales assistants' skills remain the same regardless of their appearance, and their attractive appearance cannot make the service they provide inherently better. But who defines the essential purpose or activity of a firm or enterprise? And why is it necessarily a mistake, or indefensible, to define the purpose of a particular restaurant as providing the experience of eating fine food served by attractive waiters, or to define the purpose of a particular store as selling high-quality goods served by attractive sales assistants?

[22] Hamermesh, *Beauty Pays*, 110.

Without independent criteria for determining the essential purpose or activity of a job, Hamermesh will be hard-pressed to find grounds for denying that any provision of a good or service that is conducive to satisfying the preferences of customers, clients, or audiences to interact with, or observe, those who have a particular sort of appearance, provides them with an inherently better experience, and that any appearance discrimination which involves selecting on that basis is therefore socially productive. For this reason, his resistance to the idea that selecting which tennis games will be played on the most prestigious court at a tournament, or selecting which of those games will be shown on live television, on the basis in part of the players' appearance, can be socially productive seems hard to defend. If spectators or television audiences place inherent value on the experience of seeing players who are both skilled at tennis and physically attractive, then it is beside the point to observe that '[t]he quality of tennis is generally no better when provided by Maria Sharapova than by a less good-looking, equally able competitor'.[23]

The notion of 'an inherently better experience' struggles to do the work that Hamermesh needs it to do in distinguishing justified from unjustified appearance discrimination. We might instead adopt a direct utilitarian approach that applies what Peter Singer calls 'the principle of equal consideration of interests', giving equal weight to each person's interests, irrespective of their race, gender, or attractiveness, and as a result assesses acts of discrimination in terms of the way in which they benefit or harm individuals.[24] According to this view, discrimination in general, and appearance discrimination in particular, is permissible, and indeed required, when it produces the greatest amount of overall benefit, all things considered, but impermissible when it does not do so.[25]

In assessing the morality of appearance discrimination, however, this approach runs up against some familiar problems. It seems to require us to give weight to morally objectionable preferences. Suppose that many members of a society regard those with a dark skin tone as inferior, and do not want to have to interact with them because they see them as unclean or impure. As a result, employers, even when they don't share these attitudes,

---

[23] Hamermesh, *Beauty Pays*, 120.
[24] See P. Singer, 'Is Racial Discrimination Arbitrary?', *Philosophia* 8 (1978): 185–203; see also R. Barro, 'So You Want to Hire the Beautiful, Well, Why Not?', *Business Week*, 16 March 1998, available at: https://scholar.harvard.edu/files/barro/files/98_0316_hire_bw.pdf. Accessed 2 May 2023.
[25] See Singer, 'Is Racial Discrimination Arbitrary?', especially 196–202.

would prefer not to appoint people with a dark skin tone to positions within their workplaces, because doing so is bad for business. In assessing whether it is morally permissible for them to discriminate against applicants with a dark skin tone, should we, as the principle of equal consideration of interests would suggest, simply weigh the benefits to the employer, the benefits to the employees who would not otherwise be appointed, and the benefits to those customers and clients who purchase goods and services from this company, against the harms caused to those with this skin tone who are excluded from these jobs?[26] Surely the benefit that customers and clients with such attitudes would receive from being served or assisted by employees with a light skin tone, rather than being served by those with a dark skin tone who they regard as impure and inferior, should not even be weighed in the balance. But from a utilitarian perspective, it is not easy to justify filtering out these preferences when considering whether selecting on the basis of skin tone would produce the greatest overall benefit. In so far as the belief that people with a dark skin tone are unclean or impure has a metaphysical character, it need not rest on any false factual beliefs.

Perhaps utilitarians should nevertheless simply exclude morally obnoxious preferences when calculating the total benefits that would be produced by employers using different selection criteria. But even when appearance-related preferences are not themselves morally objectionable, we might think there can be strong reasons not to count them. Suppose that a selector working for a company would prefer to appoint attractive candidates because he or she gets pleasure from looking at them. Should that preference be given any weight at all in determining whether it is permissible for him or her to discriminate in favour of attractive candidates? Do our worries about selectors discriminating in this way reduce to worries about whether such a practice will produce the most overall preference satisfaction or well-being? Is it simply that the interest the selector has in discriminating in favour of those he or she finds attractive is outweighed by the interest that customers and clients have in receiving higher-quality goods and services, combined with the interest that the unattractive have in being appointed to such jobs, and the interest that the employer has in making higher profits?

This book approaches the issue of when appearance discrimination is justified in a way that differs from both the libertarian and utilitarian

---

[26] This seems to be Singer's approach: see Singer, 'Is Racial Discrimination Arbitrary?', 188, 200–1.

approaches I have outlined. The challenges they face may not be insuperable but they do motivate the search for an alternative. Accordingly, I develop a different account of what makes discrimination wrong (when it is wrong) that I argue applies in each of the three contexts I explore. I combine my application of this general theory with considering the extent to which appearance discrimination and racial discrimination are comparable. Arguing by analogy, I maintain that there are some important similarities between the two forms of discrimination that support the conclusion that appearance discrimination is often morally problematic. Although this argument by analogy is logically unnecessary for the case I develop against appearance discrimination, it is nevertheless illuminating and, I hope, has persuasive power.

1.3 My Normative Framework

There are different senses in which discrimination in general, and appearance discrimination in particular, might be wrong. Alan Gibbard distinguishes between an objective sense and a subjective sense: 'An act is wrong in the objective sense if it is wrong in light of all the facts, knowable and unknowable, whereas it is wrong in the subjective sense if it is wrong in light of what the agent had good reason to believe.'[27] The objective sense weakens the connection between wrong-doing and blameworthiness: many acts that are wrongful in this sense are not blameworthy because the agent could not have known all of the relevant facts or was excusably ignorant of some of them. In discussing the wrongfulness or permissibility of acts of discrimination on the basis of appearance, I shall throughout this book employ the objective sense unless I indicate otherwise.[28]

There are many theories of what makes discrimination wrong, when it is wrong. In Chapters 2 and 3 I shall defend in some detail a pluralist theory

---

[27] A. Gibbard, *Wise Choices, Apt Feelings: A Theory of Normative Judgment* (Oxford: Oxford University Press, 1990), 42. The objective sense corresponds to what Derek Parfit calls the fact-relative sense. See D. Parfit, *On What Matters. Volume One* (Oxford: Oxford University Press, 2012), 150–1.

[28] The objective sense of wrongness is not the sense that we use in many ordinary contexts, and it may strike some as counterintuitive. For example, in this sense Hitler's parents acted wrongly in conceiving him. But it is nevertheless a perfectly legitimate sense and it is useful precisely because it allows us to bracket issues of culpability: even though Hitler's parents were not blameworthy in conceiving him, they would have been had they known what he would go on to do.

that draws upon several of them. I now propose to outline that theory, locating it in relation to some broader issues within normative theory. Readers who are primarily interested in the question of when it is wrong to treat a person differently on the basis of their appearance, and have less interest in the strengths and weaknesses of different general theories of what makes discrimination wrong, can learn here all they need to know about the theory that I shall employ. If you are in this camp, you do not need to read Chapters 2 and 3 to understand my argument. Those who have greater interest in recent debates about what makes discrimination wrong will find a fuller defence of my favoured pluralist theory in these chapters.

Discrimination might be regarded as wrong (when it is wrong) independently of its causal consequences, or it might be regarded as wrong (when it is wrong) in virtue of its causal consequences. I shall say that discrimination is *non-contingently* wrong when it is wrong independently of its causal consequences and that it is *contingently* wrong when it is wrong in virtue of its causal consequences. The theory I defend regards discrimination as potentially wrong in either of these ways, or both of them.

According to a pluralist theory of this kind, there are ways of treating people as equals that matter independently of the outcomes that they bring about. The version I defend proposes that an act of discrimination may be wrong in virtue of the *disrespect* that act involves independently of whether it causes harm to its victims, for example, a discriminatory act may send out a demeaning or degrading message about the inferior moral status of the victims, or the group to which they belong, even if no one picks up that message and it makes no difference to anyone's well-being. So too I claim that an act of discrimination may be wrong in virtue of the *deliberative unfairness* involved in a selection decision when selectors do not give due weight to the interests of each of the candidates, for example, because they are influenced by some personal preference they have concerning the size or shape of the candidates' noses. An act of discrimination in a selection process may be wrong because it is unfair independently of whether its unfairness affects the outcome of the decision, and therefore independently of whether it harms any of the candidates. (For example, when a selector on a committee is influenced by his dislike of a candidate's nose and as a result votes against her appointment, he acts unfairly even if it makes no difference to the committee's decision.) This does not involve denying that, normally at least, disrespectful acts and unfair processes of deliberation will adversely affect the interests of those who are the victims, for example, by denying them career opportunities about which they care deeply, and therefore harm them; and nor need it involve denying that discrimination is more wrongful when it does harm those who suffer it. Indeed, the harm caused might be thought to aggravate the wrong involved in the disrespect or the unfairness; even though its wrongness is not conditional on harm occurring, when harm does occur, then it increases the severity of the wrong-doing.

But discrimination may be morally troubling even when it is not disrespectful (or indeed unfair). Benjamin Eidelson gives the example of racial profiling based on accurate statistical data that imply members of some racial group are more likely to commit a particular sort of crime: '…in principle a policy of considering race in allocating scrutiny could avoid treating anyone as less than a full and equal person.'[29] Whether racial profiling that is not disrespectful is nevertheless wrong will depend upon the nature and magnitude of the benefits and burdens it produces and how they are distributed, and its impact on the perceived moral status of the racial groups that are given special attention. More generally, when an act of discrimination is assessed in terms of its consequences, it may be wrong either because it contributes to *creating an unjust distribution of benefits and burdens* or because it contributes to *lowering the perceived moral status of the members of a group*. It may do so by reinforcing the power structures that help to sustain an unjust distribution or to lower the perceived moral status of a group. When an act of discrimination is disrespectful or involves unfairness, the unjust consequences it generally creates may not only aggravate the wrongfulness involved in the disrespect or unfairness but also be an independent wrong-making feature.

I shall not argue for the truth of any particular theory of distributive justice, but I make two assumptions that are compatible with a range of such theories. First, I shall assume that there are demanding limits to what can count as just inequality. Second, I shall assume that personal responsibility for outcomes often makes a difference to whether those outcomes are just. There is a range of possible accounts of when inequalities are unjust and what makes them so that are compatible with these assumptions. For example, these assumptions are compatible with the following accounts: responsibility-sensitive forms of egalitarianism such as luck egalitarianism; responsibility-sensitive forms of prioritarianism that give significant extra weight to benefitting the worse off;[30] sufficientarian approaches, provided

---

[29] B. Eidelson, *Discrimination and Disrespect* (Oxford: Oxford University Press, 2015), 174.

[30] For the distinction between equality and priority, see D. Parfit, 'Equality and Priority', in A. Mason (ed.), *Ideals of Equality* (Oxford: Blackwell, 1998).

they have a reasonably high sufficiency threshold and are sensitive to responsibility-related considerations;[31] and what I have elsewhere called 'quasi-egalitarian' principles that object to inequality of a certain degree or kind independently of its consequences, again so long as these principles are made sensitive to responsibility-related considerations.[32] For the most part, I shall not presuppose the truth of any particular one of these theories, although in places I employ arguments that are more congenial to some of them rather than others, for example, in Chapter 9 I shall use the device of 'hypothetical insurance', which is in tension with egalitarian approaches that require full compensation for disadvantages that a person faces for which he or she is not responsible, and which is also hard to reconcile with a prioritarian approach. Refraining from endorsing a particular theory of justice does at times create some indeterminacy with regard to what conclusions we ought to draw in specific cases of appearance discrimination, but in such cases I try to make it clear how the adoption of one theory rather than another would affect these conclusions.

I shall judge whether an act of discrimination is wrong in virtue of the role it plays in creating an unjust distribution of benefits and burdens by considering its effect on opportunities for well-being and the distribution of these opportunities among persons. But I do not take myself to be settling the deeper issue of what is the appropriate currency of justice, that is, whether it is welfare, capabilities, primary goods, or resources.[33] In assessing the effects of discrimination on well-being, I shall treat each person's interest in autonomous agency as particularly important because of the instrumental role it plays in facilitating flourishing lives. As John Stuart Mill argued, since we are diverse in terms of our sources of fulfilment, the chances of a person finding a life in which they can flourish are greatly increased when they are in a position to make their own choices from an adequate range of options. But I shall remain uncommitted on the issue of how, exactly, a theory of distributive justice should give due weight to our interest in autonomous agency, for example, whether it should recognize a right to autonomy or endorse a lexically prior principle to protect it, or

---

[31] For an exploration and defence of the idea of sufficiency, see L. Shields, *Just Enough: Sufficiency as a Demand of Justice* (Edinburgh: Edinburgh University Press, 2016).
[32] A. Mason, *Levelling the Playing Field. The Idea of Equal Opportunity and Its Place in Egalitarian Thought* (Oxford: Oxford University Press, 2006), 125–9.
[33] For a helpful overview of these currencies, see M. Clayton and A. Williams, 'Egalitarian Justice and Interpersonal Comparison', *European Journal of Political Research* 35 (1999): 445–64.

whether its protection can be adequately secured by some overarching principle that governs benefits and burdens more generally.

1.4 Discrimination, Structural Injustice, and Individual Wrong-Doing

It might seem to some that my approach to morally assessing the disadvantages experienced by people as a result of their appearance is misconceived. Rather than framing the moral problem in terms of concepts such as 'respect', 'deliberative fairness', 'discrimination', and 'wrong-doing', I should be viewing it through the lens of concepts such as 'oppression', 'group stigmatization', and 'structural injustice'. In short, my approach to understanding what is morally objectionable about the disadvantages suffered by various groups, including those with facial differences and people regarded as overweight, is too individualistic. Iris Marion Young, for example, argues that '[o]ppression, not discrimination, is the primary concept for naming group-related injustice. Whilst discriminatory policies sometimes cause or reinforce oppression, oppression involves many actions, practices, and structures that have little to do with preferring or excluding members of groups in the awarding of benefits.'[34] (Young also contends that framing the issues in terms of the concept of discrimination focuses attention on the perpetrator rather than on the victims and their situation.)

In proposing that acts of discrimination may be wrong in virtue of reinforcing the power structures that help to sustain an unjust distribution or lower the perceived moral status of a group, my account recognizes that any plausible theory of unjust disadvantage and how it is sustained and reproduced needs to give a key role to the idea of structural injustice, that is, injustices that are located in or facilitated by social structures. According to my account, part of what makes appearance discrimination morally problematic is that it reinforces and reproduces social structures. By social structures, I mean power relations that inhere in a network of intersecting institutions and practices that are governed by formal and informal rules. These structures facilitate the disadvantaging of particular groups of people

---

[34] I. M. Young, *Justice and the Politics of Difference* (Princeton, NJ: Princeton University Press, 1990), 195. See also I. M. Young, *Responsibility for Justice* (Oxford: Oxford University Press, 2011), especially ch. 2. For a discussion of the importance of focusing on structural injustice in the context of beauty requirements, see H. Widdows, 'Structural Injustice and the Requirements of Beauty', *Journal of Social Philosophy* 52 (2021): 251–69.

and may mark them out as inferior, including people with specific appearance features, such as short height, or a shape that is taken to signify excessive weight, or facial features that are regarded as ugly. (Different social structures may of course interact in a way that reinforces or aggravates the disadvantages faced by groups of people: for example, a social structure that facilitates the disadvantaging of those with a particular appearance feature, and marks them out as inferior, may interact with a structure that facilitates the disadvantaging of a racial minority and marks them out as inferior.)[35] As Young herself proposes, a full understanding of group disadvantage requires us to identify social structures *and* the individual actions that create and sustain those structures in part through direct and indirect discrimination.[36] This leaves open the issue of who, if anyone, should be blamed and who should be assigned the responsibility to transform these structures.

It is true, however, that I focus on individual wrong-doing. Does this mean that I am putting the emphasis in the wrong place, or that I must inevitably misunderstand structural injustices or neglect some of the ways in which they are generated and reproduced? There are different ways in which this concern might arise. From a political perspective, it might be thought that my approach encourages mere 'finger-pointing', that is, criticizing and blaming individuals for their wrong-doing in a way that is at best counterproductive and at worst unfair or inappropriate, because it ends up targeting those who are either blameless or less blameworthy than others because of their lack of power. Indeed, when we contribute to structural injustice, we sometimes, perhaps often, do so in a way that is not blameworthy.[37] We may be unaware of the consequences of our actions, or be unaware of the way in which they combine with the intended or unintended consequences of other people's actions to create systematic disadvantages for the members of a group. If our ignorance is non-culpable, then we cannot legitimately be blamed for what we do. As a result, it might be argued that rather than seeking to blame individuals, what is really needed is a collective response to the structural injustices that are suffered by people who are disadvantaged by their appearance, perhaps through the operation of

---

[35] Again, this is an illustration of what Crenshaw refers to as intersectionality: see Crenshaw, 'Demarginalizing the Intersection of Race and Sex: A Black Feminist Critique of Antidiscrimination Doctrine'.
[36] See Young, *Responsibility for Justice*, ch. 4. Heather Widdows seems to me to neglect the latter: see her 'Structural Injustice and the Requirements of Beauty'.
[37] See Young, *Responsibility for Justice*, ch. 2.

appearance norms that are racially biased, or gender-biased, or biased against those with certain disabilities.[38]

In response, I would emphasize to begin with that it is not part of the point of this book to berate people who are engaged in wrongful appearance discrimination. Indeed, my adoption of Gibbard's objective sense of 'wrong' is in part designed to push to one side questions about culpability. In his objective sense, we can act wrongly without being blameworthy, for even those who are unaware that what they are doing contributes to reinforcing structural injustices, and are not blameworthy for their ignorance, may nevertheless be acting wrongly in this sense. Rather than seeking to blame individuals, I hope to encourage reflection on the ways in which we may each be involved in appearance discrimination and the extent to which our involvement in it is potentially morally problematic. Furthermore, it is important to be clear that my account is non-individualist in allowing that adequately addressing the wrongs involved in, or caused by, appearance discrimination may require collective action rather than mere changes in individual behaviour. Indeed, the kind of collective action I argue is required is not limited to enacting legislation to forbid individuals from engaging in it: resistance to appearance-related injustices may require acting collectively to try to re-shape appearance norms and to reduce the importance that people place upon their own and other people's appearance.

But it is true that we may sometimes contribute to a structural injustice in a way that does not involve any wrong-doing, not even blameless wrong-doing. Contributing to such an injustice is not always reasonably avoidable: however we behave, we may end up being complicit in some form of injustice, and perhaps the best we can do is to choose the least unjust alternative. For example, a father who tries to persuade his 15-year-old daughter to wear less revealing clothing in order to avoid attracting unwanted attention from older men may reinforce a structure of gender injustice that is complicit in victim blaming, but to the extent that his advice his heeded, his actions may serve to protect her from harm. When under circumstances such as these we minimize harm in a way that makes the outcome as least unjust as it could be, even though we contribute to structural injustice, our actions not only are blameless but involve no wrong-doing. It is important not to lose sight of such cases in focusing on individual wrong-doing. But

---

[38] For a version of this critique, see Widdows, 'Structural Injustice and the Requirements of Beauty', 262–4.

even though my approach does not foreground them, it need not deny their existence or fail to give them due weight.

It might be thought that my approach is further limited by another consideration, namely, that in order to behave wrongly by contributing to an unjust outcome, such as the unjust disadvantages experienced by those who are made worse off by their appearance, our acts (or omissions) must make a difference (or be capable of making a difference) to that outcome. But, generally speaking, it is not anyone's particular actions that cause the injustice, and there is nothing we could do, as individuals, to prevent the injustice from being brought about. What we do often makes no serious difference to whether an unjust outcome is brought about or to the degree of injustice it involves because our contribution is so small. But even if an individual's actions make no serious difference to whether an unjust outcome is brought about, he or she may be acting wrongfully because what he or she does plays a small part in producing that outcome and is wrongful because *its moral significance derives from that contribution*. I shall return to this issue in Section 3.1.

1.5 Outline of the Argument

Let me now sketch the book's argument. In Part I of the book, comprised of Chapters 2 and 3, I shall develop the theory of what makes discrimination wrong (when it is wrong) that informs what follows. Those who are less interested in these deeper issues may decide to skip this Part or skim through it. The subsequent chapters should nevertheless be intelligible even though my reasons for adopting the particular theory of discrimination that I do will be more opaque.

In Chapter 2, I distinguish between two types of discrimination using racial discrimination as a reference point: first, discrimination that is rooted in prejudices broadly understood, including psychological associations that link membership of a racial group with undesirable character traits; and second, discrimination that is rooted in non-rational responses, that is, responses for which the agent has no motivating reason. Discrimination of both of these types can be wrong for various reasons. In order to identify these reasons, I develop the pluralist theory of what makes discrimination already outlined, which gives independent weight to three potential sources of wrongness: disrespect, deliberative unfairness in a selection process, and unjust effects. Chapter 2 focuses on the first two of these, which

I characterize as sources of non-contingent wrongness, because when discrimination is wrong because of its disrespectfulness or its deliberative unfairness, then it is wrong independently of its causal consequences. Chapter 3 focuses on the way in which discrimination may have unjust effects, which I regard as a potential source of its contingent wrongness, because when discrimination is wrong for this reason, it is wrong in virtue of its causal consequences. I explain each of these potential sources of the wrongness of discrimination, examine how they interact with each other, and resist various attempts to reduce the wrongness of discrimination to the presence of a single feature.

In Part II of the book, I apply this theory of what makes discrimination wrong to three different contexts of appearance discrimination. Chapter 4 applies it to the context of employment, in particular to decisions concerning who to hire and promote, but it does so whilst considering the extent to which appearance discrimination is analogous to racial discrimination. I argue that there are some important similarities between the two; indeed, I propose that in some cases racial discrimination may be a distinctive kind of appearance discrimination, one that has distinctive origins, is sustained in distinctive ways, and has distinctive effects. These similarities between appearance discrimination and racial discrimination are persuasive in justifying the conclusion that appearance discrimination is wrong in a range of employment decisions, either because it is disrespectful, or because it involves unfairness in selection decisions, or because it has unjust consequences. Even though appearance is a diverse category, and some aspects of appearance involve a degree of choice, it is often wrong for much the same reasons that racial discrimination is wrong.

There are nevertheless important differences between appearance discrimination and racial discrimination that limit the analogy between the two. Appearance discrimination is sometimes rooted in moral judgements about appearance that are reasonable in the sense that they don't deny the fundamental moral equality of persons and are not based on prejudices, but it is hard to find comparable cases of racial discrimination. For example, discrimination against those with tattoos may be rooted in reasonable moral judgements about the sanctity of the natural body. Differences such as these are related to the fact that some aspects of a person's appearance are more under his or her control than his or her racial membership. Even though I argue that the degree of control that a person has over his or her appearance does not have as much significance for the moral assessment of appearance discrimination as it might initially seem, it has some impact on its moral permissibility, especially when we consider cases that involve 'reaction qualifications', that is, qualifications that count as such because of the responses of those with whom the successful candidate will interact in the course of performing the duties associated with the role. Whilst there is generally a strong moral reason not to take into account reaction qualifications rooted in a preference on the part of customers or clients to deal with (or not to deal with) those from a particular racial group, there is often no moral reason not to take into account reaction qualifications rooted in a preference on the part of customers or clients to deal with (or not to deal with) those with a particular appearance. This normative difference, and the explanation for it, is explored in Chapter 5.

In Chapter 6, I move on to consider appearance discrimination in the context of personal relationships, in particular, friendship and romantic partnership. Contrary to one commonly held view, moral considerations are relevant to the assessment of the choices that people make concerning what personal relationships to form, cultivate, and sustain. These decisions can be disrespectful because they may fail to take due account of the moral standing of persons by reducing them to their appearance. This happens when, say, appearance is treated as the only factor that matters in selecting a romantic partner, for example, when potential partners are rejected simply because they fall below some threshold of attractiveness. Decisions about whether to form, cultivate, or sustain a personal relationship can also be harmful in virtue of the role that they play in reducing access to the goods involved in these relationships, which figure as part of many people's conceptions of a life well-lived. Furthermore, in so far as appearance norms are biased against disadvantaged groups, appearance discrimination that tracks these norms may exacerbate the disadvantages members of these groups experience and contribute to lowering their perceived moral status. Although I argue that there are duties not to discriminate on grounds of appearance in the personal sphere, I maintain that they are limited by a personal prerogative that permits individuals to discriminate on these grounds in the context of deciding whether to form a personal relationship of a particular type when they would otherwise struggle to obtain the goods that this type of relationship can provide, or when not doing so would make it impossible for them to form and sustain a relationship of this type.

The third context of appearance discrimination that I shall explore is the ordinary practice of judging and commenting upon people's appearance, which is sometimes called 'everyday lookism'. Social media have amplified the adverse effects of the acts involved in this practice, and cumulatively their consequences can be severe. In Chapter 7, I argue that these acts may be wrong because they are demeaning, or because the appearance norms in which they are rooted are biased in a way that results in everyday lookism exacerbating the unjust disadvantages experienced by various socially salient groups. In a manner that is partly independent, everyday lookism may also be oppressive in virtue of how the costs of complying with appearance norms (or attempting to do so), and the costs of not doing so, combine to impair the autonomy of those governed by them. When everyday lookism is oppressive, the harms that flow from it, especially body anxiety and other adverse psychological effects, such as damage to self-esteem and self-confidence, may also be unjust.

The final part of the book, Part III, considers the issue of how we should respond to appearance discrimination, both when it is morally permissible and when it is morally impermissible. Chapter 8 examines the case for seeking to prevent it, by legislating against it or regulating the practices in which it occurs. I argue that there is a strong argument for legislating against some appearance discrimination in the context of decisions about who to hire or promote. In the other contexts, the case for legislation is much less strong. For example, in relation to discrimination that takes place in the personal sphere, it would be unfeasible to legislate against it in a way that would make its enforcement publicly checkable and respect defendants' right to privacy.

In practice, appearance discrimination will occur, either because it is unfeasible to prevent it or there are good reasons not to seek to do so, or because legislation does not always in practice prevent it from happening. Chapter 9 addresses the question of how we should respond to it when it does occur and contributes to creating unjust outcomes. I argue that compensation, involving measures that provide some recompense to people who experience unjust disadvantages as a result of appearance discrimination, or that provide some remedy for such disadvantages, has a legitimate role to play. In order to determine what level and kinds of compensation are justified, I propose that we should make use of a Dworkinian hypothetical insurance model. Hypothetical insurers would seek to protect themselves against some of the adverse effects that flow from possessing appearance features that others find deeply unappealing, such as facial differences, and the insurance they would purchase might justify the provision of state-funded cosmetic surgery in these cases. In the context of employment, insurers would treat unattractiveness as they do lack of talent, that is, seek to mitigate its worst effects on their career and earning prospects. In response to the potential adverse effects of lack of opportunities to form personal relationships, insurers would protect themselves against social isolation in a way that would justify state-funded or subsidized interventions to create opportunities for social interaction.

Compensation, as a strategy, has its limits, however. Other measures may be more appropriate or more effective at counteracting or reducing the disadvantages that people experience over time as a result of their appearance, and indeed may be morally required in practice. I argue that in order to deal in the most effective way with the unjust disadvantages that result from appearance discrimination, we need to act individually and collectively to reduce the importance of appearance in our societies, and to make appearance norms less demanding and more inclusive, so that it is easier and less costly for those with different kinds of appearance to comply with them.

PART I
WHAT MAKES DISCRIMINATION WRONG?

2
Non-contingent Wrongness

In order to provide a full answer to the question of whether, or when, appearance discrimination is wrong, we need a general theory of what makes discrimination wrong. There is no shortage of such theories. In navigating through them, it is worth making two distinctions, prefigured in the Introduction. First, a distinction between theories that imply that discrimination is non-contingently wrong, that is, wrong independently of its causal consequences (for example, because it is disrespectful or unfair), and those that hold that discrimination is contingently wrong, that is, wrong in virtue of its causal consequences (for example, because it has unjust effects). Second, a distinction between monist theories of what makes discrimination wrong, which maintain that there is only one potential source of its wrongness, that is, only one type of ultimate reason to which appeal can be made in judging that discrimination is wrong, and pluralist theories, which maintain that there are several potential sources of the wrongness of discrimination, that is, more than one type of ultimate reason to which appeal can be made in judging that discrimination is wrong. Pluralist theories can allow that there are a number of non-contingent sources of wrongness, or a number of contingent sources of wrongness, or a mixture of both.

I shall defend a pluralist theory that allows that discrimination may be wrong for either non-contingent or contingent reasons, or both: it may be wrong because it is disrespectful or involves deliberative unfairness; or it may be wrong because it contributes to unjust effects; or it may be wrong for some combination of these reasons. This chapter focuses on the non-contingent reasons, that is, reasons that appeal to discrimination's disrespectfulness and its deliberative unfairness, whereas the next chapter focuses on the contingent reasons, that is, reasons that appeal to its contribution to unjust effects. I shall build the theory by reference to examples of racial discrimination rather than appearance discrimination, partly because we are much more confident in our intuitions about the former, and partly because, as I shall argue in Chapter 4, there is a fruitful analogy between appearance discrimination and racial discrimination. I shall focus mainly on discrimination in the context of appointments to advantaged social position, although as we shall see in later chapters, the principles I defend have more general application. As I remarked in the Introduction, those who have little interest in general theories of what makes discrimination wrong can skip this Part of the book and go straight to the later chapters, where I apply the theory that I develop to contexts in which appearance discrimination occurs. These later chapters should still be intelligible even though my detailed reasons for endorsing the particular theory of wrongful discrimination that I do will not be presented in them.

2.1 Some Preliminaries

2.1.1 'Discriminating Against' and 'Discriminating on the Basis Of'

The term 'discrimination' is used to express different concepts.[1] For the most part I shall employ the notions of 'discriminating against someone' and 'discriminating on the basis of some property or characteristic'. Rather than engaging in an extended conceptual analysis of these notions, I shall simply stipulate that A discriminates against P if and only if A treats P less favourably than Q either because P has some characteristic C that Q lacks or because A believes that P has some characteristic C that Q lacks, where Q is an actual or possible person. According to this definition, A may discriminate against P without intending to do so, and indeed without being conscious of doing so, thus it accommodates cases of non-conscious or implicit bias.[2] Furthermore, this definition allows that A may discriminate against P because she believes that P has some characteristic C even though P in fact lacks C. I shall also stipulate that A discriminates against P *on the basis of X* if and only if A discriminates against P because P has some X-type characteristic that Q lacks, or because A believes that P has some X-type characteristic that Q lacks.[3] When I refer to X-type discrimination (for example,

---

[1] See Lippert-Rasmussen, *Born Free and Equal?*, Part I, for a systematic analysis of these concepts.

[2] See J. Holroyd, 'The Social Psychology of Discrimination', in K. Lippert-Rasmussen (ed.), *The Routledge Handbook of the Ethics of Discrimination* (London: Routledge, 2017).

[3] Lawrence Blum thinks that the expression 'discrimination on the basis of X' is often misleading, on the grounds that it suggests a kind of moral symmetry that doesn't generally obtain (see L. Blum, 'Racial and Other Asymmetries: A Problem for the Protected Categories Framework for Anti-Discrimination Thought', in D. Hellman and S. Moreau (eds) *Philosophical*

racial discrimination), I mean discrimination against a person or group because of their possession of some X-type characteristic, or because they are believed to possess some X-type characteristic. Note that these definitions allow that a person may be discriminated against because he or she possesses a particular combination of characteristics, for example, because she is both Black and a woman, in other words, characteristic C, and the relevant X-type characteristic on the basis of which a person suffers discrimination, may be complex, in the way that theorists of intersectionality argue is often the case.[4]

My stipulative definition of what it is to discriminate against a person is simpler than some careful conceptual analyses that have been proposed. For instance, it does not require that C be the property of being a member of a socially salient group, that is, a group the perceived membership of which is 'important to the structure of social interactions across a wide range of social contexts'.[5] Kasper Lippert-Rasmussen may be correct that as a result such a definition departs from ordinary usage. He suggests that the restriction of the scope of discrimination to cases where there is differential treatment on the basis of membership of a socially salient group explains why we do not talk about discrimination against unqualified applicants for jobs, or against those who do not belong to our family when, for example, we take only our own children on holiday with us.[6] But it doesn't much matter in the end whether my definition adequately captures our ordinary notion of 'discriminating against'. For my purposes, what matters ultimately are the normative issues concerning whether, and when, differential treatment on the basis of appearance is wrong. My definition allows us to ask whether discrimination against someone on the basis of an aspect of their appearance is wrong without needing to worry about whether those who share this

---

Foundations of Discrimination Law (Oxford: Oxford University Press, 2013), 183–4. When we refer to discrimination on the basis of sex, this might seem to suggest that discriminating against men is just as morally problematic as discriminating against women. So too talk of discrimination on the basis of race might seem to suggest that discriminating against white people is just as morally problematic as discriminating against Black people. Blum thinks we can avoid this misleading implication by using the locution 'discrimination against P' instead of the locution 'discrimination on the basis of X'. But (as Blum would accept) there is no strict logical implication here; provided we are careful we need not fall into the trap that he has identified.

[4] See Crenshaw, 'Demarginalizing the Intersection of Race and Sex'.
[5] Lippert-Rasmussen, *Born Free and Equal?*, 30.
[6] See Lippert-Rasmussen, *Born Free and Equal?*, 34. Nor do we talk about discriminating against those drivers who are fined because they have not paid the fee to park in a carpark: see A. Sangiovanni, *Humanity without Dignity. Moral Equality, Respect, and Human Rights* (Cambridge, MA: Harvard University Press, 2017), 117. For further discussion, see Eidelson, *Discrimination and Disrespect*, 26ff.

aspect form a socially salient group, which on Lippert-Rasmussen's definition would be necessary before we could claim that they are subject to discrimination.

Even though there is often a presumption in ordinary discourse that discrimination is wrong, the definition I am adopting is morally neutral because it leaves open the question of whether A treats P wrongfully when A discriminates against P. In some cases, discrimination, understood in the way I propose, will be morally permissible. For example, if A is selecting for a job, and C is a characteristic that would make it hard for P to do that job well, in general at least, A treats P in a morally permissible way by counting P's possession of C as a reason not to appoint him or her. Furthermore, the definition that I am adopting does not prejudge the question of whether positive discrimination, that is, discrimination *in favour of* members of disadvantaged groups, is morally permissible or even sometimes morally required.

2.1.2 Non-contingent Wrongness versus Intrinsic Wrongness

As I have suggested, it is worth distinguishing between theories that imply that discrimination is non-contingently wrong when it is wrong, that is, wrong independently of its causal consequences, and those that hold that discrimination is only contingently wrong when it is wrong, that is, wrong as a result of its causal consequences. Note, however, that non-contingent wrongness is not the same as *intrinsic* wrongness. An act of discrimination is non-contingently wrong if and only if it is wrong independently of its causal consequences, whereas it is intrinsically wrong if and only if it is wrong solely in virtue of its intrinsic or constitutive properties, that is, properties that it has independently of its relationships with other things.[7] It is therefore conceptually possible, at least, for an act to be non-contingently but extrinsically wrong, for example, an act may be non-contingently wrong in virtue of the disrespect it involves, but one might take the view that its disrespectfulness makes it wrong only when it has unjust consequences. Later in the chapter, I shall also suggest that a discriminatory act may be

---

[7] For the related distinction between intrinsic and non-instrumental value, see C. Korsgaard, 'Two Distinctions in Goodness', in her *Creating the Kingdom of Ends* (Cambridge: Cambridge University Press, 1996); J. Dancy, *Ethics without Principles* (Oxford: Oxford University Press, 2004), ch. 9.

non-contingently wrong because it is demeaning, but nevertheless be extrinsically rather than intrinsically wrong because its demeaning character is determined in part by the social and historical context in which it takes place.

2.1.3 Mechanisms of Discrimination

Let me distinguish two contrasting ways in which discrimination may occur. Selectors may have a preference not to appoint those who belong to a particular racial group because of a *prejudice* about them, for example, a belief that members of this group are untrustworthy even though the evidence provides no support for that belief. Miranda Fricker characterizes prejudices as 'judgements, which may have a positive or negative valence, and which display some...resistance to counter-evidence owing to some affective investment on the part of the subject'.[8] I shall use the term 'prejudice' differently, to encompass any unwarranted belief or 'psychological association' concerning people who possess some property or characteristic, for example, the belief that women are emotionally unstable, even if the holder of it has no affective investment in that belief or association and merely subscribes to it unreflectively.

Prejudices about those who possess a particular property or characteristic may be internalized as a stereotype, that is, as a set of beliefs or associations relating to the 'normal' member of that group. These beliefs and associations may be non-conscious and people may be influenced by them when making decisions in ways that they are unaware, and indeed may in good faith mistakenly deny that they are prejudiced. In other words, prejudices may lead to implicit biases against members of groups, which in turn may result in discriminatory treatment.[9]

---

[8] M. Fricker, *Epistemic Injustice: Power and the Ethics of Knowing* (Oxford: Oxford University Press, 2007), 35.

[9] There are wide-ranging debates among psychologists and philosophers concerning the best way of conceptualizing implicit bias, and of explaining precisely how it operates in practice. For an overview of the issues, see J. Holroyd, R. Scaife, and T. Stafford, 'What Is Implicit Bias?', *Philosophy Compass* 12 (2017). Here I try to remain neutral on the question of whether we should conceptualize stereotypes as combinations of beliefs or as associations that have a different logical character, and on the issue of whether they include as part of their nature an affective dimension. For further discussion, see T. Gendler, 'Alief and Belief', *Journal of Philosophy* 105 (2008): 634–63; E. Mandelbaum, 'Attitude, Inference, Association: On the Propositional Structure of Implicit Bias', *Nous* 50 (2016): 629–58; S. Leslie, 'The Original Sin of Cognition: Fear, Prejudice, and Generalization', *Journal of Philosophy* 114 (2017): 393–421.

A prejudice may also be part of a network of beliefs and associations that involve or presuppose a belief in the moral inferiority of those who belong to a group, rather than merely a belief or non-conscious association that links the group with an undesirable property. For example, a prejudice that the members of a particular racial group are untrustworthy might be underpinned by the belief that they lack a characteristic, such as the capacity to act morally, that is required for them to be moral equals, or a belief that they lack this characteristic to the required degree, with that being thought to explain their supposed untrustworthiness.

In some cases, however, a selector's preference not to appoint those who belong to a particular racial group might not be the product, even in part, of stereotypes about the group, or beliefs about, or associations between, the group and negative qualities. Selectors may have a *non-rational response* towards people who belong to it, without having prejudices about them, that is, selectors may have responses towards members of this racial group for which they have no motivating reason, not even an unjustified reason, and which are not a product of associating negative traits with membership of it. In such cases the responses that drive the discrimination are akin to the automatic reactions that people display in response to certain phenomena, for example, the reaction of withdrawing one's hand from a hot surface, although, unlike that case, they may instead be caused by aversions or feelings that are a product of social relations. Non-rational responses may sometimes be a cause of prejudices, but they do not necessarily lead to their formation.

Consider a potential example. Selectors may experience feelings of unease or discomfort in the presence of members of a racial group—and may even feel threatened by differences in behaviour and deportment—that arise as a consequence of informal segregation that reduces the character and frequency of encounters between members of different racial groups.[10] As a result of such feelings, selectors may be biased against members of this racial group when they are assessing candidates, perhaps judging their qualifications to be less good than equivalent qualifications held by candidates from other racial groups, without having any motivating reason for their bias. We might say that they prefer not to interact with members of this group, but their preference would be revealed in their behaviour and it would not be motivating that behaviour. They do not have reasons for their

---

[10] See E. Anderson, *The Imperative of Integration* (Princeton, NJ: Princeton University Press, 2010), especially 35–8. See also Sangiovanni, *Humanity without Dignity*, 124.

behaviour, even though it can be explained by reference to their feelings and their past experience, which are themselves a product of social relations. Their biases do not operate through non-conscious associations between that group and undesirable characteristics, or through conscious generalizations.

I shall refer to the two mechanisms of discrimination that I have distinguished as 'racial discrimination involving prejudice' and 'racial discrimination rooted purely in non-rational reactions'.[11] In both of them, the discrimination involved seems to be wrong. But what makes it so, and is it wrong in both types of case for the very same reasons? The literature contains a number of theories of what makes discrimination wrong (when it is wrong) that I shall draw upon, beginning in the next section with a class of theories that suppose that discrimination is wrong when it involves disrespect.

2.2 Disrespect

Among cases of racial discrimination that involve prejudice, consider those that are rooted in a belief that the members of a racial group are inferior because they do not possess the characteristics required to be considered as moral equals. Here it seems clear that there is wrong-doing, but in what does the wrong-doing consist? One view would be that these acts of discrimination are wrongful because they are *disrespectful*, that is, they fail to respect their victims.[12] This locates a source of genuine moral concern with these acts, but it does not enable us to pinpoint it.

One way of making it more precise would be to say that an act of discrimination is wrong in virtue of being disrespectful when it involves a *false belief* about the moral status of those who are the victims of it. For example, Larry Alexander maintains that '[w]hen a person is incorrectly judged to be of lesser moral worth and is treated accordingly that treatment is morally wrong regardless of the gravity of its effects'.[13] Locating the disrespect in a

---

[11] This is somewhat misleading because 'discrimination involving prejudice' may be ultimately rooted in non-rational reactions. As I propose to understand it, the category of 'discrimination rooted purely in non-rational reactions' excludes such cases.

[12] For an overview of theories that appeal to this idea, see E. Beeghly, 'Discrimination and Disrespect', in K. Lippert-Rasmussen (ed.), *The Routledge Handbook of the Ethics of Discrimination* (London: Routledge, 2017).

[13] L. Alexander, 'What Makes Wrongful Discrimination Wrong? Biases, Preferences, Stereotypes, and Proxies', *University of Pennsylvania Law Review* 141 (1992): 149–219, at 15.

false belief about moral status has some counter-intuitive consequences, however, which can be drawn out by considering a pair of cases devised by Kasper Lippert-Rasmussen.[14] In both of these cases a scientist engages in painful and inessential experimentation on non-human animals for the benefit of humans. In the first case the person believes that non-human animals are of lesser moral status than human beings and this in part explains why he or she engages in the experimentation, whereas in the second case he or she believes that human beings and non-human animals are of equal moral status but engages in the experimentation despite that belief. Let us then suppose that the truth is that human beings and non-human animals are of equal moral status. If discrimination is wrong when it is rooted in a false belief about moral inferiority, then the discrimination involved in the first case would be worse in at least one respect, but intuitively it doesn't seem to be. (If anything, the discrimination in the second case seems more morally troubling.)

An alternative way of pinpointing the disrespect involved in acts of discrimination that seems to avoid this problem with locating it in the possession of false beliefs about moral inferiority would be to locate it in the agent's deliberations. The underlying general idea would be the same, namely, that an act of discrimination is wrong when it is disrespectful. But the distinctive thought would be that an act of discrimination is disrespectful in the relevant way when the agent who performs it does not take due account of the victims' moral status or standing.[15] He or she may do so either by *not attributing* to the victims the characteristics in virtue of which they have that standing or by *not giving due weight to the victims' possession of these characteristics*, for example, by disregarding or ignoring the victims'

---

[14] K. Lippert-Rasmussen, 'The Badness of Discrimination', *Ethical Theory and Moral Practice* 9 (2006): 167–85, at 182–4; K. Lippert-Rasmussen, 'Respect and Discrimination', in H. Hurd (ed.), *Moral Puzzles and Legal Perplexities: Essays on the Influence of Larry Alexander* (Cambridge: Cambridge University Press, 2018), 317–32.

[15] Different accounts of what provides persons with their moral standing are possible. We might think that what matters is the possession of a capacity (at or above some threshold level) to set one's own ends or lead one's own life in one's own way, or a capacity to act on the basis of reasons, including moral reasons (again, at or above some threshold level), or some combination of these capacities. In any such account, there will be difficulties in justifying the significance that is attached to a particular capacity or set of capacities, in setting the threshold, and in explaining why differences in the extent to which persons possess these capacities above the threshold do not affect one's moral status. See J. Waldron, *One Another's Equals. The Basis of Human Equality* (Cambridge, MA: Harvard University Press, 2017) for relevant discussion, especially ch. 3. I do not grapple with these issues in this book, and try to remain as neutral as possible in relation to them, but there are some places where I conveniently help myself to a particular account, one that appeals to the possession of a capacity for personal autonomy.

possession of them, or by treating them as if they lacked these characteristics or were unlikely to employ them appropriately.

The failure to be respectful in either of these ways seems to involve a distinctive kind of non-contingent wrong-doing that supplies us with a reason to object to it, even if it does not harm its victims and even if giving respect would lead to worse outcomes overall.[16] For example, suppose that a woman is rejected for a job because due weight is not given to her moral status but she is subsequently appointed to a better job elsewhere, one that she would not have applied for had she not been rejected. The discrimination she suffers seems wrongful even though it does not harm her.[17] This account of what it is to treat another with respect seems to avoid the problem raised by Lippert-Rasmussen's pair of cases, since it implies in both of them that the scientist fails to respect the non-human animals on which he or she experiments but without implying that the disrespect he or she shows to them must be worse in the case of the discrimination that involves a false belief about moral status.

According to the account I am considering, selectors show disrespect in making a decision about whether to hire a particular candidate when they do not take due account of her moral standing, perhaps by giving less weight than they should to her possession of the characteristics in virtue of which she has that standing. It might be thought, however, that this neglects a distinctive aspect of the wrong that is done to her when she is treated disrespectfully in this way. When such discrimination takes place in selection decisions, the victims are not treated as moral equals; they are treated as *morally inferior* to those who do not suffer the discrimination. They are treated disrespectfully in a way that is comparative: the selector fails to attribute to the victims the characteristics in virtue of which they have that standing whilst attributing those characteristics to others who do not suffer the discrimination; or the selector gives less weight to the victims' possession of these characteristics than to the possession of them by others who do not suffer the discrimination. In doing so, the selector is treating them in a manner that denies their *equal* moral standing. This makes the act of discrimination worse in one way than an act that involves a failure to give

---

[16] We might say that the wrong-doing consists, in part, in a failure to provide those who are wronged with recognition respect, where recognition respect is 'a disposition to weigh appropriately in one's deliberation some feature of the things in question and to act accordingly' (S. Darwall, 'Two Kinds of Respect', *Ethics* 88 (1977): 36–49, at 38. See also Eidelson, *Discrimination and Disrespect*, 103).

[17] See A. Slavny and T. Parr, 'Harmless Discrimination', *Legal Theory* 21 (2015): 100–14.

respect that is wholly non-comparative in character, for example, when it involves failing to take due account of each and every person's standing, perhaps by treating them all as if they were incapable of making their own decisions.

The account I am considering, when it incorporates the idea of comparative disrespect, seems to me to best capture the ways in which an act of discrimination may be wrongful in virtue of being disrespectful. I shall adopt it as part of a pluralist theory of what makes discrimination wrong. According to it, an agent may act disrespectfully in discriminating against the members of a group without believing that they are morally inferior because he or she may disregard their possession of the characteristics necessary to be moral equals despite attributing those characteristics to them.[18] The decision-making of selectors may even exhibit a kind of weakness of the will in the face of social expectations, for example, they may fail to attach the significance they know they should to the possession of these characteristics because they simply conform to the racist expectations prevalent in their society. Because the failure to give someone respect does not require a belief that he or she lacks the relevant characteristics, it may also be involved in acts of discrimination that are rooted purely in non-rational aversions. For example, a medical practitioner may be distracted by feelings of intense discomfort at treating a member of a racial group that they do not normally encounter that they fail to seek his or her consent for a risky medical procedure.

But is an act of discrimination that involves a failure of respect more wrongful when it is rooted in a mistaken belief about the moral standing of the members of a group? Let us suppose that a man is culpable for his mistaken belief because he has failed to consider properly the relevant arguments or evidence for their moral equality, even though these are available to him. In arriving at a conclusion here, it might seem that it matters whether we use Gibbard's objective sense of 'wrong' or his subjective sense.[19] But even the objective sense that I have so far been employing permits us to say that in a case where a man is culpable for his mistaken belief, his discriminatory act is more wrongful *because* his culpability makes a difference to our moral assessment of the act.[20] If we address the issue from the perspective of Gibbard's subjective sense of wrong, according to which we judge an act's wrongness in the light of what the agent has good reason

---

[18] See Eidelson, *Discrimination and Disrespect*, 103. [19] See Section 1.3.
[20] This would, however, compete with the different view that his act is no more wrongful, but that there is a difference in his blameworthiness.

to believe, then the wrongness of his act may be affected in a different way by his culpability for his mistaken beliefs. If he is culpable for them because he had good reason to believe that the members of the group had equal moral status, then we are entitled to draw the conclusion that his failure of respect is wrongful in the subjective sense, whereas it would not be wrongful at all in that sense if he did not have the relevant arguments or evidence available to him in the particular historical and social environment he inhabits.

Is an act of discrimination more wrongful (in either the objective or subjective sense) when it is rooted in a culpably mistaken belief in the moral inferiority of the victims than it would be if the agent believed in their moral equality, but discriminated against them because he or she conformed to the racist expectations of his or her society due to culpable weakness of the will, and as a result failed to give due weight to their moral standing? Our intuitions here seem finely balanced when all else is equal. Suppose, however, that the agent, with wilful defiance, refuses to act upon his or her correct belief in their moral equality in a way that shows contempt for their moral status rather than mere weakness of the will.[21] Other things being equal, an act of discrimination that shows contempt in this way does seem more wrongful (in both the objective and subjective senses) than one that displays mere weakness of the will, analogous perhaps to the way in which harm that is caused intentionally is more wrongful than harm that is caused recklessly but unintentionally.

Another particularly important way in which a selector may fail to treat the members of a group respectfully without believing that they lack the relevant characteristics is by not taking into account, or not giving due weight to, the meaning of his or her behaviour in the particular social and historical context in which it takes place. I regard this as the central insight of Deborah Hellman's account of what makes discrimination wrong.[22] She in effect argues that discrimination is non-contingently wrong when it demeans the victims of it, where '[t]o demean is to treat another as not fully human or not of equal moral worth'.[23] A person can treat others as if they

---

[21] Cf. Eidelson, *Discrimination and Disrespect*, 106.
[22] D. Hellman, *When Is Discrimination Wrong?* (Cambridge, MA: Harvard University Press, 2008).
[23] Hellman, *When Is Discrimination Wrong?*, 35. In fact, she regards demeaning discrimination as intrinsically wrong, but in my terms her view is better characterized as the claim that demeaning discrimination is non-contingently wrong. Andrea Sangiovanni regards the account he offers of why discrimination is wrong as relevantly similar to Hellman's because it appeals to the idea that discrimination is wrong, inter alia, when and because it expresses

lack equal moral worth without intending to do so, and indeed without believing that they have less moral value, by discriminating against them in a way that expresses the attitude, or conveys the message, that they are inferior.[24] Moreover, this can happen without the victims, or indeed any bystanders, regarding the behaviour as demeaning. Hellman maintains that in order to demean another person, you need to have sufficient power over them to be able to put them down or subordinate them through your actions. In practice the possession of that power is likely to be facilitated by the victim's being a member of a disadvantaged group, and it will be hard, perhaps impossible sometimes, to demean someone who has power over you. She argues that discriminatory treatment may be demeaning when it is placed in the context of past or present wrongful practices. As a result of these practices, and the power relations they involve, an act of discrimination may send out the message that the victims, and the group to which they belong, are inferior.[25]

Identifying the message conveyed by an act of discrimination involves interpreting the meaning of the act in the light of the past and present treatment of the group or groups to which the victims belong.[26] It might therefore be thought that when discrimination is wrong in virtue of acts of discrimination that are demeaning, then it must be contingently wrong since its wrongness depends upon the social and historical context in which these acts take place.[27] But here we should make use of the distinction between claiming that an act is non-contingently wrong and maintaining that it is intrinsically wrong. If an act of discrimination is wrong in virtue of the demeaning message it conveys, then that would seem to make it extrinsically rather than intrinsically wrong, since its wrongfulness depends on the social and historical context in which it takes place. However, it would nevertheless be non-contingently wrong since its wrongfulness is independent of its causal consequences, because the message conveyed by a practice or

---

demeaning attitudes. But Sangiovanni's account is better seen as locating the wrongness of discrimination in its unjust consequences because, according to him, discrimination is wrong because those who demean others by discriminating in ways that stigmatize, dehumanize, infantilize, objectify, and instrumentalize them set back their interest in creating and sustaining an integral sense of self. See Sangiovanni, *Humanity without Dignity*, especially ch. 3.

[24] Scanlon also expresses some sympathy for the view that 'decisions that we call discriminatory are objectionable because they involve a kind of insult—an expression of the view that certain people are inferior or socially unacceptable' (T. Scanlon, *Moral Dimensions: Permissibility, Meaning, Blame* (Cambridge, MA: Harvard University Press, 2008), 72).

[25] Hellman, *When Is Discrimination Wrong?*, 35.

[26] Hellman, *When Is Discrimination Wrong?*, ch. 3.

[27] See Eidelson, *Discrimination and Disrespect*, 74.

the individual acts that constitute it does not depend upon that message being received or even understood by those who comply with the norm—indeed those who are demeaned need not *feel* demeaned—or by those who participate in the practice of which it is part.

2.3 Deliberative Unfairness

According to the account I have been defending, an act of discrimination is wrong if it is disrespectful. An act of discrimination is disrespectful when the agent who performs it fails to take due account of the victims' moral standing, for example, by treating them as if they lacked the characteristics in virtue of which they have that standing. It might seem that *whenever* we fail to give people's interests the weight that they ought to receive, we are treating them as if they lack the characteristics in virtue of which they have their moral standing, and therefore, on the account I am defending, we are treating them disrespectfully. But sometimes the failure to give the weight we should to a person's interests does not amount to treating them as if they lack those characteristics. Suppose, for example, that a doctor is in a rush to get home and uncharacteristically ignores one of her patient's symptoms, incorrectly judging that he does not need to be tested for some disease, with the result that she misdiagnoses the cause of his illness. In consequence, she gives his interests less weight than they should receive. If this is a simple mistake, it seems incorrect to say that the doctor has treated the patient as if he lacked the characteristics on the basis of which he has his moral standing. But irrespective of whether the doctor has treated him disrespectfully, she has treated him *unfairly* when distributing medical care simply because she has not given his interests the weight that she should and she has given them less weight that the interests of her other patients.

The deliberative unfairness that is potentially involved in the allocation of a good seems key to understanding when discrimination in a selection process for jobs or other advantaged social positions is wrongful. It reflects the general idea that those involved in distributing a good deliberate unfairly when they give less weight than they should to the interests of some subset of potential recipients of it compared to the rest.[28] A process of dis-

---

[28] Compare Lawrence Blum's claim that when professors are grading work 'favoring students who meet an arbitrary criterion (e.g., that they sit [at] the front of the classroom) is a case of unfair discrimination and wrongness pure and simple' (Blum, 'Racial and other Asymmetries', 196 n. 29).

tributing a good may be unfair independently of the outcomes it produces, or tends to produce, because it gives less weight than it should to the interests of some people who would benefit from receiving that good compared to the interests of others.[29] What counts as giving due weight to the interests of potential recipients of a good may depend upon a number of factors, such as the nature of that good, its social significance, the ownership relations within which its distribution takes place and whether or not they are just, and the broader distribution of benefits and burdens to which it contributes.

Consider a homespun example of a kind that is familiar from discussions of fair distribution. Suppose that you have baked a cake for your sister's birthday, with ingredients that you bought and legitimately own. You give your brother the responsibility to cut the cake and distribute it among family members. Deliberative fairness in this context is inconsistent with your brother giving weight to his own prejudices about particular family members in allocating bits of the cake, and indeed with him giving weight to his own particular ethical judgements about whether they lead successful lives. But deliberative fairness seems consistent with your brother allocating a larger piece of cake to your sister on the grounds that it is her birthday that is being celebrated, or indeed with you instructing your brother to give you a larger slice on the grounds that you baked it and paid for the ingredients.

With respect to jobs, what counts as giving due weight to the interests of each candidate is affected by the ownership relations involved. When these relations are reasonably just at least, giving due weight to the interests of each candidate permits selectors acting on behalf of an employer to give considerable weight to the employer's interests, but seriously limits the weight that it is permissible for selectors to give to their own interests. At the minimum, it requires that a selector not be influenced by his or her own prejudices or non-rational reactions, or by his or her own particular moral and aesthetic judgements concerning the characteristics of candidates, in a way that would disadvantage some candidates. This idea is faithful to the moral phenomenology of rejection: people who believe that they have been unsuccessful in an application for a job as a result of a selector's prejudices, or his or her personal moral or aesthetic judgements concerning their characteristics, often *resent* the treatment they have received, independently of whether they end up with equivalent or better jobs elsewhere, and

---

[29] Even though a process of deliberation may be unfair independently of its outcome, it may be worse, or be more unfair, when it affects that outcome, for example, by denying a candidate a particular job opportunity.

independently of whether they belong to a group that has been systematically disadvantaged. Those who deny that an unsuccessful applicant has been treated unfairly in such circumstances will struggle to explain these reactive attitudes in a way that does not involve to some extent debunking them.

I should emphasize that by 'a selector', I mean a person occupying a particular role within an organization. A selector may also occupy other roles—for example, she may be the employer, or a potential future colleague, or both—but she need not be. Her role within a company might be simply to serve on selection committees. My claim is, in effect, that when a person is occupying the role of selector, deliberative fairness requires that she give no weight in selection decisions to her own prejudices, interests, or personal moral or aesthetic judgements about the candidates' characteristics, at least when doing so would disadvantage some of them, for otherwise she would not be giving due weight to their interests. But in so far as the selector is also the employer or a potential future colleague, then it may be that she can give significant weight to her interests as an occupant of one or both of these other roles without that meaning that she has given the interests of candidates less weight than they are due.[30]

Giving due weight to each candidate's interests may permit selectors to promote wider justice-related goals when these goals can be served by selecting on the basis of a particular attribute that cannot justifiably be regarded as a qualification. So deliberative fairness may be consistent, in principle, with selectors taking part in an affirmative action programme: giving due weight to the interests of each candidate may be consistent with the selectors giving weight to membership of a marginalized group in order to bring about greater justice for members of this group in the future, or to redress the injustices they have experienced in the past. But if selectors are to give due weight to the interests of each candidate in the context of an affirmative action programme of this kind, then at the very least this requires that their decisions not be influenced by their prejudices, their non-rational reactions, or their own personal moral or aesthetic judgements about the candidates' characteristics.

Although what counts as deliberative fairness in the process of selecting for jobs may in various ways be affected by wider considerations of justice, it is not wholly determined by reference to what constitutes a just overall distribution of benefits and burdens. On a reductive view, whether a distribution of jobs is deliberatively fair depends solely on whether it contributes

---

[30] I return to these issues in Chapters 4 and 5.

to the production of a just overall distribution of benefits and burdens, and the rules that ought to be followed in distributing jobs are identified by considering what rules, if generally followed, will tend to lead to such a distribution. On the view I am defending, deliberative fairness is an independent consideration that is conditioned by the justice of the wider practices of which it is part, including the justice of the ownership relations involved in them, but it is not wholly determined by whether or not the rules for allocating jobs contribute to, or are conducive to creating, a just overall distribution of benefits and burdens.[31] Furthermore, fairness in allocating a particular job matters independently of whether a person obtains an equivalent or better job elsewhere as a result of succeeding in a different selection process.

How does the notion of deliberative fairness that I have been unpacking relate to two other ideas that are sometimes thought to provide a moral basis for assessing selection processes for jobs, namely, the meritocratic idea that the best-qualified applicant for a job deserves it, and the idea that in a broadly meritocratic society the best-qualified applicants have a legitimate expectation that they will be appointed?

The meritocratic principle that the best-qualified applicant deserves the job can be seen as a particular way of interpreting the idea of deliberative fairness.[32] According to this principle, it is unfair when selectors are influenced by their own non-rational responses, prejudices, or personal moral or aesthetic judgements concerning the candidates, because the best-qualified candidate *deserves* to be appointed, and being influenced in these ways creates a risk that the best-qualified candidate will not receive his or her just deserts. This appeal to a pre-institutional notion of desert is controversial, however, as are other such attempts to justify the idea that the best-qualified candidate for a job has a moral claim to it or that there is a *pro tanto* moral reason to appoint him or her to it. Since I do not need to make use of this

---

[31] This is consistent with supposing that the distribution of the benefits and burdens that jobs provide (such as the job satisfaction they may involve, and the salaries they pay) is ultimately governed, morally speaking, by principles of justice that regulate the distributions of benefits and burdens more generally. So it is consistent not only with what Simon Caney calls 'Moderate Integrationism' but also with what he calls 'Strong Integrationism'. See S. Caney, 'Climate Change', in S. Olsaretti (ed.), *The Oxford Handbook of Distributive Justice* (Oxford: Oxford University Press, 2018), 664–88, at 672–3.

[32] For defences of it, see D. Miller, *Principles of Social Justice* (Cambridge, MA: Harvard University Press, 1999), ch. 8; T. Mulligan, *Justice and the Meritocratic State* (New York: Routledge, 2018), ch. 5. For relevant discussion, see N. Dobos, 'The Duty to Hire on Merit: Mapping the Terrain', *Journal of Value Inquiry* 50 (2016): 353–68; S. Segall, 'Should the Best Qualified Be Appointed?', *Journal of Moral Philosophy* 9 (2012): 31–54.

idea in what follows, I shall put to one side the issue of whether it is defensible.

The idea of legitimate expectations is also compatible with, and can inform, the notion of deliberative fairness. When there is an established practice of distributing benefits on a particular basis, and that practice is morally permissible, then the legitimate expectations that are thereby created provide a weighty reason of fairness for continuing to distribute these benefits on that basis. In any society in which there is an established practice of making appointments to jobs and other advantaged positions on the basis of qualifications, the candidates have a legitimate expectation that selection will take place on this basis, at least when there is no moral requirement that a less well-qualified candidate be appointed. When selection does not take place on this basis, for example, because of prejudices about, or non-rational responses towards, the members of a racial group, then those who are thereby disadvantaged are treated unfairly because their interests are not given the weight that they can legitimately expect them to be given. Even when racial and other forms of discrimination are common in a society, to the extent that they are frowned upon in codes of practice, and there are public declarations of commitment to selecting on the basis of qualifications, there will be a legitimate expectation that appointments are made on this basis. (Of course, this legitimate expectation may be outweighed under some circumstances, for example, when an important public purpose is served by giving weight to other considerations, such as a person's race, in the way that defenders of affirmative action may justifiably claim. In that case, deliberative fairness is consistent with selecting candidates in a manner that goes against their legitimate expectations.)

2.4 Concluding Remarks

In this chapter, I have identified two potential sources of the wrongness of discrimination: first, the way in which it may be disrespectful, and second, the way in which it may involve deliberative unfairness. These are sources of non-contingent wrongness, that is, sources of wrongness that are independent of the causal effects of discrimination. Each of them has a role to play in a pluralist theory of what makes discrimination wrong. In the next chapter, I shall examine the way in which discrimination may be wrong in virtue of its contribution to the creation of unjust effects, that is, the way in which it may be contingently wrong.

3
Contingent Wrongness

As we saw in the previous chapter, discrimination may be non-contingently wrong because it involves disrespect or deliberative unfairness. But discrimination may also, or instead, be contingently wrong because of its role in generating unjust consequences. In this chapter, I shall explore the two main ways in which discrimination may be wrong in virtue of the outcomes it promotes. First, it may contribute to creating an unjust distribution of benefits and burdens, for example, by playing a part in depriving the victims of goods that they need in order to flourish. Second, it may contribute to lowering the perceived moral status of a group, that is, it may play a part in creating a society in which the members of a group are widely regarded and treated as morally inferior.[1] Importantly, it may do so by reinforcing the power structures that help to sustain an unjust distribution of benefits and burdens or that facilitate lowering the perceived moral status of members of a group, for example, by appointing people to positions of power who share the same prejudices or have the same negative non-rational responses. My account thus makes space for the idea that acts of discrimination may be wrong in virtue of their role in creating or reinforcing structural injustices.

3.1 Individual Wrong-Doing and Blameworthiness

Generally speaking, it is not any particular person's discriminatory acts that cause an unjust outcome, and there is nothing we could do, as individuals, to prevent an unjust outcome from being brought about when it is created

---

[1] It may do so, in part, by fostering differences in social status or social standing, that is, differences in the way in which groups are ranked in a society. Differences in social status need not involve any denial of fundamental moral equality (see K. Lippert-Rasmussen, *Relational Egalitarianism. Living as Equals* (Cambridge: Cambridge University Press, 2018), 65–7.) But when these differences do not reflect differences in the contributions that people make to a society, or the efforts they expend, then they are likely to play a role in fostering a state of affairs in which the members of a group are regarded and treated not merely as socially inferior, but also as morally inferior.

What's Wrong with Lookism? Personal Appearance, Discrimination, and Disadvantage. Andrew Mason, Oxford University Press. © Andrew Mason 2023. DOI: 10.1093/oso/9780192859792.003.0003

by numerous people engaging in such acts, supported by structures that facilitate their behaviour. As I noted in Section 1.4, in these circumstances what we do, as individuals, often makes no serious difference to whether an unjust outcome is brought about or to the degree of injustice it involves. Even when that is the case, however, a person may be acting wrongfully because what they do plays a small part in producing the unjust outcome and is wrongful because its moral significance derives from that contribution.[2] But what about cases in which the outcome is overdetermined, and what a person does makes no difference at all to whether it is brought about or to the degree of injustice it involves? It may be that in the objective sense of 'wrong' that I am employing, according to which an action is wrong if it is wrong in light of all the facts, both knowable and unknowable (see Section 1.3), they do not act wrongly. There is room for doubt, however, concerning how many cases in practice fall into this category. There are many ways in which we can make a small contribution to an unjust outcome, for example, our ways of behaving may reinforce the power structures that facilitate creating or sustaining an unjust distribution or that facilitate lowering the perceived moral status of members of a group.[3] In these cases, so long as the power structures concerned are not already maximally resilient, how we are behaving does make a difference, albeit a very small one.

It is important to recall that the objective sense of moral wrongness loosens the connection between moral wrongness and culpability. Playing a part in producing an unjust outcome, where the moral significance of one's actions derives from the fact that one is doing so, need not be blameworthy in any way. A person who contributes to an unjust outcome may be unaware that their actions are playing this role or have this significance, and their ignorance may be entirely non-culpable, even though their actions are wrongful in the objective sense. The cases with which I am concerned, where people create an unjust outcome by engaging in individual acts of discrimination, often unaware of how their behaviour is playing a role in

---

[2] For relevant discussion, see T. Isaacs, 'Individual Responsibility for Collective Wrongs', in J. Harrington, M. Milde, and R. Vernon (eds), *Bringing Power to Justice? The Prospects of the International Criminal Court* (Montreal: McGill-Queens University Press, 2006), 167–90. There is an extensive philosophical literature on the morality of individual actions when they play a role in producing collective outcomes, in the context of which I am making a relatively uncontroversial move. Much of this literature is inspired by Derek Parfit's cases of *The Drops of Water* and *The Harmless Torturers*: see D. Parfit, *Reasons and Persons* (Oxford: Oxford University Press, 1984), 75–86.

[3] In these cases, we might say that our ways of behaving make us structurally complicit in injustice. See C. Aragon and A. Jaggar, 'Agency, Complicity, and the Responsibility to Resist Structural Injustice', *Journal of Social Philosophy* 49 (2018): 439–60, at 449.

generating that outcome, are very different in terms of their implications for the allocation of blame from cases of collective agency in which the participants are clearly culpable for contributing to creating an unjust outcome because they are acting together as part of a joint enterprise with the intention of realizing that outcome.[4]

But why suppose that we act wrongly when we behave in ways that contribute to the creation of injustice? It might seem obvious that we are under a general moral duty to avoid such behaviour. But there is an alternative view, namely, that we are *only* under a duty to do our bit to help reform unjust institutions, laws, and policies (and, if we are lucky enough to live within a reasonably just basic structure, we are under an obligation to support it.)[5] It is not obvious how we might resolve a disagreement between those who think we are only under a duty to play our part in reforming unjust institutions, laws, and policies and those who think that we are also under a duty to avoid behaving in ways that contribute to creating or maintaining an unjust outcome. It might be argued that we can't be under that additional duty because often we can't foresee that the ways in which we are behaving contribute to injustice. But that seems to provide grounds for restricting the duty to cases where we can foresee the contribution that an action will make to an injustice, rather than abandoning the idea that there is such a duty. It might be argued that even when we know that we are behaving in a way that contributes to injustice, it may be impossible or very difficult for others to be able to see that we are behaving in such a way, so our compliance with this duty is not publicly checkable. But unless we are seeking to enforce compliance with the duty, or provide publicly justifiable compensation for those who are adversely affected by the failure to comply with it, why should it matter for the issue of whether there is such a duty whether others would be able to tell that we had violated it?

---

[4] See, for example, C. Kutz, *Complicity: Ethics and Law for a Collective Age* (Cambridge: Cambridge University Press, 2000), especially ch. 4.

[5] I am thinking here of the natural duty of justice that Rawls defends: see J. Rawls, *A Theory of Justice*, revised edition (Oxford: Oxford University Press, 1999), 99, 293–6. But there are other forms that the alternative view I am envisaging could take. For example, it might take the form of a rejection of what Iris Marion Young calls the liability model of responsibility and an endorsement of the social connection model instead (see Young, *Responsibility for Justice*). If we do have a duty to avoid behaving in ways that contribute to creating unjust outcomes *in addition to* a duty to work to transform processes that produce unjust outcomes, we will not be able to make do with the social connection model alone. We will need to replace the liability model with some other approach that attends to the ways in which people act wrongly, even if blamelessly, in contributing to the production of unjust consequences.

The disagreement here between those who take an expansive view of our duties as citizens and those who take a narrower view may not be as crucial as it initially seems. People who believe that our sole duty as citizens is to support just institutions, laws, and policies and to play our part in reforming unjust ones, will need to acknowledge a wide-ranging derivative duty not to contribute to producing an unjust distribution, for contributing in this way will often involve a failure to play our full part in combating unjust institutions, laws, and policies. In many circumstances, effectively combating unjust institutions, laws, and policies will involve refusing to comply with them and refraining from participating in the practices they sustain, when that is feasible and we would otherwise contribute to creating unjust outcomes. So the disagreement in the end may come down to whether we have an independently justifiable duty to avoid contributing to unjust outcomes or whether a duty of this kind, perhaps more limited in scope, is derived from a duty to play our part in combating unjust institutions, laws, and policies. Whatever its ultimate justification, I am proposing that we act wrongly when we as individuals, or members of groups, behave in ways that contribute to creating or maintaining an unjust distribution, or that contribute to undermining the perceived moral status of members of a group.

We should, however, recognize that there are at least two kinds of exceptions to this principle, the first of which was foreshadowed in Section 1.4, namely, that we do not act wrongly in contributing to an injustice when we cannot avoid that happening, or we can avoid it happening only by contributing to creating an even greater injustice. Consider again the father who puts pressure on his adolescent daughter not to wear revealing clothes in order to reduce her vulnerability to harm, but by doing so contributes to promoting a culture of victim-blaming. In these kinds of cases, refraining from contributing to the lesser injustice would do no good and indeed would cause harm or increase the risk of harm. Second, we do not act wrongly when we can avoid contributing to an injustice only by incurring costs that it would be unreasonable to expect a person to bear. When this is the case, we have a personal moral prerogative to pursue our own good. In Chapter 6, for example, I shall argue that we have a moral prerogative to discriminate on grounds of race or appearance in the context of entering into a romantic partnership when it would otherwise be impossible or very difficult for us to obtain the goods that are available through such relationships.

But how are we to determine whether a person's actions contribute to creating unjust outcomes? There are two kinds of issue here. First, there is the issue of how in practice we are to trace the complex empirical connections between individual acts of discrimination and an unjust outcome in order to be justified in claiming that these acts really do contribute to creating that outcome. Second, there is the normative issue of how we are to justify the claim that a particular outcome is *unjust*. From a philosophical point of view, the second of these issues is more fundamental, so in the next two sections I shall focus on it. Section 3.4 concludes the development of my overall theory of what makes discrimination wrong by explaining the ways in which it is pluralist and defending it against the charge that some of its elements are unnecessary or redundant.

3.2 Unjust Consequences

Both direct and indirect discrimination can play a role in generating unjust consequences. In some cases, real or imagined, there may be no room for doubt, either empirically or normatively, concerning whether a series of discriminatory acts has generated an unjust outcome, for example, when a Black woman is denied a range of jobs on grounds of either her race or her sex, and she ends up living in poverty because she cannot find work. Those who discriminate against her deprive her of opportunities to obtain the goods internal to advantaged social positions, and the external goods, such as high salary and social esteem, that are attached to them. But it not always easy to establish that an act of discrimination contributes to creating or maintaining an unjust distribution. Even if we can show empirically that an act of discrimination has contributed to creating a particular outcome in which the victims have been disadvantaged, it may be hard to establish that this outcome is unjust, because judgements about whether a distribution of benefits and burdens is unjust are often complex. This is particularly the case when we are considering the effects of indirect discrimination.

Without dwelling on the difficulties surrounding how, exactly, we should analyse the notion of indirect discrimination, let me stipulate that a rule, norm, or policy indirectly discriminates against people who possess some characteristic C when the adoption of the rule, norm, or policy is not the result of any bias against people who possess C, but acting on it nevertheless on average disadvantages people who possess C compared to people who do not possess C.[6] (I shall also say that a person who acts on a rule, norm or

---

[6] For an extensive discussion of how we should define 'indirect discrimination', see Lippert-Rasmussen, *Born Free and Equal*, ch. 2.

policy indirectly discriminates against people who possess a characteristic C when he or she is not influenced by any bias against people who possess C, but acting on that rule, norm or policy nevertheless on average disadvantages people who possess C compared to people who do not possess C.) Indirect discrimination is sometimes described as 'disparate impact' and some might wonder whether its rather different character means that it is confusing to refer to it as discrimination at all. But so long as we are clear what we mean by it, there need be no confusion involved. Like the definition that I have adopted for direct discrimination, this definition of indirect discrimination is morally neutral: there is no justified automatic inference from the fact that an act or policy involves indirect discrimination to the conclusion that it is morally wrong, or to the conclusion that it is morally wrong because it has unjust consequences in particular. Whether it has unjust consequences will depend, in part, on the distribution of benefits and burdens to which it leads, including whether, and to what extent, it exacerbates the unjust disadvantages that the members of a group experience.

Suppose, for example, that a government decides to withdraw funding for medical research from a small institute that specializes in research on treatments for sickle cell anaemia, which, given racial differences in vulnerability to the disease, has a worse impact on Black people compared to white people. The funding cut is not the result of any racial bias; its aim is to concentrate funding for medical research in the hands of a smaller number of large institutes in order to make efficiency gains. This counts as a case of indirect racial discrimination, but is it morally unjustified? Answering this question involves making complex judgements that require more contextual knowledge. How large are the efficiency gains? Is research on sickle cell anaemia being conducted elsewhere, and if so, is the budget for it in proportion to the numbers affected by this disease? Could the researchers who are currently engaged in this research be relocated to one of the larger institutes the funding of which will be sustained at existing levels or increased?

In many cases, policies that involve indirect discrimination against a disadvantaged group can be changed in order to avoid imposing costs on that group, or so that members of it can relatively easily avoid incurring those costs, without thereby imposing serious costs on any other group. (This is often true of appearance codes that involve indirect discrimination on grounds of race, sex, religion, or disability, for it is often costless simply to reform these codes.) But in other cases, the costs of changing a policy may be high, even if they can be made to fall mainly on relatively advantaged groups. The judgements we need to make in order to determine whether in such cases the indirect discrimination involved is unjust, given the feasible alternatives, are often complex. Suppose, for example, that a company can employ people who need wheelchairs in order to move around only if they install a lift and provide a ramp at the front of their premises. Can that company justifiably refuse to employ people who need wheelchairs because of the costs of adapting the workplace? If not, who should bear the costs of adapting it? Should these be met wholly by the company? What if the company cannot afford to meet these costs and they have a choice between going out of business or not employing those in wheelchairs? Should the costs be met, at least in part, by society as a whole, perhaps through public subsidies to employers to be used in making their workplaces wheelchair friendly? It is clear that we cannot answer these questions fully without a reasonably well-worked out theory of distributive justice.

Different theories of distributive justice will often diverge in their implications for when discrimination, whether it is direct or indirect, contributes to creating or maintaining an unjust distribution of benefits and burdens. Some consequentialist theories hold that an act of discrimination, or a policy that permits discrimination, is unjust if it fails to maximize well-being, with potential disagreement concerning whether to conceptualize well-being as the satisfaction of preferences, or as pleasure, or as a complex good with a number of different ingredients. Other consequentialist theories have the same basic structure but maintain that in judging the consequences of an act or policy we should give additional weight to the well-being of those who are worse off, or those who are worse off through no fault of their own.[7] Yet other consequentialist theories maintain that well-being is not all that matters fundamentally and include other goods within their account of what is to be maximized, including 'impersonal goods', such as equality. Then there are a range of non-consequentialist theories that purport to draw out the implications of what it means to treat people as equals for the distribution of resources, opportunities, liberties, or well-being within a society or, indeed, across the globe.

I do not propose to try to resolve these complex issues. There is insufficient scope within a book on appearance discrimination to develop and defend a particular theory of distributive justice. What I shall go on to say

---

[7] See Lippert-Rasmussen, *Born Free and Equal?*, ch. 6, especially section 6; R. Arneson, 'Discrimination, Disparate Impact, and Theories of Justice,' in D. Hellman and S. Moreau (eds), *Philosophical Foundations of Discrimination Law* (Oxford: Oxford University Press, 2013), 87–111.

in the remainder of the book is compatible with a range of such theories, though as I indicated in the Introduction I shall make a number of assumptions. I shall assume, first, that there are demanding limits to what can count as just inequality and, second, that personal responsibility for an outcome often makes a difference to whether that outcome is just. These assumptions are compatible with responsibility-sensitive forms of egalitarianism such as luck egalitarianism, and responsibility-sensitive forms of prioritarianism that give significant extra weighting to benefitting the worse off.[8] They are also compatible with sufficientarian principles with a reasonably high sufficiency threshold, and quasi-egalitarian principles that suppose that inequalities of a certain degree or kind are non-contingently objectionable, so long as these principles give weight to considerations of responsibility.[9] I shall conduct my argument by considering the effects of discrimination on opportunities for well-being, but I do not take myself to be settling the deeper issue of whether the appropriate currency of justice is well-being, resources, primary goods, or capabilities.[10] Refraining from endorsing a particular theory of justice does at times create some indeterminacy with regard to what conclusions we are entitled to draw in specific cases of appearance discrimination, but in such cases I try to make it clear how the adoption of one theory rather than another would affect these conclusions.

Note, however, that on any of the theories of justice with which my approach is compatible, compensation might in principle be given for the burdens that result from acts of discrimination, in order to prevent them from having unjust consequences. As a result, the wrongness of such acts is conditional: in so far as they are morally objectionable only because they contribute to an unjust distribution of benefits and burdens, then they are morally permissible when compensation is provided in a way that restores a just distribution. It follows that if an agent performs them whilst there are mechanisms in place to provide full compensation, for example, a system of taxation that redresses the injustices caused by the impact of acts of discrimination of that type, then he or she acts permissibly.[11]

---

[8] For the distinction between equality and priority, see Parfit, 'Equality and Priority'.
[9] For the idea of sufficiency, see Shields, *Just Enough*. For the idea of a quasi-egalitarian principle, see Mason, *Levelling the Playing Field*, ch. 5.
[10] For an elucidation of these currencies, see Clayton and Williams, 'Egalitarian Justice and Interpersonal Comparison'.
[11] I discuss the issue of when compensation is appropriate as a response to discrimination in Section 8.1.

3.3 The Significance of Personal Autonomy

I shall also assume that any adequate theory of distributive justice will prize personal autonomy, that is, the capacity of individuals to lead their own lives in their own way, and the exercise of that capacity. Autonomy involves mental capabilities, including the capability to reflect upon one's options and decide among them; enough information to appreciate what is at stake, including the consequences of making different decisions; and an adequate range of options from which to choose.[12] A person's autonomy is impaired when their capacity to reflect upon their options is developed inadequately or reduced as a result of indoctrination or manipulation. It is also impaired when they are prevented from pursuing a conception of how to live that they have adopted with a reasonable expectation that they would be able to act in accordance with it. And it is impaired when their pursuit of that conception of how to live is burdened by a range of costs that are imposed on them as a result of the prejudices of others.

Some theories of distributive justice will attach fundamental significance to autonomy and its exercise, for example, they may see its exercise as a non-instrumentally valuable ingredient of well-being, others will regard it as instrumentally valuable in terms of its role in promoting happiness or pleasure. I shall assume that, at the very least, personal autonomy has considerable instrumental value. In practice, possessing autonomy, and being disposed to exercise it, facilitates one's flourishing. It is hard, perhaps even impossible in some cases, for a person to lead a flourishing life without possessing autonomy because, generally speaking, we need to exercise autonomy in order to be able to find a life that is fulfilling for us.[13] John Stuart Mill captures some of the plausibility of this claim when he writes:

---

[12] Tarunabh Khaitan identifies four basic goods secure access to which is necessary for well-being, viz., goods that are required to satisfy our biological needs, negative freedom, an adequate range of valuable options from which to choose, and an appropriate level of self-respect (see T. Khaitan, *A Theory of Discrimination Law* (Oxford: Oxford University Press, 2015), 95–6). These goods can be understood as conditions that are required for the exercise of autonomy. So the account of the normative foundations of discrimination law that he goes on to construct can be regarded as developing the idea that discrimination may be wrong in virtue of its unjust consequences in a way that gives a central role to the value and importance of autonomy, focusing in particular on the role that 'relative group disadvantage' can play in impairing it.

[13] See H. Brighouse, *School Choice and Social Justice* (Oxford: Oxford University Press, 2002), 68–73; I. MacMullen, *Faith in Schools? Autonomy, Citizenship, and Religious Education in the Liberal State* (Princeton, NJ: Princeton University Press, 2007), 96–103.

A man cannot get a coat or a pair of boots to fit him, unless they are either made to his measure, or he has a whole warehouseful to choose from: and is it easier to fit him with a life than with a coat, or are human beings more like one another in their whole physical and spiritual conformation than in the shape of their feet? If it were only that people have diversities of taste that is reason enough for not attempting to shape them all after one model. But different persons also require different conditions for their spiritual development; and can no more exist healthily in the same moral, than all the variety of plants can in the same physical atmosphere and climate.[14]

This instrumental argument for the value of autonomy provides a particularly powerful case for its importance when combined with the thesis of value pluralism. At a minimum, value pluralism maintains that there is an irreducible plurality of values. It can also incorporate the idea that different values may be realized in different ways of life, that very different ways of life may each have value, and that different individuals may have natures that suit them to different ways of life. Given our fallibility, it is often the case that in practice we need to exercise autonomy in order to identify what ways of life are valuable and find one that fits, to use Mill's metaphor.

The instrumental argument for the value of autonomy makes an empirical claim that ideally requires evidence to support it, but it is not easy to formulate it precisely or gather evidence that bears upon it. In fact, there are different versions of it that can be generated from the following formula: there is a probability x that a percentage y of a society will not achieve a level of flourishing z unless they possess, and exercise, autonomy. The instrumental argument seems plausible even when reasonably high numbers are substituted for x and y, and z is specified as an adequate level of flourishing. Perhaps most people can achieve an adequate level of flourishing in a variety of different lives—rather like the average person can find clothes that fit reasonably well straight "off the peg" in a range of shops—and do not need to exercise autonomy to find a valuable life in which they can achieve that level of flourishing. But there may still be a sizeable minority who can flourish to an adequate extent only in a small number of ways of life. (These people are the ethical equivalent of men taller than 6' 6", with feet that are size 13 or larger, who struggle to find clothes and shoes that fit unless they have them made to measure.) They might not be able to flourish

---

[14] J. S. Mill, 'On Liberty', in M. Warnock (ed.), *Utilitarianism* (London: Collins, 1962), 197.

simply by conforming to their family or community's conception of how to live—and indeed might be seriously damaged if they were indoctrinated to accept its tenets and the assumption that it is the only valuable way to live.[15] Perhaps this is true of many gay men and lesbians who are born into homophobic communities or ways of life.

There are different ways in which a theory of distributive justice might give due weight to our interest in autonomous agency. We might think that its importance is sufficient to justify an independent principle the satisfaction of which is more urgent than principles governing other goods, so that in cases of conflict the former takes priority. We might suppose that there is a right to autonomy because our interest in it is sufficiently great to place others under a duty to respect it. Alternatively, we might think that our interest in autonomous agency can be adequately protected by an overarching principle governing the distribution of all of the various benefits and burdens that lie within the scope of distributive justice, so long as the weight that interest is given reflects its vital role in our flourishing. I shall leave unresolved the issue of which of these approaches is the best.

How does the value of autonomy impact upon our judgements about the permissibility of discrimination in employment decisions? When, say, racial discrimination in these decisions is rife, those who suffer it will have reduced opportunities to obtain the goods internal to advantaged social positions, and the external goods, such as high salary and social esteem, that are attached to these positions, and some may find it altogether impossible to obtain such goods. These goods are likely to be important for a person to realize his or her conception of how to live. People may also suffer damage to their self-esteem and self-confidence as a result of being stigmatized, that is, marked out as inferior, in a way that detrimentally affects their capacity to pursue those conceptions. The damage that the victims of racial and other forms of discrimination suffer to their interest in autonomous agency makes it contingently wrong when it contributes to creating an unjust overall distribution of benefits and burdens.

The value of autonomy might seem a rather blunt weapon to use in identifying acts of discrimination that are wrongful in the context of employment. When less well-qualified candidates are rejected in favour of the best-qualified candidate, then so too their interest in autonomous agency is set back, but surely appointing the best-qualified is morally permissible, in

---

[15] See H. Brighouse and A. Swift, *Family Values. The Ethics of Parent-Child Relationships* (Princeton, NJ: Princeton University Press, 2014), 167.

general at least. What this shows is that we have to consider the impact of different acts of discrimination on each person's autonomy, and on the distribution of benefits and burdens in general, in order to judge whether these acts have unjust consequences. When less well-qualified applicants for jobs are rejected, then their autonomy is potentially impaired in a serious way. But, in general at least, everyone, even the less well-qualified, benefits to some extent from a policy of appointing the best-qualified candidates, unlike a policy of not appointing those from a racial minority. Furthermore, arguably we should give greater weight to damage to autonomy when it is a product of wrong-doing. If those who are subject to racial discrimination are disadvantaged in the competition for advantaged social positions as a result of deliberative unfairness, then the harm they suffer as a consequence, especially in terms of its adverse effect on their autonomous agency, should be judged to be greater as a result of being a product of wrong-doing.

In a manner that is consistent with my approach, Sophia Moreau argues that discrimination is wrong when it impairs the victims' deliberative freedom in a way that violates their right to that freedom.[16] Deliberative freedom involves 'the freedom to deliberate about one's life, and to decide what to do in light of those deliberations, without having to treat certain personal traits (or other people's assumptions about them) as costs, and without having to live one's life with these traits always before one's eyes.'[17] She argues that people have a right to deliberative freedom that is violated in cases when, as a result of the attitudes, assumptions, and prejudices of others, 'normatively extraneous features', such as their race or gender, impact upon their decisions concerning, for instance, what jobs to seek. When a woman is routinely subject to discrimination on grounds of race or gender in selection processes, then she will need to factor in whether her race or gender will be a barrier to the pursuit of her preferred career. Respecting her right to deliberative freedom requires that her decisions on this matter should not be burdened by having to take into account how the attitudes, assumptions, and prejudices that others have about her race or gender will affect her career opportunities.

[16] S. Moreau, 'What Is Discrimination?', *Philosophy and Public Affairs* 38 (2010): 143–79. In her more recent book-length treatment of the issues, she argues that impairing deliberative freedoms is just one of the ways in which discrimination may be wrongful or wrong its victims: see S. Moreau, *Faces of Inequality: A Theory of Wrongful Discrimination* (Oxford: Oxford University Press, 2020), especially ch. 3.
[17] Moreau, *Faces of Inequality*, 84.

Moreau's approach faces the challenge of providing an account of what makes a feature or trait normatively extraneous, that is, what makes it true of a trait or feature that in a range of decisions a person who possesses it ought not to have to take into account various costs, related to the attitudes, assumptions or prejudices of others concerning it. In the article in which she first presented her account, she maintained that there is no single criterion for determining whether a feature or trait in normatively extraneous in this sense.[18] In her more recent book, however, Moreau drops the language of 'normatively extraneous features' and suggests instead that we can understand when a person's right to deliberative freedom is violated by reference to the idea that there are certain kinds of cost the imposition of which fails to respect a person as a being who is equally capable of autonomy.[19]

Moreau does not see the wrongness of discrimination that violates a right to deliberative freedom as rooted in the harm it causes and the unjust distribution of benefits and burdens to which it contributes. Indeed, it might seem that when the wrongness of discrimination that violates a right to deliberative freedom is understood in the way she is now suggesting, then it is better conceived as a respect-based consideration rather than a harm-based consideration that relates to the unjust consequences of discrimination. But it seems to me that no violence is done to her theory by regarding the impairment of deliberative freedom as a kind of harm that is suffered by those who experience discrimination. Moreau's reasons for resisting that reconceptualization seem to me to be unpersuasive.[20] It is true that in the cases with which she is concerned what matters to the victims of discrimination is that they are rendered unable to decide for themselves whether to take advantage of an opportunity, or doing so becomes more costly than it would otherwise be, so it is the adverse impact of discrimination on their deliberative freedom that they care about. But this adverse impact might nevertheless be best construed as a harm. Thinking of the impairment of deliberative freedom as an important harm is plausible if we see the right to that freedom as a component of a broader right to autonomy that is grounded in the vital importance of exercising autonomy for finding and leading a life in which one can flourish. We might then suppose that we

---

[18] Moreau, 'What Is Discrimination?', 157.
[19] See Moreau, *Faces of Inequality*, 89–90.
[20] See S. Moreau, 'Discrimination and Freedom,' in K. Lippert-Rusmussen (ed.), *The Routledge Handbook of the Ethics of Discrimination* (London: Routledge, 2017), 167–8.

have a right to deliberative freedom that is grounded in the weighty interest that each of us has in autonomy and which is violated by some impairments of that freedom.

3.4 Pluralism and Reductionism

As I highlighted in the introduction to Chapter 2, we can distinguish between monist and pluralist theories of what makes discrimination wrong when it is wrong. According to monist theories, there is a single wrong-making feature that explains why discrimination is wrong, whereas according to pluralist theories there are several different wrong-making features, any one of which may explain why discrimination is wrong in a given case, or which may combine to explain its wrongness, with each making an irreducible contribution to that explanation, even when the wrongness of the discrimination is over-determined.

The theory I have been defending seems deeply pluralist, for it allows that discrimination may be wrong for either non-contingent or contingent reasons, or both: it may be wrong independently of its consequences because it involves disrespect or deliberative unfairness, or it may be wrong because of its role in generating unjust consequences. It might be argued, however, that the pluralism here does not go as deep as it might seem, on the grounds that the disrespect and unfairness that are sometimes involved in acts of discrimination are best regarded as impersonal 'bads' to be minimized or distributed justly. Even if, as I have claimed, the victims of discrimination need not be made worse off by being treated disrespectfully or unfairly, it might be argued that the disrespect (or the disrespectful acts) and the unfairness (or the unfair deliberation), should be regarded as bad consequences that have to be taken into account in determining what course of action will produce the best consequences all things considered, or the most just distribution. Similarly, it might be thought that 'relating to others as moral equals' and 'deliberating fairly' are important goods, of impersonal value, that also need to be taken into account in making such judgements.[21]

---

[21] For relevant and instructive discussion, see G. Elford, 'Relational Equality and Distribution', *Journal of Political Philosophy* 25 (2017): 80–99; Lippert-Rasmussen, *Relational Egalitarianism*; A. Moles and T. Parr, 'Distributions and Relations: A Hybrid Account', *Political Studies* 67 (2019): 132–48; P. Tomlin, 'What Is the Point of Egalitarian Social Relationships?', in

I do not want to deny that the wrongness of the disrespect or deliberative unfairness that is sometimes involved in discrimination might be outweighed by sufficiently beneficial consequences. The disrespectfulness or unfairness of an act of discrimination makes it *pro tanto* wrong, not necessarily wrong all things considered. But it seems to me to be a mistake to think that whether an act of discrimination is wrong all things considered is determined by some overall assessment of goods and 'bads' that includes giving weight to the badness of disrespectful acts and deliberative unfairness, and the goodness of relating to others as equals and deliberating fairly. The non-contingent reasons I identify are, in my view, best conceived as agent relative reasons, that is, very roughly, as reasons the full specification of which makes an essential reference to the agent for whom they are a reason. I have a reason not to act disrespectfully, or not to deliberate unfairly, and that reason is not properly characterized as a reason to minimize disrespect (or disrespectful acts) or to minimize deliberative unfairness (or deliberatively unfair acts), nor indeed is it derived from some more general reason to produce the best or most just consequences. It is a reason *for me* not to act disrespectfully or deliberate unfairly, rather than a reason for me to minimize the number of disrespectful acts or amount of deliberative unfairness in the world or to produce the most just consequences. There may be situations where I can minimize overall disrespect by acting disrespectfully, if, for example my acting disrespectfully would somehow be a spur to others to act respectfully, but if I have an agent relative reason not to act disrespectfully, how I should act isn't settled by the fact that by acting disrespectfully I could minimize the total amount of disrespect (or total number of disrespectful acts) or produce the most just consequences. Most of my argument in the rest of the book does not stand or fall, however, with this claim that reasons of respect and reasons of deliberative fairness are agent relative.

My theory allows that when an act of discrimination is wrong for multiple reasons, these reasons may interact with each other in such a way that its wrongness cannot be understood simply by aggregating them. When an act of discrimination plays a role in generating unjust consequences, then this may aggravate the wrongness of any disrespect it involves or any deliberative unfairness that preceded it in a selection process; so too when an act of discrimination is disrespectful, or deliberatively unfair, then that may aggravate the wrongness that is involved in contributing to unjust

A. Kaufman (ed.), *Distributive Justice and Access to Advantage: G. A. Cohen's Egalitarianism* (Cambridge: Cambridge University Press, 2015).

consequences. But might the different kinds of reasons that I have identified interact in a deeper way? Might it be the case that discrimination that involves a failure to respect its victims is wrong *in virtue of that failure of respect* only if it contributes to creating unjust consequences? Or might it be the case that discrimination that contributes to creating unjust consequences is wrong *in virtue of doing so* only if it is disrespectful?

These positions may seem incoherent, but they are intelligible in the light of two related distinctions that we have already encountered: first, the distinction between claiming that an act is non-contingently wrong, that is, wrong independently of its consequences, and claiming that it is intrinsically wrong, that is, wrong in virtue of its intrinsic properties, independently of its relationship to anything else, and second, the distinction between claiming that an act of discrimination is unconditionally wrong and claiming that it is conditionally wrong. It might be said that an act of discrimination is never intrinsically wrong in virtue of the disrespect it involves, since its wrongness is conditional on its playing a role in generating unjust consequences, but it can nevertheless be non-contingently wrong in virtue of that disrespect when it plays such a role. So too, it might be said that an act of discrimination is never unconditionally wrong in virtue of its role in generating unjust consequences, since its wrongness is always conditional on its being disrespectful. Neither position seems intuitively plausible, however.

In order to see the counter-intuitiveness of the idea that an act of discrimination that is disrespectful can be wrong in virtue of its disrespectfulness only if it plays a role in generating unjust consequences, consider a woman who is unaware that she has been denied a job as a result of discrimination on grounds of her racial inferiority but is appointed to another equally good or perhaps better job. Not only does she obtain an equally good or better job elsewhere, she does not suffer from any loss of self-confidence or self-esteem, and she does not feel stigmatized.[22] Yet the discrimination still seems wrong in virtue of its disrespectfulness. Or suppose that a selection committee appoints a member of a racial group who is the best qualified for the position, but does so on the basis of a majority vote, with those in the minority privately regarding her as morally inferior in virtue of her membership of that group, and voting against her appointment on that basis. Don't their votes wrongly discriminate against her even though she is appointed? In both cases it would seem that she is treated

---

[22] See Slavny and Parr, 'Harmless Discrimination'.

wrongfully, with a lack of equal respect, because she is treated as if she has an inferior moral status, even though she does not suffer harm as a result.

In order to see the counter-intuitiveness of the idea that an act of discrimination that plays a role in generating unjust consequences can be wrong in virtue of that role only if it is disrespectful, consider acts of discrimination that are rooted in evidence-based statistical generalizations about the behaviour of members of a group that is stigmatized or disadvantaged, when for some reason it is unfeasible or too costly to determine whether an individual member of that group conforms to the generalization. Racial profiling is in principle a potential example.[23] When it is used in policing, it may generate unjust consequences or contribute to doing so (for example, because it contributes to stigmatizing the members of a racial group yet does not, as it turns out, create much in the way of overall benefit) without necessarily being disrespectful, and it may be wrongful in virtue of its effects.

As both Lawrence Blum and Sophia Moreau note, there has been a tendency to adopt monist theories or, at least, to avoid fully fledged pluralist theories.[24] For example, Richard Arneson endorses a 'desert-catering prioritarian consequentialist' account that implies that discrimination is wrong, and only wrong, when it fails to maximize well-being after additional weight has been given to benefits to those who are undeservedly worse off.[25] Hellman too seems to be a monist, for she argues that only discrimination that offends against the norm of equality is wrongful discrimination.[26] Even Moreau herself strikes me as insufficiently pluralist because it seems that she in effect denies that acts of discrimination can be non-contingently wrong.[27]

Monist theories can be hard to argue against because, from the perspective of a pluralist theory, it is common for the wrongness of discrimination

---

[23] See Eidelson, *Discrimination and Disrespect*, ch. 6.
[24] Blum, 'Racial and Other Asymmetries', 195–8; Moreau, *Faces of Inequality*, 22.
[25] See R. Arneson, 'Discrimination, Disparate Impact, and Theories of Justice'. Kasper Lippert-Rasmussen also endorses a desert-prioritarian account but adds that '[t]hese accounts may not offer a satisfactory, complete account of the sources of wrongness of discrimination and I have indicated that unfairness may play a role as well. So in this sense I am open to a pluralist account of the wrongness of discrimination' (Lippert-Rasmussen, *Born Free and Equal?*, 183).
[26] Hellman's argument here has a whiff of circularity about it, however: she contends that a form of discrimination can be wrongful but not count as wrongful discrimination if it is wrongful for a reason that 'does not have anything to do with failing to treat each person as a person of equal moral worth' (See Hellman, *When Is Discrimination Wrong?*, 15–21, at 17.)
[27] See Moreau, *Faces of Inequality*, 10.

to be over-determined, that is, for there to be multiple reasons why it is wrong. As a result, monists can often provide an explanation of the wrongness of a discriminatory act in a way that may appear adequate but, from the point of view of a pluralist theory, will fail to provide a *full* account of the reasons why that act is wrong. There are nevertheless potential test cases, some of which I have already put to work, where our intuitions seem to favour particular judgements about the permissibility or impermissibility of discriminatory acts, but those judgements diverge from what is implied by specific monist theories of what makes discrimination wrong. Monists, however, argue that these test cases are at best inconclusive because they do not demonstrate what their critics suppose they do. Indeed, monists sometimes use 'debunking arguments' which try to show that, given a theory of what makes discrimination wrong at the fundamental level, and an account of the best way in practice of minimizing wrongful discrimination given our biases and the limitations in our knowledge, we should expect there to be some divergences between our intuitions about particular cases and that theory. Let me illustrate.

Those who defend the idea that discrimination may be non-contingently wrong sometimes describe acts of discrimination that they think involve harmless wrong-doing and which appear to be inconsistent with a monist theory of why discrimination is wrong that appeals solely to the harm it causes, and the role of that harm in creating an unjust distribution of benefits and burdens. Recall the case already described of the woman who is unaware that she has been denied a job as a result of discrimination on grounds of her racial inferiority but is appointed to another equally good or perhaps better job elsewhere. She suffers no harm but is treated disrespectfully, and therefore wrongly. Consequentialists who think that well-being, or the opportunity to acquire it, is all that matters fundamentally would defend the idea that a discriminatory act is wrong only when it causes harm and reject these apparent counterexamples. They can distinguish between the criterion of right action they endorse and the secondary principles that ought to serve as a practical guide in decision-making. The latter are justified in so far as the adoption of these secondary principles is, on balance and over time, likely to lead to better consequences than any other approach, such as simply applying, on a case-by-case basis, the consequentialist criterion of right action. Once this distinction has been drawn, consequentialists of this kind can allow that we may come to treat these secondary principles, including principles that regard discrimination as non-contingently wrong, as unconditionally applicable, thereby generating intuitions that diverge from the criterion of right action, including the intuition that discrimination may be wrong even when it causes no harm. But in fact, they claim, these intuitions are a product of the secondary principles that we internalize as a result of our moral education, and that we come to regard as having unconditional authority. In reality, however, any authority they possess derives from the fact that in general, and for the most part, conforming to these principles generates the best consequences.[28]

These consequentialists sometimes argue in addition, or instead, that harmless acts of discrimination that involve failing to respect the moral status of the victims reflect badly on the character of the discriminator, but that there is no moral reason to object to the acts themselves, and that ultimately we have a moral reason to object to discrimination only if it has harmful effects of one kind or another.[29] Neither of these strategies strikes me as successful, however. There is a danger of begging the question here, but our intuitions about cases of harmless discrimination that involve giving insufficient weight to moral status don't seem to be simply a product of the internalization of secondary principles, and these cases seem to concern wrong-doing not merely bad character. There are cases of harmless discrimination that seem to be morally objectionable simply because they are disrespectful and regardless of whether they cause harm.[30]

If it is implausible to deny the existence of cases of harmless discrimination the wrongfulness of which is best captured in terms of the idea of a failure of respect, is it implausible too to deny the existence of cases of wrongful discrimination that are rooted in harms, and the unjust distribution of benefits and burdens in which they are supposedly implicated, that involve no failure of respect? I think so. There are acts of discrimination that seem wrongful because of the harm they cause, and the unjust distribution of benefits and burdens to which they contribute, but which don't involve any disrespect. Consider, again, a policy of racial profiling where the discrimination involved is a good faith attempt to bring about a valuable outcome even though it involves an error in balancing the costs and benefits involved in pursuing that policy.

---

[28] Arneson, 'Discrimination, Disparate Impact, and Theories of Justice', 94–7.
[29] See Lippert-Rasmussen, *Born Free and Equal?*, 160, 173; Arneson, 'Discrimination and Harm', 157–8.
[30] Slavny and Parr, 'Harmless Discrimination'.

Even if an adequate theory of what is wrong with discrimination needs to invoke principles concerned with the way in which it can be disrespectful, and principles that are concerned with the way in which it can play a role in generating unjust consequences, do we really need further principles that are concerned with the way in which it can be unfair in virtue of bias in the selection decisions through which advantaged social positions are distributed? Or might our worries about the fairness of these decisions be captured fully in terms of the unjust consequences caused by biased decision-making and the forms of disrespect involved in it? Some might argue that deliberative fairness in making decisions about the allocation of advantaged social positions is determined by reference to the consequences of such decisions, in particular, whether the rules that are followed in these processes promote just outcomes, as determined by independent principles of justice that apply more broadly to the distribution of benefits and burdens.

It is not hard, however, to construct examples where selectors who are filling jobs are negatively influenced by their prejudices, or their non-rational reactions, or their own personal moral or aesthetic judgements about the characteristics of candidates, but in a way that does not involve any disrespect and does not cause any harm, yet seems to involve wrongful discrimination because it is unfair. Consider a variant of the example described earlier in which members of an appointing committee are influenced non-consciously by negative stereotypes concerning women from a particular ethnic minority and, as a result, give somewhat less weight to the qualifications of an applicant than they would otherwise do, but she is nevertheless appointed to the position because she is still judged to be the best qualified. No harm is caused to the woman who suffers discrimination, and there has not been any failure to provide her with respect, but nevertheless the evaluation of her qualifications involves deliberative unfairness. In response, it might be said that our intuitions here are a product of the legitimate expectations we form as a result of codes of practice that endorse selection on the basis of candidates' qualifications alone, together with the lingering effects of a meritocratic principle that many have internalized but for which it is hard to provide a convincing philosophical defence. However, the widespread intuition that it is simply unfair when candidates are rejected as a result of a selector's prejudices, non-rational reactions, or personal aesthetic or moral judgements about their characteristics, resists being debunked in this way. Even if this intuition cannot be successfully defended by appealing to ideas of desert, it cannot be easily dismissed.

3.5 Concluding Remarks

Each of the elements of the pluralist theory of what makes discrimination wrong (when it is wrong) that I am advocating would benefit from further refinement and defence. But this is a book on the ethics of appearance discrimination in particular, rather than one on discrimination in general, so my defence of a general theory of what makes discrimination wrong when it is wrong is necessarily incomplete. I shall conclude this chapter by summarizing my view. Discrimination, whether involving prejudice or rooted purely in non-rational aversions, may be wrong for at least three different sorts of reason: it may be wrong because it fails to treat the victims of it with respect even if it does not harm them; it may be wrong because the deliberation it involves unfairly disadvantages them in a selection decision even if they are selected; it may be wrong because it has unjust consequences in virtue of contributing to the creation of an unjust distribution of benefits and burdens or contributing to lowering the perceived moral standing of members of a group (including reinforcing the power structures that facilitate these outcomes.) In the next Part of the book, I shall apply this theory to various contexts in which appearance discrimination takes place, beginning in Chapter 4 with discrimination in employment decisions. I shall approach appearance discrimination in this context partly by considering the extent to which racial discrimination and appearance discrimination are analogous, that is, the extent to which the reasons we have for thinking that racial discrimination is wrong are relevant to the moral assessment of appearance discrimination.

PART II
CONTEXTS OF APPEARANCE DISCRIMINATION

4
Appearance, Race, and Employment

In this chapter I explore the issue of when and why appearance discrimination is wrong in the context of employment decisions. Rather than addressing this issue head-on, by simply applying the pluralist theory of what makes discrimination wrong that I developed in the previous two chapters, I shall instead explore it through an examination of the relationship between appearance discrimination and racial discrimination. There is a morally significant analogy between the two since, like racial membership, many appearance-related characteristics are such that we have very little control over them, the possession of some of these characteristics is stigmatized, and discrimination on the basis of them has a considerable impact on people's chances of occupying advantaged social positions. I shall make prominent use of the pluralist theory I have defended, but by applying it in the light of a comparison between appearance discrimination and racial discrimination, I aim to illuminate the moral concerns we ought to have about appearance discrimination when it occurs in decisions about recruitment and promotion.

I argue that there is no morally relevant difference between appearance discrimination and racial discrimination in a range of employment decisions where we judge the latter to be wrong.[1] In doing so, I take seriously the idea that since races don't exist in the way that is often supposed, some of what is classed as racial discrimination *is* a distinctive kind of discrimination on the basis of appearance. In Section 4.1, I suggest that it is an empirical rather than merely conceptual question what proportion of racial discrimination is appearance discrimination, but that we should leave open the possibility that a significant amount of it is best interpreted in this way. I propose that, when racial discrimination is a distinctive form of appearance discrimination, it casts light on the moral assessment of other forms of appearance discrimination and that, even when it is not, the issue of when

---

[1] There may be other analogies that also cast light on the morality of appearance discrimination: for example, there may be a significant analogy between appearance and talent or ability: see Hamermesh, *Beauty Pays*, 102–3. See also Section 9.2.

What's Wrong with Lookism? Personal Appearance, Discrimination, and Disadvantage. Andrew Mason, Oxford University Press. © Andrew Mason 2023. DOI: 10.1093/oso/9780192859792.003.0004

appearance discrimination is morally permissible is illuminated by reflecting on when and why racial discrimination is wrong. Like racial discrimination, appearance discrimination in hiring or promotion can be wrong because it is disrespectful, or because it involves deliberative unfairness in the decision-making process, or because it plays a role in generating unjust consequences.

The analogy between racial discrimination and appearance discrimination might seem inappropriate, however, and in any case to have serious limits. Racial discrimination, it might be said, is a much more serious moral problem than appearance discrimination, and that comparing appearance discrimination to racial discrimination trivializes the latter. Furthermore, it might be thought that it is a mistake to regard them as analogous because people have much more control over aspects of their appearance than they do their racial membership. In response, I shall argue in Section 4.2 that even though racial discrimination is in various ways a more serious problem than appearance discrimination, appearance discrimination itself is far from trivial; and in Section 4.5 I shall contend that it is unclear whether the differences between them that relate to the control we have over our appearance compared to our racial membership have as much moral significance as it might initially seem.

So, my overall aim in this chapter, and indeed the next, is to use the normative framework described in Section 1.3, and developed in Chapters 2 and 3, to explore the moral permissibility of appearance discrimination in the context of employment, whilst at the same time reflecting upon the extent and limits of the analogy between appearance discrimination and racial discrimination. I shall do so in a way that is sensitive to the different possible origins of appearance discrimination, in particular, whether it is rooted in prejudices, non-rational reactions, aesthetic judgements, or moral judgements; that takes into account the different parties who may have these prejudices or non-rational reactions, or form these aesthetic or moral judgements, such as, selectors, employers, customers, or clients; and that factors in the extent to which the appearance features to which these parties are responding are under the control of the people who possess them. Accordingly, in Section 4.3 I shall explore the moral permissibility of selectors' decisions being influenced by their prejudices or non-rational reactions concerning appearance features over which we *lack* control, whereas in Section 4.4 I shall explore the moral permissibility of selectors' decisions being influenced by either their own or their employers' aesthetic judgements concerning such features. In Section 4.5, I shall examine the moral permissibility of selectors' decisions being influenced by their own or their employers' prejudices, non-rational reactions, or aesthetic or moral judgements concerning appearance features over which we *possess* control. In doing so, I conceive of selectors as occupying a distinctive role within an organization, one that involves making decisions over job appointments and promotions, and which differs from the roles of employer, co-worker, customer, or client—although the same individual may occupy more than one of these roles at any one time or at different times.

My discussion is not intended to cast doubt on the possibility that in some cases appearance features might be genuine qualifications for a job or justifiably influence employment decisions. In Sections 4.4 and 4.5, I consider the way in which employers' moral and aesthetic values concerning aspects of appearance may permissibly influence a job appointment when they are seeking to express these values through their organizations. In the next chapter, I shall consider some ways in which the preferences of customers and clients concerning the appearance of employees may permissibly influence selection decisions by generating legitimate 'reaction qualifications'. Furthermore, how people dress or present themselves may provide evidence of dispositions and traits that can justifiably be regarded as qualifications for a job, for example, dressing in a suit for an interview may signal a willingness to comply with convention, or having a neat appearance may provide evidence of industriousness.[2]

4.1 Racial Discrimination and Its Relationship to Appearance

There is a puzzle concerning the nature of racial discrimination that affects how we should understand its relationship to appearance discrimination and the extent to which there is a morally significant analogy between the two. Those who engage in so-called racial discrimination often suppose that human beings belong to different races in a way that cannot be sustained

---

[2] See Rhode, *The Beauty Bias*, 108. There is evidence that a range of personality traits are reliably correlated with visual self-presentation: see L. Albright, D. Kenny, and T. Malloy, 'Consensus in Personality Judgements at Zero Acquaintance', *Journal of Personality and Social Psychology* 55 (1988): 387–95; P. Borkenau and A. Liebler, 'Trait Inferences: Sources of Validity at Zero Acquaintance', *Journal of Personality and Social Psychology* 62 (1992): 645–57; L. Naumann, S. Vazire, P. Rentfrow, and S. Gosling, 'Personality Judgements Based on Personal Appearance', *Personality and Social Psychology Bulletin* 35 (2009): 1661–71.

empirically. The study of human genetics shows that what are regarded as separate races differ with respect to a small number of genes that influence features of appearance such as skin colour, but genes do not in general line up in a way that would support the idea that races are natural kinds.[3] From a biological point of view, differences in skin colour are no more significant than differences in eye colour. Furthermore, there is no reason to think that the genetic differences that underlie differences in skin colour generate differences in ability, behaviour, or character of a kind that might, with any degree of plausibility, be thought to justify racial discrimination. How then should we understand what is ordinarily regarded as discrimination on the basis of race if in an important sense there are no races? Can there be any such thing as racial discrimination, properly so called?

According to the definition provided in Section 2.1, X-type direct discrimination occurs when A discriminates against B because of B's possession of some particular token of X, or because A *believes* that B possesses some particular token of X. This formulation allows that even when A is mistaken in thinking that B belongs to some biological racial kind, because there are none, he can be viewed as engaged in (direct) racial discrimination if he treats B less favourably as a result of his belief that B belongs to that racial kind. Indeed, this formulation allows that A may be involved in racial discrimination, even if there is no plausible sense of 'race' in which races can be justifiably held to exist, simply by regarding B as a member of a particular race and treating B unfavourably as a result. Nevertheless, we might think that there are ways of conceiving of race that enable us to make better sense of what we ordinarily regard as racial discrimination because they correctly identify genuine features of the world to which people are in fact responding when they engage in it.

There are several possibilities worth considering here: first, race might be conceived in such a way that it maps on to something of biological significance, even though it is not regarded as a natural kind distinguished by intrinsic biological properties; second, even if race is not regarded as having biological significance, it might be thought to correspond to real differences in visible physical features, ancestry, and geographical origin; third, races or racial groups might be thought of as social constructions, that is, as causal

---

[3] See I. Hannaford, *Race: The History of an Idea in the West* (Washington, DC: The Woodrow Wilson Center Press, 1996); Luigi Luca Cavalli-Sforza, *Genes, Peoples, and Languages* (Berkeley: University of California Press, 2001).

products of social or cultural processes, practices, or institutions.[4] I don't plan to provide a full philosophical assessment of these accounts. Instead, I shall examine each of them in turn in order to see whether they can help to identify the features of the world to which people are responding when they engage in what we ordinarily think of as racial discrimination. I shall then consider the implications of my discussion for how we should understand the relationship between racial discrimination and appearance discrimination.

According to the most promising version of the first approach, races are understood as breeding populations that share a common geographical origin, that is, they are conceived as populations with a common geographical origin that, reproductively speaking, are largely separate from each other, either as a result of the physical distance between them or because of legal, social, or cultural norms that reduce their interactions.[5] This has the virtue of providing a basis for the existence of different races that has biological significance, but it does so at some cost: the groupings that constitute races on this account are unlikely to correspond to any great extent to races as they are ordinarily understood, not least because racial membership, on this approach, has nothing inherently to do with appearance.[6] As a result, many cases of discrimination that are conventionally regarded as racial in character will not count as racial discrimination on this conceptualization, and it does not seem to provide us with the basis for a plausible account of the features that people are in fact responding to when they are involved in what we ordinarily regard as racial discrimination.

The second approach, which holds that even though the concept of race is not of biological significance, it nevertheless corresponds to real differences in visible physical features, ancestry, and geographical origin, invokes what we might call a 'folk' account of race. As Michael Hardimon argues, this account can, in principle at least, keep apart the idea of racial membership from the kinds of beliefs about races that fuel racist practices. It employs a core concept of race, rather than a particular conception of it that

---

[4] I do not claim that these exhaust the possibilities, but for my purposes they capture the most important approaches, and different versions of them are available.

[5] See R. Andreasen, 'A New Perspective on the Race Debate', *British Journal for the Philosophy of Science* 49 (1998): 199–225; Q. Spencer, 'How to Be a Biological Racial Realist', in J. Glasgow, S. Haslanger, C. Jeffers, and Q. Spencer, *What Is Race? Four Philosophical Views* (Oxford: Oxford University Press, 2019), 73–110.

[6] Indeed, some defenders of this account make no claim that it does; see Andreasen, 'A New Perspective on the Race Debate', 219. See also J. Glasgow, 'On the New Biology of Race', *Journal of Philosophy* 100 (2003): 456–74 at 459–60; J. Glasgow, 'Is Race an Illusion or a (Very) Basic Reality?', in Glasgow et al., *What Is Race?*, 111–49, at 120–3.

imports problematic views about the nature of race and its significance.[7] According to this core concept, a person's membership in a racial group is determined by their possession of various visible physical features, by their ancestry (for example, by the fact that their parents belonged to that racial group), and by the geographical location from which their ancestors originated. This folk account of race has some overlap with a biological account that sees races as breeding populations that share a common geographical origin, but it is compatible in principle with a degree of intermixing depending on the particular interpretation that is employed of what it means to have a shared ancestry, and it adds to such an account the idea that members of the same race must share visible physical features.

The folk account seems to provide us with the basis for a plausible understanding of the features to which those who engage in what we ordinarily regard as racial discrimination are responding, for instance, it attaches significance to the sharing of visible physical features. In reply, it might be said that there are no visible physical features that distinguish all and only people we would conventionally regard as members of the same racial group, for example, there are no visible physical characteristics that separate Black people from white people. As Naomi Zack puts the point, 'The visual and cultural markers for membership in the black race differ too greatly for there to be any physical traits shared by all black individuals, likewise for whites'.[8] But in order to make sense of the idea of visible racial markers, we do not need to suppose that there are visible physical features possessed by all of the members of a racial group that distinguish them from other races. It is enough that there be a set of characteristic such features, including skin tone, the possession of some of which, to a sufficient degree, is adequate to provide one of the bases for racial classifications.[9] We might then suppose that it is, at least in part, differences in these physical features to which people are responding when they engage in what we ordinarily regard as racial discrimination.

The third approach, which views races or racial groups as a product of social or cultural processes, practices, or institutions, is widely endorsed in the academic literature on race. Even if the notion of race does not capture anything of biological significance, it is plausible to think that racial groups

---

[7] See M. Hardimon, 'The Ordinary Concept of Race', *Journal of Philosophy* 100 (2003): 437–55, at 439–40, 449–51.

[8] N. Zack, 'Life after Race', in N. Zack (ed.), *American Mixed Race: The Culture of Microdiversity* (Lanham, MD: Rowman and Littlefield, 1995), 297–307, at 303.

[9] Hardimon, 'The Ordinary Concept of Race', 444–5.

exist as social constructions. According to this approach, people may belong to the same racial group because they possess particular features that in their social environment mark them out for different treatment, with the result that they often come to regard themselves and each other as co-members of that group and indeed may develop a distinctive shared way of life. On this view, racial groups are real enough—unlike races when they are understood as natural kinds—but they are created by social processes, practices, and institutions.[10] Like the folk account of race, this 'social constructionist' approach potentially provides us with the basis for a plausible account of what people are responding to when they are engaged in what is ordinarily regarded as racial discrimination: they can be seen as responding to particular features the possession of which marks out a person for differential treatment, whether this treatment is favourable or adverse. Social constructionist approaches may vary in terms of their accounts of which features people are responding to in a given social context or society, and they can allow that different people within a particular social context or society may be responding to different features. For some people who are involved in racial discrimination, it might be that it is, at root, appearance alone to which they are responding; others may be responding instead to the presumed ancestry or geographical origin of their victims, for which they regard appearance features as evidence.[11]

I am not planning to evaluate the suitability of these different accounts of race for all of the various purposes that might be served by them. But both the second and third accounts can provide a plausible basis for identifying the features of the world to which people are responding when they engage in what we ordinarily regard as racial discrimination, for they can give a

---

[10] Within social constructionist accounts, a distinction can be drawn between those that see racial groups as necessarily hierarchically organized, and those who think that, in principle, at least they could exist as different ways of life even in the absence of hierarchies between them: see S. Haslanger's and C. Jeffers's contributions to J. Glasgow et al., *What Is Race?* For relevant discussion, see also L. Blum, 'Racial Groups: The Sociohistorical Consensus', *The Monist* 93 (2010): 298–320; J. Glasgow, *A Theory of Race* (London and New York: Routledge, 2009); P. Taylor, 'Appiah's Uncompleted Argument: W. E. B. Du Bois and the Reality of Race', *Social Theory and Practice* 26 (2000): 103–28; S. Haslanger, 'Gender and Race: (What) Are They? (What) Do We Want Them To Be?', *Nous* 34 (2000): 31–55; C. Jeffers, 'The Cultural Theory of Race: Yet Another Look at Du Bois's "The Conservation of Races"', *Ethics* 123 (2013): 403–26.

[11] Linda Alcoff remarks that '[i]t is an indisputable fact about the social reality of mainstream North America that racial consciousness works through learned practices and habits of visual discrimination and visible marks on the body' (L. Alcoff, *Visible Identities: Race, Gender, and the Self* (Oxford: Oxford University Press, 2006), 196). But she also points out that many believe that there is a fact of the matter concerning one's racial identity, determined by one's ancestry.

role to differences in visible physical features, ancestry, and geographical origin. Both of these accounts permits us to suppose that, in a significant range of cases, direct racial discrimination might *be* discrimination on the basis of appearance features, particularly skin tone, because in such cases it is these features alone to which people are responding.

The idea that direct racial discrimination is sometimes a type of appearance discrimination might seem to misunderstand its distinctive character. But this idea is compatible with there being particular histories to be uncovered concerning the origins of racial discrimination (or, indeed, the origins of specific forms of it), its effects, the lived experience of those who encounter it, and how it is sustained. It might nevertheless be argued that equating racial discrimination with appearance discrimination, even in a limited range of cases, collapses an important distinction between racism and colourism. But I don't think it does. When racial discrimination is a type of appearance discrimination, the visual characteristics that form its basis may extend beyond skin tone and include hair texture and facial features, such as the size and shape of one's nose or lips. In so far as some cases of racial discrimination are based solely on skin tone, then they are examples of colourism, a specific kind of appearance discrimination.[12] But colourism may also take place between those of the same race, and when it does it has its own characteristic origins, effects, lived experiences, and mechanisms through which it is maintained and reproduced.[13]

What should we take away from this discussion of race and racial discrimination and how it relates to appearance discrimination? To begin with, it is worth noting that if what is conventionally regarded as direct racial discrimination is sometimes best seen as a distinctive form of discrimination on the basis of appearance, then there is at least some appearance discrimination that may be wrong for the reasons canvassed in Chapters 2 and 3: when appearance discrimination that is also racial discrimination occurs in the context of appointments to advantaged social positions, it may be disrespectful, involve deliberative unfairness in selection decisions, or play a role in generating unjust consequences. But both in principle and in practice, racial discrimination may take different forms. Some cases,

---

[12] For a useful overview of the diverse forms that colourism takes, and the way in which it interacts with gender, see the Introduction to N. Khanna (ed.), *Whiter: Asian American Women on Skin Color and Colorism* (New York: New York University Press, 2020).

[13] For example, in societies with a history of slave ownership, colourism may be a product of the better treatment received by mixed-race children who were the offspring of Black slaves who had non-consensual relationships with white slave owners or overseers. See E. Dabiri, *Don't Touch My Hair* (London: Allen Lane, 2019), 14.

perhaps many, might indeed be best understood as discrimination on the basis of appearance (perhaps with those who share that kind of appearance mistakenly being believed to be of a particular biological kind). But other cases might be best understood as discrimination on the basis of ancestry or geographical origin, for example, on the basis of being descended from those of African origin (perhaps with people who have that ancestry and origin mistakenly being believed to be of a particular biological kind). This is not merely a matter of the intentions or beliefs of the discriminator; rather it has to do with the best interpretation of what discriminators are in fact responding to, taking into account their beliefs and intentions, how they would behave if they came to regard their beliefs as false, and what features of the world their discriminatory behaviour is tracking.

4.2 Concerns about the Analogy between Racial and Appearance Discrimination

Drawing an analogy between appearance discrimination and racial discrimination might seem at best inappropriate and at worst to trivialize racial discrimination. Racial discrimination, it might be said, is a much more serious problem. Of course, if a significant amount of racial discrimination is a form of appearance discrimination, then this to some extent undercuts that criticism. But even if very little or no racial discrimination can be properly understood as appearance discrimination, it seems to me that the analogy between the two has an important role to play: appearance discrimination is not itself a trivial problem and indeed poses a challenge that is global in its reach.

Appearance discrimination is especially troubling in the sphere of employment. Studies reveal how the appearance of candidates affects their chances of being selected for interview, their chances of being appointed and, for those appointed, their chances of being promoted as their careers progress.[14] In a study in Israel that involved sending out pairs of identical CVs to companies that had advertised vacancies, one with a picture attached

---

[14] C. Marlowe, S. Schneider, and C. Nelson, 'Gender and Attractiveness Biases in Hiring Decisions: Are More Experienced Managers Less Biased?', *Journal of Applied Psychology* 81 (1996): 11–21; B. Ruffle and Z. Shtudiner, 'Are Good-Looking People More Employable?', *Management Science* 61 (2015): 1760–76; F. Bóo, M. Rossi, and S. Urzúa, 'The Labor Market Return to an Attractive Face: Evidence from a Field Experiment', *Economics Letters* 118 (2013): 170–2; J. Biddle and D. Hamermesh, 'Beauty, Productivity, and Discrimination: Lawyers' Looks and Lucre', *Journal of Labor Economics* 16 (1998): 172–201.

to it of an attractive or plain-looking man or woman and the other without any picture on it, it was found that attractive men were significantly more likely to be invited for interview than the men with CVs without a picture, and more than twice as likely to be called for interview as plain-looking men. The results were different for women, however. Women candidates *without* pictures had the highest number of invitations for interview, 22% higher than plain-looking women and 30% higher than attractive-looking women.[15] This evidence would suggest that rather than being advantaged by their looks, attractive women are disadvantaged by them in the competition for jobs. But studies in other countries have reached different conclusions. A positive correlation between attractiveness and invitations to interview for both men and women was found in a study in Argentina in which researchers sent out fake CVs with pictures, half of them of attractive individuals and the other half of plain-looking people. The attractive candidates received 36% more call-backs than the plain-looking ones, with no significant overall gender difference.[16] In a study of the impact of managerial experience, gender, and attractiveness on appointments, it was found that all managers, regardless of their level of experience, were biased towards more attractive candidates, with this effect being especially pronounced in the case of attractive men.[17]

Partly as a result of the bias that is shown to attractive candidates in the process of selection, appearance has a profound effect on earnings over the course of people's lives. According to Daniel Hamermesh, studies of earnings in the US that involve rating photographs on the basis of looks provide evidence that below average-looking women earn 4% less than average-looking women, whereas above average-looking women earn 8% more than those who are average-looking; below average-looking men earn 13% less than average-looking men, whereas above average-looking men earn 4% more than average-looking men. In other words, the overall beauty premium for good-looking women is 12%, whereas for men it is 17%.[18] Over their careers, the good-looking on average earn $230,000 more than the below average-looking and $90,000 more than those with average looks.[19]

Similar results have been obtained outside the US. A study in Britain that looked at the impact of height and weight on earnings found that the shortest men and women, that is, those in the bottom 10% of the height

---

[15] Ruffle and Shtudiner, 'Are Good-Looking People More Employable?'.
[16] Bóo et al., 'The Labor Market Return to an Attractive Face'.
[17] Marlowe et al., 'Gender and Attractiveness Biases in Hiring Decisions'.
[18] See Hamermesh, *Beauty Pays*, 45–6.   [19] See Hamermesh, *Beauty Pays*, 47.

distribution for each sex, suffer an earnings penalty.[20] Relatively short men, that is, those in the bottom 10–19% of the distribution, experienced an earnings penalty of 3.8% compared to men of average height, whereas the shortest men experienced an earnings penalty of 4.3%. Relatively short women, in contrast, received a premium of 5.1% compared to women of average height, but the shortest women had a 5% penalty. With respect to weight, women suffered greater penalties than men. Indeed, women in the top 20% in terms of weight experienced an earnings penalty of 5.3% compared to those of average weight. The picture is much the same in other European countries. A study that investigated the link between weight and earnings using data drawn from the European Community Household Panel, focusing on a group of southern European countries (Greece, Italy, Portugal, and Spain) and northern European ones (Austria, Belgium, Denmark, Finland, and Ireland), found that a 10% increase in the average body mass index reduced the per hour earnings of men by 1.86% and of women by 3.27%.[21] Overall, the data reveals the deep effect that height and weight has on earnings, and provides indirect evidence of the complex sex-biased character of appearance norms governing both, and of the way in which these norms influence recruitment and promotion decisions.

Appearance discrimination in employment seems to be as pervasive as other forms of discrimination, including racial discrimination, and its effect on earnings seems to be just as pronounced. According to a study conducted by Rebecca Puhl, Tatiana Andreyeva, and Kelly Brownwell that took self-reported perceptions of discrimination as evidence of it, '[d]iscrimination due to weight/height is common among Americans, with prevalence rates among women close to the prevalence of race discrimination. Weight/height discrimination is the third most common type of discrimination among women, and the fourth most prevalent form of discrimination reported by all adults. Weight/height discrimination occurs in employment settings...virtually as often as race discrimination, and in some cases even more frequently than age or gender discrimination.'[22] With respect to the

---

[20] B. Harper, 'Beauty, Stature and the Labour Market: A British Cohort Study', *Oxford Bulletin of Economics and Statistics* 62 (2000): 771–800.
[21] When looking at the results from North and South Europe separately, it appears that the impact of a high BMI on income is concentrated in the southern European countries that are included in the study: see G. Brunello and B. d'Hombres, 'Does Body Weight Affect Wages? Evidence from Europe', *Economics and Human Biology* 5 (2007): 1–19.
[22] R. Puhl, T. Andreyeva, and K Brownell, 'Perceptions of Weight Discrimination: Prevalence and Comparison to Race and Gender Discrimination in America', *International Journal of Obesity* 32 (2008): 992–1000, at 998.

effects of attractiveness on earnings, Daniel Hamermesh notes that 'African American men's earnings disadvantage, adjusted for the earnings-enhancing characteristics that they bring to labor markets, is similar to the disadvantage experienced by below-average compared to above-average-looking male workers generally'.[23]

Of course, there are differences between appearance discrimination and racial discrimination that are morally relevant. Racial membership is commonly transmitted from one generation to another, even when parents belong to different racial groups, whereas the inheritance of appearance-related characteristics is less reliable.[24] The way in which racial discrimination contributes to and reproduces structural disadvantages, in part through practices of segregation, gives rise to distinctive problems in tackling it. But appearance discrimination also raises serious moral concerns and these concerns are illuminated, at least to some extent, by the similarities between it and racial discrimination. In the next section I focus on some paradigmatic cases of appearance discrimination in employment—ones that are not also examples of racial discrimination—in order to identify the main reasons why it is often wrong through a comparison with racial discrimination.

4.3 Prejudices or Non-rational Responses in Relation to Appearance Features over Which People Lack Control

It is helpful to recall the very different aspects of appearance that may form the basis of appearance discrimination. First, there are appearance features over which a person has no choice, or very little choice, for example, his or her skin tone or height.[25] Second, there are appearance features over which a person has significant but restricted choice. This involves a diverse set of characteristics. Some of these features may be such that the cost or difficulty of not acquiring them, or getting rid of them once acquired, is high,[26] for

---

[23] Hamermesh, *Beauty Pays*, 161.
[24] See X. Liu, 'Discrimination and Lookism', in K. Lippert-Rasmussen (ed.), *Routledge Handbook of the Ethics of Discrimination* (London: Routledge, 2017), 284.
[25] Leg-lengthening surgery is available in some countries but it is risky, expensive, and painful. See https://www.bbc.co.uk/news/world-55146906, accessed 5 July 2022.
[26] For the distinction between cost and difficulty, see G. A. Cohen, *On the Currency of Egalitarian Justice and Other Essays in Political Philosophy* (Princeton, NJ: Princeton University Press, 2011), 16. Cohen's examples provide us with an intuitive grasp of this distinction: 'It is costly, but not difficult, for me to supply you with a cheque for £500.... It is extremely difficult

example, for many middle-aged people, wrinkled skin falls into this category. It also includes features of appearance that a person had unrestricted choice over acquiring, even though it would now be costly or difficult to get rid of them, for example, a large tattoo that he or she was gifted. And it includes features of appearance that a person has unrestricted choice with respect to retaining them, even though he or she had very little, if any, choice over their acquisition, for example, a skin tag that he or she could easily arrange to have removed, without pain, through inexpensive minor surgery. Third, there are appearance features over which a person has unrestricted choice in relation to both acquisition and retention, in that he or she could have refrained from acquiring them, and could now get rid of, without great cost or difficulty in either case, for example, bodily adornments that can be easily removed.

The analogy between appearance discrimination and racial discrimination becomes less strong as we progress through these cases. In the remainder of this section and the next one, I shall focus on appearance discrimination that involves features of the first type, together with features which are such that the cost or difficulty of not acquiring them, *and* of getting rid of them once acquired, is considerable. I shall refer to these as appearance features over which we lack control. I shall include height and facial differences in this category, and also body shapes that are regarded as signifying excessive weight, since for many people avoiding such a shape would require continual rigorous dieting.[27] In this section, I shall examine discrimination on the basis of appearance features over which we lack control when it is fuelled by selectors' prejudices or non-rational reactions, whereas in the next section, I shall examine discrimination on the basis of such features when it is fuelled by selectors' (or employer's) aesthetic

---

for me to transport you to Heathrow on the back of my bicycle, but it is not costly, since I love that kind of challenge, and I have nothing else to do today' (ibid.).

[27] With respect to weight, '[g]enetically determined set-points work to keep bodies within a predetermined range; furthermore, when dieters reduce their calorific intake and increase their exercise, their metabolism slows down to compensate and makes any weight loss difficult to sustain' (D. Rhode, 'The Injustice of Appearance', *Stanford Law Review* 61 (2009): 1033–1101, at 1050). See also L. Wang, 'Weight Discrimination: One Size Fits All Remedy?', *Yale Law Journal* 117 (2008): 1906–8. Wang's reasons for resisting regarding weight discrimination as a form of appearance discrimination seem weak. She assumes without argument that if weight discrimination were a form of appearance discrimination, it would be fuelled by a visceral reaction against fat people as opposed to mistaken views about a person's weight being within their control (see ibid., 1918). It is best to think of the appearance discrimination that takes place against people regarded as fat as relating primarily to their body shape and size, rather than their weight as such: see Section 1.1.

judgements. In Section 4.5, I shall explore appearance discrimination that involves appearance features where the cost and difficulty of not acquiring them is low, and/or the cost and difficulty of getting rid of them once they have been acquired is low. I shall refer to these as appearance features over which we possess control; I shall include tattoos, hairstyles, beards, and bodily adornments in this category.[28] Again, I shall consider discrimination on the basis of such features when it is fuelled by selectors' prejudices, non-rational reactions, or aesthetic judgements before then considering cases where it is fuelled by selectors' (or employer's) reasonable moral judgements, that is, moral judgments that do not deny the fundamental equality of persons.

Consider then the prejudices that are sometimes harboured in relation to features of people's appearance over which they lack control. Like racial discrimination, appearance discrimination on the basis of such features may occur as a result of generalizations that are not supported by the available evidence, for example, the generalization that people who are overweight are lazy or lacking in self-discipline,[29] or that short men are domineering or aggressive because they suffer from inferiority complexes. Furthermore, like racial discrimination, appearance discrimination on the basis of these features may occur as a result of psychological associations between them and character traits or abilities. In general, attractiveness tends to be associated with a range of desirable character traits, and with greater competence across a range of activities, for men at least.[30] A selector who has these asso-

---

[28] I include tattoos, hairstyles, and beards in this category because I am restricting what counts as a cost in the relevant sense. I am only counting costs that would be incurred by a person in acquiring or getting rid of an appearance feature regardless of whether she endorses some particular moral or aesthetic vision that values or disvalues it. So the relevant costs include the physical pain and financial expense that would be involved in acquiring or getting rid of an appearance feature, but not, for example, the feelings of frustration, dissatisfaction, or guilt that might be experienced as a result having to rid oneself of an appearance feature that expresses one's moral or political values. So even if, say, shaving off one's beard would involve acting against what one sees as a religious requirement, it would not be costly in the relevant sense to do so. This restriction I am placing on what counts as a cost is solely for the purpose of classifying appearance features in terms of the control we possess over them.

[29] See J. Agerström and D. Rooth, 'The Role of Automatic Obesity Stereotypes in Real Hiring Discrimination', *Journal of Applied Psychology* 96 (2011): 790–805; Wang, 'Weight Discrimination', 1916–18.

[30] K. Dion, E. Berscheid, and E. Walster, 'What Is Beautiful Is Good', *Journal of Personality and Social Psychology* 24 (1972): 285–90; A. Eagly, R. Ashmore, M. Makhijani, L. Longo, 'What Is Beautiful Is Good, but...: A Meta-Analytic Review of Research on the Physical Attractiveness Stereotype', *Psychological Bulletin* 110 (1991): 109–28; S. Lee, M. Pitesa, M. Pillutla, and S. Thau, 'When Beauty Helps and When It Hurts: An Organizational Context Model of Attractiveness Discrimination in Selection Decisions', *Organizational Behavior and Human Decision Processes* 128 (2015): 15–28; Stockemer and Praino, 'Blinded by Beauty?'; S. Banducci, J. Karp,

ciations may not be aware that they influence his or her deliberations in appointment decisions.

There may be differences here concerning how those with prejudices explain the supposed truth of the unwarranted generalizations they make, but in general at least these differences alone do not seem to be relevant to judging the wrongness or otherwise of the discrimination that occurs as a result of them. For example, people with prejudices about the behaviour of members of a racial group often regard this behaviour as a *causal consequence* of race or membership of that group, for instance, they may believe that Black people are untrustworthy *because* of their genetic makeup or *because* of their upbringing within the Black community. With prejudices about appearance, it is common for an appearance feature to be regarded as a *product* of a particular character trait, for example, people who are regarded as overweight are sometimes thought to be overweight *because* they are lazy or lacking in self-discipline. Despite this difference, prejudices about features of appearance may operate in much the same way as racial prejudices, for example, as stereotypes or associations that influence behaviour non-consciously, and the different types of causal relationship that are thought to obtain do not seem to affect the moral assessment of the discriminatory behaviour to which the prejudices give rise.

The reasons for thinking that racial discrimination is wrong when it involves prejudices about the members of a racial group may also be reasons for thinking that appearance discrimination is wrong when it involves prejudices about appearance features over which people lack control. Sometimes selectors' prejudices about an appearance feature may result in them treating a candidate *disrespectfully*, that is, failing to take due account of his or her moral standing. This may happen when the aspect of appearance that is the basis of the prejudice interacts in some way with membership of a disadvantaged group based on another characteristic. As a possible example, consider the way in which a selector may treat an interviewee as 'dumb' because she has natural blond hair and he associates such hair in women with stupidity. In this case, it is being a natural blond-haired woman—a combination of membership of a disadvantaged group and an appearance feature—that is the object of prejudice and the basis of the discrimination she experiences. This is potentially disrespectful in so far as she

M. Thrasher, and C. Rallings, 'Ballot Photographs as Cues in Low-Information Elections', *Political Psychology* 29 (2008): 903–17; Ritts, Patterson, and Tubbs, 'Expectations, Impressions, and Judgments of Physically Attractive Students'.

is being treated as if this combination of features means that she is likely to exercise inappropriately the capacities in virtue of which she has her moral status.

Appearance discrimination fuelled by prejudices may also be disrespectful when the appearance feature that elicits the prejudice is itself stigmatized. Consider, for example, the practice of 'fat shaming', which denigrates people regarded as overweight. As part of that practice, those regarded as obese are treated not merely as aesthetically unappealing but as morally flawed because they are seen as lazy or lacking in self-control despite many of them having little or no control over their weight. These prejudices may be internalized by selectors and influence appointments to advantaged social positions. Attributing a moral flaw to a person is not the same as regarding them as lacking a characteristic that is necessary for their equal moral worth. But in so far as a capacity to act autonomously, that is, to act in pursuit of one's own goals, is one of the characteristics that gives a person their moral status, when a person is treated as if they lack that capacity, or as if they lack the ability to make appropriate use of it because they have no self-control, then they are being treated disrespectfully. Much the same is true of shortness of height in men, which is also stigmatized in virtue of the prejudices that surround it. Men who are short are regarded not merely as unattractive, but also as possessing inferiority complexes that are likely to make them lose control and become aggressive. Again, these prejudices may be internalized by selectors in a way that influences their decisions in recruitment processes and discrimination rooted in them may be disrespectful.

In both cases I have described, selectors with prejudices about appearance features do not take due account of the moral standing of some of the candidates for a job. Furthermore, in both cases, because of a history of disadvantage, and the power relations that obtain, the acts of discrimination involved may be demeaning because these acts send out the message to others that the candidates concerned lack the capacities or characteristics required in order to be moral equals, or at least, that these candidates are likely to make inappropriate use of the relevant capacities or characteristics, similar in this way to some acts of racial discrimination that convey the message that members of a particular racial group are morally inferior. Just as the lack of respect that occurs in some forms of racial discrimination rooted in prejudice makes it wrong, so too the lack of respect that occurs in some forms of appearance discrimination rooted in prejudice makes it wrong.

Even though it is hard to demean someone over whom you lack power, is it impossible to do so? It might be thought that fat shaming is one way in which the less powerful can sometimes demean the more powerful. Consider, for example, employees who joke about the size of their boss. Hellman might resist the idea that their behaviour could be demeaning. She wants to distinguish between mere disrespect, which may take the form of insults, and demeaning behaviour properly so-called.[31] Only the latter puts a person down in the relevant sense since merely disrespectful behaviour does not amount to treating a person as if they lacked equal moral worth. On this view, the difference between merely disrespectful and demeaning behaviour may lie in the power relations that obtain rather than in the content of what is said. But even if fat shaming is demeaning only if the person who engages in it has power over the victim, that need not require the victim to be a member of *some other* disadvantaged group. Since those regarded as obese are themselves a stigmatized group as a result of prejudices that are held about them and the treatment they receive, slim people may possess sufficient power to demean a man who is obese even when they have less power along other dimensions, for example, when the slim person is a female employee and he is the boss.

What should we say about non-rational responses (that is, responses that do not have a motivating reason) that are directed towards people with a particular appearance feature, a feature over which most or all of them lack control? Suppose, for example, that some selectors simply respond more favourably to those they regard as good-looking: they find themselves preferring a good-looking candidate without having a reason why; they may even prefer a good-looking candidate because they give more importance to his or her achievements than these merit as a result of being influenced by his or her appearance.[32] Just as the non-rational negative responses that are sometimes involved in racial discrimination need not be based on any general beliefs or stereotypes about members of the racial group that is being victimized, so too favourable responses towards the attractive, or negative responses to the unattractive, need not be based on any general beliefs or stereotypes about the attractive or the unattractive. These responses may be

---

[31] Hellman, *When Is Discrimination Wrong?*, pp. 29, 36.
[32] Deborah Rhode cites evidence that '[a]ppearance...skews judgements about competence and job performance....Resumes get a more favourable assessment when they are thought to belong to more attractive individuals' (D. Rhode, *The Beauty Bias. The Injustice of Appearance in Life and Law* (Oxford: Oxford University Press, 2010), 27).

a product of socialization, or even perhaps a result of how we are 'wired', and they can generate biases in the context of selection decisions.

Sometimes, at least, a selector who discriminates in favour of those he finds attractive, or against those he finds unattractive, as a result of non-rational responses towards them, may fail to give respect to the victims of such discrimination. He may fail to take due account of their moral standing by allowing these responses to influence his behaviour, whether culpably or not. Indeed, discriminatory acts that are a product of non-rational responses may be disrespectful in virtue of sending out a demeaning message. For example, selectors may show disgust towards a candidate's facial scarring, perhaps avoiding making eye contact with him or her, in a way that is demeaning because in their society it conveys the message that he or she, and others with facial differences, are morally inferior, whether they intend to convey this message or not.[33]

Discrimination on the basis of appearance features over which people lack control may also be wrong when it is a product of prejudice or is rooted purely in non-rational responses on the grounds that it involves *deliberative unfairness*. In the process of selecting for jobs and other advantaged social positions, those whose qualifications are given less weight as a result of a selector's prejudices about their appearance, or a non-rational response to it, are unfairly disadvantaged regardless of whether they end up being appointed, and regardless of whether the selector is blameworthy. It is unfair when selectors' prejudices or non-rational responses relating to (say) the height or body shape of candidates influence their decisions. When this happens, the victims' interests are not being given due weight in the selection process. The discrimination they suffer may also be unfair because their legitimate expectation that appointments will be made on the basis of qualifications have been frustrated. Even if direct appearance discrimination is rife in a society, when there are public declarations of commitment to appointing on the basis of qualifications, then there is a legitimate expectation that selection decisions will be made on that basis rather than on the basis of appearance when appearance cannot be construed as a qualification.

---

[33] Interpreting his experiences through the lens of Erving Goffman's *Stigma: Notes on the Management of Spoiled Identity*, James Partridge writes that his scars 'were marks that not only rendered me unusual, odd, an outsider, alienated but also, critically, degraded me to a lower moral order' (J. Partridge, *Face It. Facial Disfigurement and My Fight for Face Equality* (Pebble Press, 2020), 63).

Appearance discrimination involving prejudices or rooted purely in non-rational responses may also be wrong when it relates to features of appearance over which people lack control on the grounds that it plays a role in producing *unjust consequences*. When selectors are influenced by the same prejudices, or share the same non-rational responses, the victims of appearance discrimination may find it much harder to secure particular kinds of advantaged social positions, and in that way be prevented from obtaining the internal and external goods made available by these positions. (When groups marked out by their appearance become stigmatized, such as people who are regarded as overweight or who have facial differences, then acts of discrimination against them may even contribute to lowering their moral standing.) Appearance discrimination rooted in prejudices or non-rational reactions may therefore generate significant inequalities, with people who possess particular appearance features, such as short height, or a body shape regarded as signifying excessive weight, losing out.

Whether the inequalities involved here are judged to be unjust will depend to a considerable extent on the particular theory of justice that is endorsed.[34] It is nevertheless plausible to think that appearance discrimination rooted in prejudices or non-rational reactions is wrong when it relates to features of appearance over which people lack control and contributes to creating sizeable inequalities. Appearance discrimination of this kind may have a serious impact on its victims' interest in autonomous agency, since the fulfilment of their plans may rely on possessing or realizing the internal or external goods provided by particular kinds of jobs, their access to which is restricted. They may want to pursue self-realization through their work, or take advantage of leisure opportunities that the remuneration attached to these jobs would make possible. Their interest in autonomous agency may also be set back because their deliberative freedom is impaired. When discrimination against those with particular appearance features over which they lack control is widespread and rooted in prejudices or non-rational reactions, victims of it may be forced to take into account how these prejudices and non-rational reactions affect their access to advantaged social positions and to factor that into their decision-making about which jobs to apply for.

---

[34] See Sections 3.1 and 3.2.

4.4 Aesthetic Judgements Concerning Appearance Features over Which People Lack Control

What should we say about cases in which a selector rejects candidates not because he or she has a prejudice about their appearance, or a non-rational response to it, but simply because he or she finds their looks aesthetically unappealing, yet they lack control over their looks? Here we seem to bump up against one limit of the analogy between racial discrimination and appearance discrimination. There are cases of racial discrimination that are rooted in aesthetic judgements, but they seem to be cases of appearance discrimination as well. For example, a candidate for a job might be rejected because a selector regards his or her dark skin tone as aesthetically unappealing. This seem to be a case of *both* direct racial and direct appearance discrimination; or, at least, if it is not direct racial discrimination, then it is direct discrimination on the basis of skin colour.

It might be thought that aesthetic judgements concerning a person's looks simply *are* non-rational responses that are a product of either hard-wired preferences or internalized appearance norms that reflect or express collective tastes. But even if aesthetic judgements are non-cognitive because they merely express brute preferences or collective tastes, the responses they evoke are not best conceived as non-rational. A response is non-rational if and only if it is not motivated by a reason, but if aesthetic judgements are motivated by preferences or tastes, then these preferences and tastes can be construed as motivating reasons even if they cannot be rationally justified. In any case, according to at least some philosophical analyses of aesthetic judgement, these judgements need not be *merely* the expression of non-cognitive preferences or tastes. They may be more or less justifiable in virtue of being appropriately sensitive to aesthetically relevant features of the world. In so far as aesthetic judgements can be justifiable because they track aesthetically relevant properties, appearance norms that express aesthetic judgements may also be justifiable from an aesthetic point of view.

Discrimination on the basis of aesthetic judgements, concerning appearance features over which people lack control, may be wrong because it involves deliberative unfairness. For the kind of reasons given earlier, when a selector making an employment decision is influenced by his or her own aesthetic judgements concerning the appearance of candidates, perhaps fuelled by widely endorsed appearance norms, then it is difficult to justify. It is hard to see how deliberative fairness can permit the selector's aesthetic preferences, that is, the preferences of the person who is responsible for choosing, or playing a part in choosing, an employee, to be given any weight at all, qua occupant of that role. In so far as these preferences are given some weight, then that would seem to be unfair because the interests of at least some candidates, namely, those who lack the relevant appearance feature, have been given insufficient weight. But what if the selector is also the employer, or the employer authorizes the selector to choose on the basis of a particular aesthetic vision that they want their company to reflect and express, perhaps because they believe that this will make their business more successful?

In this case, it would seem that giving due weight to the interests of each of the candidates is consistent with giving some weight to the employer's interests, including their interest in developing or making profitable a company with a particular aesthetic vision. Indeed, since the employer's interest in autonomous agency would be at stake here, this may permit a significant amount of weight to be given to their aesthetic judgements, and consequently justify a significant amount of appearance discrimination, in so far as they are making a genuine attempt to present a particular aesthetic vision through their employment practices, rather than simply letting their prejudices or non-rational responses influence their selection policy.[35]

But even if deliberative fairness permits significant weight to be given to the aesthetic judgements of the employer, there may be other objections to appearance discrimination fuelled by these judgements. Appearance discrimination rooted in aesthetic judgements may be wrong because of its role in producing unjust consequences. Suppose that an employer authorizes a selector to reject candidates with various appearance features over which they lack control, because she wants her company to express a particular aesthetic vision. She may be acting wrongly when the policy she has adopted reflects a society-wide pattern of decision-making that is shaped by commonly endorsed appearance norms and has adverse effects on those who possess these appearance features. Her employment policy may contribute to creating an unjust distribution (for example, when acts of discrimination of this type lead to large earnings differentials between those with a body shape regarded as signifying excessive weight and those with

---

[35] There are also a range of difficult questions concerning what weight deliberative fairness permits selectors to give to the aesthetic preferences or judgements of customers and clients, particularly when doing so can contribute to the success of a business. I shall explore the issue of when appearance discrimination that is rooted in the aesthetic judgements of customers or clients (rather than merely those of the selector or employer) is morally permissible in the next chapter.

other body shapes) or to lowering the moral standing of members of a group (for example, when acts of discrimination of this type lead to those with darker skin tone being regarded as morally inferior).

Of particular concern here is the way in which appearance discrimination may be fuelled by appearance norms that set demanding aesthetic standards, but which people lack control in relation to satisfying and which are biased against a disadvantaged group. The operation of these norms has a worse effect on that group even when the individuals who endorse them and act on them are not themselves biased against it. Employment decisions influenced by biased appearance norms of this kind may contribute to structural injustices by exacerbating the disadvantages experienced by members of a group. Consider some different ways in which appearance norms may be biased against a group and be implicated in creating or sustaining structural injustices.

As we have already seen, appearance norms may be *racially biased* because they are harder or more costly for members of one racial group to comply with compared to others. This includes not only norms that favour lighter skin tone over darker skin tone but also norms that regard broad noses as ugly or tight curly hair as messy. When appearance discrimination is a product of acting in accordance with a racially biased appearance norm in a way that does not involve any racial bias on the part of those engaged in it (that is, their behaviour is not motivated by racial prejudice or caused by non-rational negative responses to the members of a racial group), then it constitutes indirect rather than direct racial discrimination. In so far as their behaviour plays a role in creating or maintaining an unjust distribution of benefits and burdens, it is nevertheless wrongful.

Appearance norms may be *gender biased* because they are harder or more costly for one gender to comply with compared to the other. These include gender-specific norms that make demands on one gender but not the other (for example, norms requiring women but not men to wear makeup, and norms that forbid men from wearing makeup), and gender-differentiated norms that make greater demands in various respects on one gender compared to the other (for example, norms governing weight or body shape, which make greater demands on women).[36] When

---

[36] The gender-biased character of many appearance norms, and the way in which these norms tend to make much greater demands on women than men, has been a central theme of feminist thought. For an exemplar, see N. Wolf, *The Beauty Myth. How Images of Beauty Are Used against Women* (London: Chatto and Windus, 1990).

discrimination is influenced by these norms, then it constitutes direct discrimination on the basis of gender and may contribute to creating or sustaining unjust inequalities.

Appearance norms may be *biased against people with a disability*, for example, norms that value symmetrical bodies or faces may have a worse effect on those with particular physical disabilities. So too appearance norms may be *biased against people who are economically deprived*, for example, norms with which it is expensive financially to comply have a worse effect on those who do not have very much money. When appearance norms are biased against people with particular disabilities, or against the economically deprived, the indirect discrimination fuelled by them may also contribute to creating or sustaining unjust inequalities.

Many appearance norms are also what might be called 'naturally biased' because, independently of whether they are biased in other respects, they place greater demands on people whose appearance is, as a result of their physical constitution, further away from the ideal that the norm specifies, that is, whose genes or biological makeup mean that it is harder or more costly for them to comply with the norm. Some are born with the potential to acquire the looks that these norms prize without needing to make much effort or incur many costs, for example, some boys are born with the potential to become tall, and thus in later life (assuming adequate nutrition and nothing untoward happens to them) they will fare better when judged against a norm that regards tall men as better-looking. When appearance discrimination is fuelled by naturally biased appearance norms, does it discriminate wrongly in virtue of playing a role in generating unjust consequences?

On some theories of distributive justice, that would seem to follow. Luck egalitarians, for example, should have moral qualms about appearance discrimination when it is fuelled by naturally biased appearance norms, on the grounds that the acts of discrimination it involves make some worse off than others through no fault of their own, at least in so far as those made worse off do not receive compensation for the disadvantages they experience. As we have seen, there is empirical evidence that significant economic benefits flow to people regarded as more attractive when judged against these norms. This evidence does not distinguish between inequalities that arise as a result of appearance features being reasonably regarded as qualifications for advantaged social positions and those that do not arise in this way, nor does it distinguish between the different possible origins of appearance discrimination, such as whether it is rooted in prejudices, non-rational reactions or aesthetic judgements. But it provides some grounds for thinking that people who are perceived as better-looking when judged against naturally biased appearance norms are systematically being rewarded with economic benefits, and the sizeable inequalities thereby created ought to be of concern from a luck egalitarian point of view, especially when these inequalities are worsened by the impact on employment opportunities of prejudices and non-rational reactions concerning various appearance features. Other theories of distributive justice should also have qualms about appearance discrimination that is informed by naturally biased appearance norms to the extent that these acts contribute to the creation of inequalities of a particular size or character, for example, when they contribute to creating inequalities in which those who are worst off are unable to lead flourishing lives.

4.5 Choice and the Limits of the Analogy between Race and Appearance

In the previous two sections of this chapter, I have focused on features of a person's appearance over which he or she lacks control. I argued that in cases where appearance discrimination relates to these features, the analogy between the wrongness of appearance discrimination and the wrongness of racial discrimination is forceful, although it reaches a limit in cases where discrimination is rooted in aesthetic judgements. When we consider other features of appearance over which people have much more control, the analogy between the wrongness of appearance discrimination and the wrongness of racial discrimination seems to reach another limit. There is a very restricted role for choice when it comes to racial membership, whereas we have a much greater degree of control over some appearance features, and this seems to make a difference to our judgements about the permissibility of cases of appearance discrimination that are based on these features.[37] So what should we say about discrimination based on appearance features over which we possess control, that is, appearance features where

---

[37] It is controversial whether one's race can be chosen or is simply a given. Since it is mistaken to regard race as a natural biological kind, membership of a racial group may depend in some way, or to some degree, on a person's identifications. For relevant discussion, see R. Tuvel, 'In Defence of Transracialism', *Hypatia* 32 (2017): 263–78.

the cost and difficulty of not acquiring them is low, and/or the cost and difficulty of ridding oneself of them once they have been acquired is low?

It might be argued that those who grow beards, or have visible tattoos or piercings, should know that some have prejudices about these features of appearance, or have a non-rational negative response to them, or find them aesthetically unappealing. If an aspect of a man's appearance is under his control, then wouldn't it be fair to require him to bear the costs of it, even if it expresses his own aesthetic vision, or his self-chosen identity in some other way? In this respect, isn't it similar to an expensive taste, one that may mean that a person has to forego various opportunities because of the prejudices, non-rational aversions, or aesthetic sensitivity of others, including selectors, towards this aspect of his or her appearance?

As we shall see later in this section, the fact that an appearance feature was chosen may make a difference to our judgements concerning whether discriminating on the basis of it contributes to creating an *unjust outcome*. But it is not clear that it makes any difference to how much weight *deliberative fairness* requires selectors to give to a candidate's interest in not being subject to discrimination on the basis of that feature in an appointment process. Deliberative fairness requires due weight to be given to the interests of each candidate. But that does not seem to permit a selector to discount (or give less weight to) candidates' interest in not being subject to discrimination on the basis of an appearance feature simply because that feature is under their control and he has a non-rational reaction to it, a prejudice about it, or regards it as aesthetically unappealing.

When a candidate has made a relatively trivial choice to acquire an appearance feature, in the sense that it does not reflect or express any deeply held moral or aesthetic beliefs, it seems wrong, because unfair, that she should be disadvantaged in the process of selection merely as a result of a selector's prejudices about it, non-rational responses to it, or aesthetic judgements concerning it. When a candidate's appearance is a product of her deeply held beliefs about how she should present herself to the world, it seems even harder to deny that she is treated unfairly if her prospects of being appointed to a job are negatively affected by the prejudices, non-rational reactions, or aesthetic responses of selectors in relation to it. If she is rejected as a result, she is unfairly treated in the selection process because her interests are not given due weight. So, even though the analogy between the wrongness of racial discrimination and the wrongness of appearance discrimination reaches a limit in cases where a person has control over an appearance feature that forms the basis of the discrimination she experiences, in one respect at least this limit does not seem to be significant for our moral assessment of that discrimination.

So too when selectors make *moral* judgements about an appearance feature over which a person possesses control. Suppose, for example, that a selector believes that tattoos disrespect one's body, or that makeup exhibits an excessive concern for one's appearance, or that people who do not make the best of their looks are failing in their moral duty to themselves, and these beliefs then influence his selection decisions. In cases such as these, the selector's judgements are not based on prejudices in my narrow sense and are reasonable in the minimal sense that they don't deny the fundamental equality of persons. Here the analogy between racial discrimination and appearance discrimination is again unhelpful because it is hard to provide coherent descriptions of relevantly similar cases involving race. In practice, moral judgements about race tend to involve prejudices or a denial of moral equality, for example, the moral judgement that members of a particular racial group are untrustworthy. But even though the analogy with racial discrimination is unhelpful in these cases, we should surely conclude that it is unfair when a selector's decision-making is influenced by his own particular moral judgements concerning an appearance feature, on the grounds that this gives insufficient weight to the interests of some candidates.

Cases where selectors act on their own personal moral or aesthetic judgements concerning an appearance feature over which the candidates have control are important, but it might be thought that they are not as significant, either in theory or in practice, as cases where a selector is acting on the moral or aesthetic judgements of his employer, or the selector *is* the employer. In these cases, it would seem that deliberative fairness permits considerable weight to be given to the interests of the employer, especially when her deeply held moral convictions are at stake. Indeed, it might be argued that when an employer has a reasonable moral objection to an appearance feature, she is permitted to discriminate on the basis of it, or to authorize those who select on her behalf to do so, not least because by employing people with it she might be taken to be endorsing her employees' choices, for example, to be approving of their tattoos or implants. Those who work for an employer represent her business, and she might think that her choice of employees sends out a message about her values or the values to which her business is committed. Indeed, if her business is committed to an ethical doctrine that condemns body art or body modifications, such as tattoos, piercings, or implants, then it might seem that she is permitted to discriminate on these grounds when selecting for roles within it because of the message that not doing so would convey. Note, however, that even here deliberative fairness does not seem to permit us to give less weight to a candidate's interest in not being subject to discrimination on the basis of an appearance feature simply because he chose that feature; rather it permits us to give weight to the employer's interest in expressing a particular moral ethos or vision through her business.

The message that an employer sends out by their choice of employees will be affected by what forms of discrimination are legally permitted. In a society where discrimination against those with tattoos or body implants is prohibited, when an employer hires a person with them, this need not send out a message that the employer approves of body art or body modifications. But what if there is no legislation in place? And even if there is legislation in place, mightn't an employer reasonably regard himself, or his organization, as implicated in supporting or promoting a way of life by hiring people committed to it and paying them a salary, perhaps in a way that undermines its ethos? That might be thought to be the case with employing someone who has visible tattoos or noticeable body implants.

Deliberative fairness therefore seems to permit employers in their selection policies to give considerable weight to their own interests when these interests relate to their desire to run a business with an ethos that expresses certain values. It permits an employer to authorize a selector to choose employees on the basis of reasonable moral or aesthetic judgements concerning appearance features that are under their control, when an employer has a genuine desire for his or her company to express a particular moral or aesthetic ethos that reflects these judgements. But there is undoubtedly some balancing to be done here: there is a danger of giving too much weight to the interests of the employer relative to the interests of the candidates, including the candidates' interest in self-expression and autonomous agency more generally. Compare the issue of whether a company with a religious ethos that frowns upon abortion or adultery is morally permitted to discount candidates that have had abortions or that are in adulterous relationships. It is at least questionable whether deliberative fairness would permit a company to engage in such a practice, even though appointing candidates who have behaved in these ways conflicts with its ethos.

When is appearance discrimination that reflects an employer's reasonable moral judgements concerning an appearance feature that is under a person's control wrongful in virtue of contributing to the production of unjust consequences? Sometimes it may be wrongful for much the same reason that discrimination relating to appearance features over which people lack control is wrongful, namely because it exacerbates an unjust disadvantage that has some other basis. For example, consider workplace appearance codes that are gender-differentiated and place greater burdens on women than men, such as a code which requires women to wear makeup or high-heeled shoes. Even when these codes are not particularly costly or difficult for women to comply with, they may nevertheless be wrongful because they contribute to creating an unjust distribution of benefits and burdens.

When people experience discrimination in employment that relates to appearance features over which they have control, but not in a way that is connected to their membership of a disadvantaged group, there may nevertheless be reasons for worrying about its consequences. Discrimination against people with visible tattoos, for example, may set back a person's interest in living in accordance with his or her own moral and aesthetic values. That interest may be setback considerably when employers routinely impose workplace appearance codes that forbid visible tattoos perhaps because, like others in their society, they have internalized an appearance norm that disapproves of them, whether for aesthetic or moral reasons. But what weight should we give to a person's interest in being able to modify or adorn their body in accordance with their own conception of how to live when judging whether appearance discrimination in employment contributes to the production of unjust consequences? And what significance should we attach to the fact that an appearance feature has been chosen, in making these judgements? Our answers to these questions will be determined, or at least deeply influenced by, the particular theory of justice we endorse.

One crucial issue here concerns the currency of justice, that is, how we should compare people's situations in judging whether one individual is made worse off than another, in a way that is relevant from the point of view of justice, as a result of experiencing discrimination. Suppose that, at the fundamental level, well-being is the appropriate currency. In judging whether a practice of appearance discrimination in employment, relating to an appearance feature over which people have control, contributes to creating or maintaining an unjust distribution, we will then need to consider the impact of that practice on the levels of well-being of all those affected by it, including employers, candidates with and without that feature, and those who will interact with the successful candidates in the performance of their jobs. In a judgement of this kind, the candidates' interests in being able to modify or adorn their bodies in accordance with their own conception of how to live should surely be given considerable weight, especially when such a practice is widespread.

If, however, an adequate theory of justice should give weight to personal responsibility for outcomes, as one of my framing assumptions requires, then it might seem that the appropriate currency of justice is *access* to well-being, or the opportunity to acquire well-being, rather than well-being itself. If so, then the deficits in well-being experienced by people who have been discriminated against in employment decisions as a result of their choice to modify or adorn their bodies in a particular manner, in full knowledge that doing so may adversely affect their chances of employment, would not seem to be relevant to determining whether they have been unjustly disadvantaged. In such cases, the impediment to employment they face as a result of their choices would not count as a restriction on their access to well-being, properly understood.

A more nuanced position here would allow that a person's access to well-being would be restricted, in a way that is relevant from the point of view of justice, if he or she is put in a position in which self-chosen aspects of his or her appearance are an obstacle to securing employment opportunities when these aspects reflect deeply held moral or aesthetic commitments. For example, to the extent that a man's tattoos reflect a commitment to body art and its value, we might think that even though they are self-chosen, it would be unjust for him to have to bear the costs of appearance discrimination when that would mean that he is deprived of a range of employment opportunities that others enjoy. A position of this kind could find support in G. A. Cohen's defence of subsidizing expensive tastes with which a person identifies, that is, expensive tastes that are informed by his or her valuational judgements.[38]

On the other hand, if the relevant currency is resources rather than (access to) well-being, and we use Ronald Dworkin's envy test to determine when someone has been disadvantaged in a way that is relevant to the just distribution of benefits and burdens, then we may reach different conclusions.[39] The person who has chosen a particular feature of appearance, a facial tattoo say, as a form of self-expression presumably prefers that tattoo and their more restricted set of employment options to being without that tattoo and having a wider range of employment options. According to this view, they do not, therefore, experience any relevant disadvantage when

---

[38] See G. A. Cohen, 'Expensive Taste Rides Again', in J. Burley (ed.), *Dworkin and His Critics* (Malden, MA: Blackwell Publishing, 2004), 3–29, especially 7–8, 10–13, 20–2.

[39] See R. Dworkin, *Sovereign Virtue. The Theory and Practice of Equality* (Cambridge, MA: Harvard University Press, 2002), 67–71, 85–6.

they suffer from discrimination on the basis of their tattoo. From this perspective, the desire for a facial tattoo in a society where these elicit disapproval, either because they are thought to be aesthetically unappealing or because there are thought to be moral objections to modifying one's body in this way, can be regarded as an expensive taste that can legitimately affect distributive outcomes. In a book on appearance discrimination, I cannot hope to resolve to anyone's satisfaction these issues concerning the currency of justice, but much turns on them when we are considering aspects of people's appearance that are under their control.

4.6 Concluding Remarks

When appearance discrimination is rooted in features of a person's appearance over which he or she lacks control, it may be wrong for much the same kinds of reasons that racial discrimination is wrong. It may be wrong in some cases because it is disrespectful. It may be wrong because it has unjust consequences in virtue of contributing to the creation of an unjust distribution of benefits and burdens or contributing to lowering the perceived moral standing of a group. Furthermore, it is wrong when it is rooted in the selector's own prejudices, non-rational reactions, or aesthetic judgements because it is deliberatively unfair in virtue of giving insufficient weight to the interests of at least some of the candidates. Deliberative fairness nevertheless permits selectors to give weight to their employer's interest in expressing her own moral and aesthetic vision for her company, provided that this vision is compatible with the fundamental equality of persons.

In cases where a person suffers discrimination on the basis of a feature of appearance over which he or she has control, the issues are harder to resolve. When selectors are influenced in their decisions by their own prejudices, non-rational responses, or moral or aesthetic judgements, then there is still a strong case for holding that this is deliberatively unfair, although again deliberative fairness permits considerable weight to be given to the interests that employers may have in running a company with a particular moral and aesthetic vision. In judging whether a practice of appearance discrimination contributes to an unjust distribution of benefits and burdens, we need to be guided by particular theories of justice and these diverge on the issue of whether the outcomes experienced by those who suffer discrimination as a result of self-chosen features of their appearance are potentially unjust.

Although I have addressed the issue of how the interests of the employer can influence the permissibility of appearance discrimination, I have put to one side the question of how the interests of customer, clients, and co-workers may affect it. What weight, if any, are selectors permitted to give to the appearance-related moral and aesthetic judgements of those with whom the successful candidate will interact in carrying out the role that is being filled, such as customers or clients, and indeed prospective colleagues? This takes us into the realm of what are often called 'reaction qualifications' and suggests that there may be further limits to the analogy between the wrongness of appearance discrimination and the wrongness of racial discrimination. It is to this issue that I turn in the next chapter.

5
Appearance as a Reaction Qualification

In the previous chapter, I focused on cases where discrimination has its origins in selectors' or employers' prejudices, non-rational responses, or moral or aesthetic judgements concerning appearance.[1] But there is another class of cases that are particularly important, where what is at issue is whether a selector (acting on behalf of an employer) is morally permitted to give weight to the preferences of customers, clients, and co-workers concerning the appearance features of the employees with whom they will interact, or to give weight to their responses to these features, when these features would otherwise have nothing to do with a person's ability to do the job.

Alan Wertheimer refers to the diverse array of people with whom an employee will interact in the course of doing his or her job as 'the recipients' and characterizes qualifications rooted in their preferences and responses as 'reaction qualifications'.[2] For example, when customers—a group of recipients—prefer sales assistants to be polite, and shop at a store in part because of the politeness of its staff, then a willingness to behave politely is a reaction qualification for the job of sales assistant in it. But when is counting a reaction qualification morally objectionable and when is it unobjectionable? And what are the implications of our view on this matter for whether we are permitted to treat the possession of some appearance feature as a qualification when recipients would prefer to deal with employees who have that feature?

It is clearly unobjectionable to count some reaction qualifications. If customers really do prefer sales assistants to behave politely, and it makes a difference to where they shop, then it is surely morally permissible for a selector to count a willingness to behave politely as a qualification for the

---

[1] This chapter draws upon my 'Appearance, Discrimination, and Reaction Qualifications', *Journal of Political Philosophy* 25 (2017): 48–71, although I have reframed my position somewhat and refined it.

[2] See A. Wertheimer, 'Jobs, Qualifications, and Preference', *Ethics* 94 (1983): 99–112.

job. But there are also cases in which counting reaction qualifications is equally clearly objectionable, including cases of racial discrimination. Suppose that customers would prefer not to be served by Black people because they believe that they are untrustworthy, and they respond more favourably to white shop assistants. As a result, white assistants achieve better sales figures. There is an unproblematic sense in which 'being white' is a qualification for the job of sales assistant, but selectors have a weighty moral reason not to count it when deciding who to employ and employers have a weighty moral reason not to require selectors take it into consideration.

But what about cases in which appearance or aspects of appearance are reaction qualifications? Suppose that clients or customers prefer to deal with good-looking employees or respond more favourably to them, with the result that good-looking employees are beneficial for businesses. Suppose that television viewers prefer to see good-looking reporters on their screens and choose the news programmes they watch partly on that basis. Would there be any moral reason for selectors not to take into account these preferences or responses when appointing to such positions? There is also a wide range of difficult cases in which an unconventional appearance, rather than good looks as such, provokes a negative response in customers and clients, for example, facial tattoos or piercings, and hairstyles that involve dreadlocks, braids, or bright colours. In these cases, is there any moral reason not to allow that response to count against applicants with such an appearance?

My aim in this chapter is to develop a framework that explains what makes a reaction qualification illegitimate or illegitimate and apply it in the context of appearance discrimination. Reflecting on these issues reveals a significant disanalogy between appearance discrimination and racial discrimination. Whilst there is generally a strong moral reason not to take into account reaction qualifications rooted in a preference on the part of customers or clients to deal with (or not to deal with) those who belong to a particular racial group, there is often no moral reason not to take into account reaction qualifications rooted in a preference on the part of customers or clients to deal with (or not to deal with) those with particular appearance features.

5.1 Core Cases and Key Cases

Let me stipulate that a reaction qualification is *legitimate* if and only if there is no weighty moral reason for selectors not to count it, whereas it is *illegitimate* if and only if there is such a reason for them not to count it. Drawing the distinction in this way leaves open the possibility that even though a reaction qualification is illegitimate, there are cases in which counting it is morally justified *all things considered*. I shall return to this issue in Section 5.7. It also leaves open the possibility that some reaction qualifications may be legitimate even though there is a weak moral reason for selectors not to count them. These non-weighty reasons would need to be taken into account in making all things considered judgements about whether selectors are justified in counting a reaction qualification.

Before we can determine when, if at all, a person's appearance can be a legitimate reaction qualification, it is instructive to begin with some cases that are not appearance related but in response to which we are relatively confident in our judgements, the first two of which I have already mentioned. I shall refer to them as *core cases*:

Normal Customers. Customers prefer to be served by sales assistants who behave politely, and they buy more goods from them. As a result, when stores are hiring, they give preference to applicants who are willing to behave politely.

Prejudiced Customers. A department store's customers are prejudiced against people who belong to a particular racial group. They prefer not to be served by them because they believe members of this group are dishonest or untrustworthy and they would shop elsewhere were the store to employ them as sales assistants. As a result, the store has a policy of not employing members of this group.

Female Patients. The female patients registered at a medical practice would prefer to consult a doctor of the same sex about gynaecological problems and are reluctant to make appointments with male doctors, even though they don't deny that the medical skills of male doctors are just as good. The practice is recruiting a new doctor and has few female doctors, so treats being female as a qualification.

In relation to *Normal Customers*, there is a consensus that there is no moral reason not to count a willingness to behave politely as a qualification for the job, in other words, that it is a legitimate reaction qualification, whilst in relation to *Prejudiced Customers*, it is almost universally agreed that there is a weighty moral reason for the store to refrain from counting membership in a favoured racial group as a qualification for working there, in other words, that it is an illegitimate reaction qualification. I shall treat these judgements as fixed points in our deliberations: any adequate account of how we should distinguish illegitimate from legitimate reaction qualifications will need to be able to make sense of our judgements about these cases. The other core case is more contentious but nevertheless commands reasonably widespread agreement: under the circumstances described it is generally agreed that being female is a legitimate reaction qualification for the job. But even among those who agree with this verdict, there may be considerable disagreement over the reasons for it. Any adequate theory of reaction qualifications should be capable of illuminating these reasons.

With respect to features of appearance, however, we are often much less confident concerning whether they are legitimate reaction qualifications in particular cases, and those who share the same intuitions are likely to disagree even more markedly over the reasons for their judgements. Consider the following, which I shall call *key cases*:

Good Looks. Many customers automatically respond more favourably to good-looking sales assistants, sometimes by purchasing goods that they would not otherwise buy. In consequence, retailers treat good looks as a qualification for being a sales assistant.

Dress Code. The customers of a café prefer to be served by attractive women wearing short skirts and low-cut tops. They derive pleasure from looking at them and this is the main reason why they frequent the cafe. In order to keep their customers happy, it is part of the hiring policy of the café that the women they employ must be sexually appealing and willing to dress in this way.

Facial Differences. As a result of an accident, a lawyer has extensive facial scarring that makes many of those who look at him recoil in horror. In consequence, clients would prefer not to be represented by him, judges would prefer him not to work in their courts, and members of the public would prefer not to serve on juries when he is representing a client. Law firms are reluctant to hire him as a result.

Tattoo. A man has a large facial tattoo. He values body art and thinks that his tattoo is an important form of self-expression. Some people have an automatic negative reaction to it, however, and try to avoid having to interact with him. Employers are unwilling to hire him as a result of the response his tattoo elicits from customers and clients.

Dreadlocks. A man who is seeking work as a tree surgeon has dreadlocks. He is rejected by a company because their clientele is conservative and will disapprove, sometimes to the extent of seeking the services of another company. He regards his dreadlocks as an important part of his identity, so he is unwilling to cut them off.

Hijab. The clients of an agency prefer not to be assisted by Muslim women wearing headscarves, and some will go to another agency to avoid having to interact with Muslim women dressed in this way. It is not because they have anything against Islam, but they do not like overt displays of religious commitment outside of religious settings. As a result, the agency will not hire women who wear the hijab.

What I propose to do in the remainder of the chapter is develop and defend a general account of what distinguishes illegitimate from legitimate reaction qualifications that makes sense of our verdicts in the core cases described initially and that also illuminates the key cases that concern aspects of appearance.

5.2 The Symmetric Theory

It might seem that an adequate theory of legitimate and illegitimate reaction qualifications should exhibit a certain kind of symmetry. If there is no weighty moral reason for a *selector* not to discriminate against a candidate on some ground, there is no weighty moral reason for a selector not to take into account a reaction qualification that is rooted in the preferences of *recipients* based on the same ground. On the other hand, if there is a weighty moral reason for a selector not to discriminate against a candidate on some ground, there is also a weighty moral reason for a selector not to take into account a reaction qualification that is rooted in the preferences of recipients based on the same ground.

This kind of symmetry has a degree of intuitive appeal.[3] Consider some of its implications. If there is a weighty moral reason for selectors not to favour a woman candidate just because they find her sexually appealing, then so too there is a weighty moral reason for selectors not to favour a woman candidate just because their clientele would find her sexually appealing. If there is a weighty moral reason for selectors not to discriminate against people they regard as overweight on the basis of the prejudice

---

[3] It is endorsed by Kasper Lippert-Rasmussen: see Lippert-Rasmussen, *Born Free and Equal?*, 239.

that they are lazy, so too there is a weighty moral reason for selectors not to take account of reaction qualifications that are grounded in the same prejudice held by recipients. This kind of symmetry is also plausible in relation to the justification of employer dress codes or appearance codes that are grounded in the preferences of recipients. If there is a weighty moral reason for an employer not to insist that women who work for him must wear low-cut tops or high-heeled shoes just because he likes women to dress in this way, so too there is a weighty moral reason for an employer not to impose an appearance code of this sort just because customers like women to be dressed in this way.

The symmetric theory can be combined with the pluralist theory of what makes discrimination wrong when it is wrong that I defended in Chapters 2 and 3, and indeed this pluralist theory can help to explain why the symmetric theory holds in a range of cases. When a recipient has a non-rational response to those who belong to a particular racial group, or does not want to interact with them because he has prejudices about them, then he may be behaving disrespectfully by not taking due account of their moral standing, for example, by disregarding or ignoring their possession of the characteristics in virtue of which they have that standing, or by treating them as if they lacked these characteristics or were unlikely to utilize them appropriately. There is a powerful moral reason not to count a reaction qualification grounded in the disrespectful attitudes or behaviour of the recipients, even though there may be sound business reasons for a selector, seeking to further her employer's interests, to want to do so. Even if the selector and her employer do not share the same prejudices or non-rational responses, counting a reaction qualification grounded in the disrespectful attitudes or behaviour of recipients would be to condone that wrongful behaviour or these wrongful attitudes. In other words, reaction qualifications of this kind are illegitimate because there is a powerful moral reason not to condone disrespectful behaviour or attitudes.

Furthermore, when reaction qualifications that are grounded in the prejudices or non-rational negative responses of recipients concerning those who belong to disadvantaged groups are counted in a selection process, then the candidates for jobs who lose out as a result are potentially harmed in a manner that contributes to creating an unjust distribution of benefits and burdens, in much the same way as when selectors have the same prejudices or non-rational responses and let them influence their decisions about who to employ. If the prejudices that recipients harbour about members of a disadvantaged group, or their non-rational negative responses to them, ground reaction qualifications for a particular type of job, then the weighty interest that members of this group have in autonomous agency is set back when as a result they are rejected from jobs of this type, for they may be deprived of the internal and external goods associated with these jobs, and these goods may be important for realizing their conception of how to live. As a result, counting reaction qualifications grounded in the prejudices or non-rational negative responses of recipients relating to members of disadvantaged groups runs the risk of contributing to creating an unjust distribution of benefits and burdens. It may also contribute to lowering the standing of members of a stigmatized group, for example, when clients would prefer not to deal with Black employees because they think they are untrustworthy, this may contribute to stigmatizing Black people and to fostering a culture in which they are regarded and treated as morally inferior.

Preserving the kind of symmetry described might seem appealing, but it has some counterintuitive consequences that come into view when we consider its potential implications for discrimination on the basis of appearance that is grounded in recipients' moral or aesthetic judgements concerning appearance, and which also suggest another important limit to the analogy between the wrongness of appearance discrimination and the wrongness of racial discrimination. It seems to me that there is a weighty moral reason for selectors not to take into account their own appearance-related moral or aesthetic judgements in making appointment decisions, but often there is no weighty moral reason for selectors not to take into account reaction qualifications rooted in customers' or clients' moral or aesthetic judgements concerning appearance. So, for example, if a selector believes that tattoos disrespect one's body, there is a weighty moral reason for her, qua selector, to bracket that view when making appointment decisions. But if potential customers hold such a view, then there is no weighty moral reason for her not to take into account their preferences not to deal with those who have tattoos in deciding who to appoint when it derives from that view. As a result, a range of reaction qualifications grounded in the preferences of recipients for particular appearance features are potentially legitimate. The analogy between appearance discrimination and racial discrimination reaches another important limit here, for there seem to be very few cases in which reaction qualifications involving race are legitimate. Counting them would either condone the disrespect that the recipients' behaviour often involves or play a role in generating unjust consequences because it worsens the position of members of an unjustly disadvantaged group, or both.

This is merely an intuition, and it may not be universally shared. What we need is a theory of legitimate reaction qualifications that captures what is appealing in the kind of symmetry I have described between legitimate reasons for selectors to discriminate and legitimate reaction qualifications but explains how classes of exceptions to it may arise. A key part of the explanation is provided by the idea of deliberative fairness to which I appealed in Chapters 2 and 4, namely, that selectors fail to give due weight to the interests of a candidate, and thereby treat him or her unfairly, when their decisions are influenced by their own prejudices or non-rational responses, or by their own particular moral or aesthetic judgements. But giving due weight to the interests of candidates, and treating them fairly, permits a selector to take into account the interests of recipients (and indeed to take into account her own interests *qua* recipient if she will interact with them as fellow workers) since these affect what counts as giving due weight to the interests of candidates. One important interest that is at stake here is the recipients' interest in autonomous agency. The importance of this interest means that selectors are permitted to give significant weight to recipients' preferences concerning appearance when these are a product of their reasonable moral judgements since then they are an expression of their autonomous agency. As a result, there is potentially a wide range of reaction qualifications related to features of appearance that there is no weighty moral reason for a selector not to count. In the next section, I shall organize these thoughts into the basis of an overall theory of when reaction qualifications are illegitimate.

5.3 A Theory of Illegitimate Reaction Qualifications and Its Application to the Core Cases

Drawing in part upon the discussion so far, I propose that an adequate theory of illegitimate reaction qualifications will involve at least three elements. A reaction qualification is illegitimate if counting it would:

(1) condone the disrespectful behaviour or attitudes of recipients, *or*
(2) give insufficient weight in the process of selection to the interests of some of the candidates, *or*
(3) tend to worsen the disadvantages that are experienced by members of an unjustly disadvantaged group.

This theory exhibits a kind of symmetry with the theory of what makes discrimination wrong that I defended in Chapters 2 and 3. Condition (1) relates to the first potential source of reasons for why discrimination may be wrong, that is, respect for persons; (2) relates to the second potential sources of reasons, that is, deliberative unfairness in the process of selection; and (3) relates to the third potential source of reasons that is, the unjust consequences to which discrimination may contribute. The main case for (1) has in effect already been presented, so I shall focus mainly on (2), whilst also giving some more indication of how (3) is to be interpreted.

In Section 2.3, I argued that deliberative fairness, that is, giving due weight to the interests of each candidate, imposes some constraints on selectors' decision-making, but the constraints I defended there do not help in determining when condition (2) above is met. Crucially, we need to know when giving weight to the interests of recipients, by counting a reaction qualification that is rooted in their preferences, means that insufficient weight is being given to the interests of some of the candidates.

Even if deliberative fairness does not in general *require* a selector to give weight to the preferences of recipients, it surely *permits* him or her to do so when authorized by an employer, at least in so far as their preferences are not disrespectful and do not express demeaning attitudes. But the preferences of recipients may conflict with the interests of some candidates. Counting a reaction qualification will tend to adversely affect the interests of candidates who lack it, for example, if customers, in general, would prefer not to have to deal with assistants who have unusual facial features, such as a large birthmark, then counting a reaction qualification grounded in that preference will adversely affect the interests of candidates with facial differences. But not counting such a reaction qualification will also adversely affect the interests of customers who would prefer not to interact with assistants with facial differences. Since deliberative fairness permits a selector to give some weight to the interests of recipients, it must permit him or her to *balance* the interests of candidates against those of recipients. It is very difficult, however, to provide a precise set of rules for determining when counting a reaction qualification would give insufficient weight to the former. The best I can do here is to identify a range of relevant considerations.

What constitutes giving due weight to the interests of the candidates, when balancing them against the interests of recipients, will depend in part on the *number* of recipients who would be adversely affected by not counting a reaction qualification rooted in their preferences or responses compared to the number of candidates who would be adversely affected by counting it. If most potential customers would prefer not to deal with assistants with facial differences, perhaps because they have internalized appearance norms that regard unsymmetrical faces, scarred faces, or faces with birthmarks, as unsightly, then this would provide some grounds for regarding it as fair to count a reaction qualification rooted in this preference, whereas if most potential customers are unconcerned about whether or not they are served by assistants with facial differences, then this would provide some grounds for regarding it as unfair to count a reaction qualification that is rooted in the preference of the remaining customers not to have to deal with assistants with such differences.

What it means to give due weight to the candidates' interests may also be affected by whether a reaction qualification is *grounded in a prejudice or false belief*. For example, suppose that members of the public would prefer police officers to be tall on the grounds that they provide better protection against criminals, but there is compelling evidence that well-trained short police officers provide no less protection. In that case, the genuine interests of members of the public might be better served by selectors not favouring tall candidates, and deliberative fairness, that is, giving due weight to the interests of each candidate, might give selectors a strong reason not to count this preference for tall police officers. In other words, it might justify regarding a reaction qualification rooted in this preference as illegitimate on the grounds that counting it would be unfair, since doing so would adversely affect short people who want a career in the police force without furthering the interests of citizens in being protected against criminals.

What counts as giving due weight to the interests of a candidate may be affected by whether a feature towards which customers or clients respond negatively can be justifiably regarded as *chosen* by her. A candidate may lack a reaction qualification as a result of a choice she is making, even though the cost or difficulty of her acquiring that qualification is not unreasonably large, so her interests would not be setback to any great extent by counting it. To illustrate, consider a man who has a body odour that others find repellent, but he is unwilling to wear a deodorant that would eliminate or mask the smell, even though doing so would cause him no harm. It would surely be permissible to regard his body odour as counting against appointing him to a job that required him to deal with co-workers, customers, or clients, or in favour of insisting that he agree to use a deodorant before appointing him to it.

The issues here are more difficult when an appearance-related characteristic expresses a candidate's reasonable conception of how to live, or some deeply held reasonable commitment. In this type of case, it seems that her interest in not being disadvantaged by it should be given considerable weight because it reflects her autonomous agency. For example, if a man has a beard because he believes that it is required by his religious commitments, then his interest in not being disadvantaged by it in the process of selection, as a result of prejudices that customers or clients have about beards or non-rational responses that they have to them, should be given considerable weight.

In response, might it be argued that growing a beard is nevertheless a choice, and one of the costs of that choice is the negative reactions that facial hair provokes in some others. Since it is just to require people to bear the costs of their choices, it might be thought that deliberative fairness permits us to give less weight to candidates' interest in not being disadvantaged by their beards compared to the interests of customers and clients in not having to deal with those who have beards. But this misunderstands the relevance of choice in determining whether due weight has been given to the interests of candidates in forming judgements about deliberative fairness. It might be morally permissible, or even morally required to hold people responsible for their choices when making judgements about the just overall distribution of benefits and burdens. But as we saw in Section 4.5, the extent to which candidates are responsible for their appearance features, and the extent to which recipients are responsible for their non-rational responses, is not directly relevant to judgements about deliberative fairness. Let me explain further.

In making selection decisions, deliberative fairness requires giving due weight to the interests of each of the candidates. The responsibility of candidates for their appearance features matters in so far as it is relevant to determining their interests, including crucially their interest in autonomous agency. So, if a candidate's tattoos reflect her commitment to body art, the interest in autonomous agency they express should be given weight in determining whether deliberative fairness permits us to count a reaction qualification rooted in recipients' non-rational negative responses to them, even though she chose to have them done. Furthermore, the extent to which recipients can educate their non-rational responses is relevant to determining whether due weight has been given to the interests of each candidate, for it is relevant to determining whether the negative effects on recipients of an employee's appearance features, such as her tattoos, poses a serious threat to their interests because these effects cannot reasonably be avoided. If recipients' can easily educate their negative non-rational responses, or these responses are likely to be transitory, then they do not pose a significant threat to their interests, whereas if these responses are strong, cannot be educated, and are likely to be enduring, then they do pose such a threat, and therefore deliberative fairness permits attaching importance to them in assessing whether due weight has been given to the candidates' interests. But, again, their significance does not consist in allowing us to make judgements about the responsibility of recipients for their non-rational responses to appearance features.

It also makes a difference whether recipients' responses are rooted in a reasonable conception of how to live to which they are committed. If, for example, a company's clients object to being assisted by scruffy employees because they think that people have an obligation to make the best of themselves, or to be aesthetically appealing objects, then deliberative fairness permits selectors to give this significant weight when balancing candidates' interests against recipients' interests, because in this case the recipients' interest in autonomous agency is at stake, to some extent at least, in a way that it is not when recipients' merely have a mild negative non-rational response to employees with a particular appearance feature.

That completes my brief survey of a range of considerations that are relevant in determining whether counting a reaction qualification would give insufficient weight to the interests of some of the candidates, which, according to condition (2) would make it illegitimate. In relation to (3), what matters is whether counting a reaction qualification would worsen the position of members of an unjustly disadvantaged group. To illustrate, suppose that customers prefer not to be served by those with afro hairstyles. Even if that preference is not rooted in racial prejudice, counting a reaction qualification grounded in it would worsen the position of members of racial groups whose hair tends to be naturally suited to such styles. If these racial groups are unjustly disadvantaged independently, then, according to (3), such a reaction qualification would be illegitimate. Of course, it may not always be clear whether a particular group is unjustly disadvantaged. To return to an earlier example, are people with facial differences an unjustly disadvantaged group? In so far as they are, reaction qualifications grounded in the preference of customers not to deal with those with facial differences are illegitimate.

5.4 Application of the Theory to the Core Cases

Now consider how my theory, as outlined, bears upon the three core cases I identified at the beginning of the chapter. *Normal Customers* is a relatively straightforward case for the theory. A reaction qualification rooted in a preference to be served by sales assistants who behave politely would clearly be legitimate because it doesn't meet any of the three conditions for regarding it as illegitimate. Counting it would not condone disrespectful attitudes or behaviour; it would seem to give due weight to the interests of the candidates since for the most part they can choose to behave politely without any great cost or difficulty; and it would not worsen the disadvantages that are experienced by members of an unjustly disadvantaged group.

The account I am proposing also illuminates *Prejudiced Customers*. When customers prefer not to be served by a member of a particular racial group because they believe that members of this group are less trustworthy or honest, whilst the available evidence supports the conclusion that dishonesty or untrustworthiness is no more prevalent in that group than it is in their own group, then a reaction qualification rooted in their preferences is illegitimate, potentially for multiple reasons. Counting it would seem to condone disrespectful attitudes or behaviour, so it seems to be illegitimate according to (1). It would seem to be illegitimate according to condition (2) because counting it would give insufficient weight to the interests of candidates from members of this racial group since the genuine interests of customers in being served by honest and trustworthy assistants would not be set back by discounting it. And it would be illegitimate according to condition (3) if the racial group is unjustly disadvantaged independently. If more than one the conditions is met, the illegitimacy of this reaction qualification will be over-determined.

Consider a variant of *Prejudiced Customers*, concerning which we might justifiably reach a different verdict in relation to condition (2). As in the original case, the customers of a department store have prejudiced beliefs about those from a particular racial group and will shop elsewhere if the store employs members of that group. But the proportion of customers that are prejudiced in this way is sufficiently large that the store will go out of business if it doesn't conform to their wishes. The store's owners are not themselves prejudiced, but there is no legislation in place that prohibits counting reaction qualifications that are grounded in such prejudices, and they have reason to think that their competitors will (continue to) give weight to qualifications of this kind when selecting employees. So they count these qualifications because they fear, with good reason, they will not otherwise be able to survive given market conditions.

This is a difficult case. Under the circumstances described, a reaction qualification rooted in the recipients' prejudices may satisfy condition (2) because giving due weight to the interests of candidates permits the interests of the employer to be taken into account. One of the crucial issues here concerns what costs we can fairly ask employers to bear in resisting racial prejudice. In cases where an employer's business would merely be less profitable as a result of hiring members of this racial group, then it seems that there is a strong moral reason, a reason of fairness, not to count reaction qualifications rooted in recipients' prejudices. But when the employer's livelihood would be under threat, we might justifiably think that fairness permits him to give weight to these reaction qualifications, at least in cases when it would be difficult or impossible for him to earn a living through other means. Counting a reaction qualification in this case would nevertheless still seem to fall foul of conditions (1) and (3) because doing so would seem to condone the disrespectful attitudes of recipients and tend to worsen the disadvantages that are experienced by members of an unjustly disadvantaged group.

My account also has plausible implications for a rather different case that is related to *Prejudiced Customers*, which I shall call *Segregated Customers*. In this variant, the customers of a shop prefer not to be served by the members of a particular racial group, but they do not regard them as having an inferior moral status, nor do they harbour prejudices about them. They merely feel uncomfortable or anxious being served by members of this group since they do not encounter many in their daily lives, largely as a result of segregation in neighbourhoods, schools, and workplaces that is now sustained by patterns of uncoerced choice. Their discomfort is not rooted in negative beliefs about the group or the members of it, and nor do they possess any reasons for these feelings of discomfort, though their feelings are explicable by reference to their experience of segregation. Again, according to (1), a reaction qualification grounded in their feelings would be illegitimate if their visible discomfort sends out the message that they regard members of this racial group as morally inferior, even though in fact they attribute equal moral status to them. Such a reaction qualification would also be illegitimate according to (2) if counting it would, as it seems, harm candidates from this group in a way that gives insufficient weight to their interests. And it would be illegitimate according to (3) if the racial group to which these people belong is unjustly disadvantaged. This matches and explains the intuitions that I think are shared by many in relation to this case.

Finally, consider the other core case that I am regarding as a test of a successful theory of reaction qualifications, namely, *Female Patients*. These patients' preferences to be treated by female doctors need not involve denying or disregarding the equal standing of male doctors, and counting a reaction qualification grounded in them would not tend to exacerbate the disadvantages experienced by members of an unjustly disadvantaged group, at least if transwomen doctors are counted as female by patients. In consequence, conditions (1) and (3) do not create any problem for treating being female as a qualification. The preference that female patients have for being examined by a female doctor need not involve any prejudice against male doctors or in favour of female doctors. Their preference may be rooted in reasonable religious doctrines that prohibit being unclothed in front of members of the opposite sex who are not close family members, or in social norms governing intimate contact, or in justified concerns about unwanted male attention or objectification in a society where that is common. As a result, counting a reaction qualification rooted in the preferences of female patients would give the interests of male doctors sufficient weight, so condition (2) does not pose any problem. It follows that a reaction qualification of this kind can be legitimate according to my account, which again makes good sense of a widely shared judgement.

5.5 Application of the Theory to the Key Cases Involving Appearance

Let me now consider the application of my theory to the key cases involving appearance that I described earlier. In the case of *Good Looks*, the customers in question are not characterized as having any general beliefs about good-looking people; they simply respond more favourably to good-looking assistants. In other words, their responses are non-rational because they are not motivated by reasons. The customers' responses do not relate to their conception of how to live, so if a selector does not count a reaction qualification grounded in them, this would not set back in any significant way their interest in autonomous agency. In contrast, counting a reaction qualification grounded in these responses would seem to give the interests of candidates who lack good looks too little weight, and it would therefore be illegitimate according to condition (2). The same conclusion would follow in the different case where customers prefer to be served by good-looking assistants because they believe that they are more competent: when customers' preferences are rooted in prejudices about the unattractive, then counting a reaction qualification grounded in them would seem to give insufficient weight to the interests of candidates regarded as unattractive.

But in determining whether the interests of candidates have been given sufficient weight should we take account of the choices that candidates may make to improve their looks and the way in which the availability of these choices affect their interests? Most people have some degree of control over their looks: perhaps they can improve them by taking more trouble over how they dress, using cosmetics, or at the extreme, by surgery. But there are limits to these improvements and they are often costly or difficult to make: '[w]hile looks can be altered by clothing, cosmetics, and other short-term investments, the effects of these improvements are minor. Even plastic surgery doesn't make a huge difference.'[4] When we take into account this evidence, it is implausible to suppose that candidates have sufficient choice in relation to their looks for it to make a difference to the conclusion that when selectors count a reaction qualification that is grounded in customers' non-rational responses towards good-looking assistants, they give insufficient weight to the interests of candidates who lack good looks.

Note, however, that variants of *Good Looks* are possible for which my theory might have different implications. Suppose that many of a store's customers attach value to the experience of shopping in a prestigious retail outlet and being served by glamorous and attractive assistants. In that case, the customers' preference for being served by good-looking glamorous employees would express their conception of how to live, so counting a qualification that is grounded in it would not seem to treat unfairly candidates who lack these looks, at least if enough customers share this conception of how to live. In determining what it is to give due weight to the interests of candidates, selectors are permitted to take into account the customers' interest in autonomous agency. So counting a reaction qualification grounded in customers' preference for being served by glamourous attractive assistants need not fall foul of (2).

Is the sensitivity that my account displays to whether recipients' responses are grounded in reasons that express their conception of how to live an

---

[4] Hamermesh, *Beauty Pays*, 35–6.

unappealing feature of it? My account draws upon ideas concerning deliberative fairness that are independently plausible. When we reflect upon *Good Looks* and its variants, it seems clear that we should be concerned about how candidates for jobs can be disadvantaged in the process of selection by giving weight to recipients' non-rational responses or their prejudices about the unattractive. But in cases where recipients' responses are rooted in their conceptions of how to live, then the disadvantage that some candidates experience as a result of grounding a reaction qualification in these responses does not seem unfair, in light of the interest that the recipients have in autonomous agency.

There may also be reasons for thinking that when selectors count reaction qualifications rooted in customers' preferences for the good-looking, this exacerbates existing unjust disadvantages experienced by people regarded as unattractive, in which case these qualifications would be illegitimate according to condition (3). Those regarded as unattractive seem to suffer from a widespread but unfair bias against them in various contexts simply because people favour the good-looking or are influenced by stereotypes or associations concerning the attractive or the unattractive, such as an association between attractiveness and greater competence, and as a result the opportunities of people regarded as unattractive are adversely affected in a systematic way. Furthermore, to the extent that who counts as good-looking is determined in part by gender-specific norms that place greater burdens on women than men, or by racially biased standards that it is tougher for some racial groups to meet, then selecting on the basis of looks will tend to exacerbate the existing unjust disadvantages experienced in various contexts by women and members of these racial groups.

In *Dress Code*, the preference of the men who go to the café to be served by attractive women in short skirts and low-cut tops is arguably disrespectful because it objectifies women in a way that fails to take due account of their moral standing and treats them as if their proper role is to be sexually appealing objects. As a result, a dress code grounded in those preferences would be illegitimate because counting it would condone disrespectful attitudes. It would also potentially be illegitimate according to condition (3) when we take into consideration the role that this dress code would play in promoting stereotypes that reinforce gender disadvantage.[5]

---

[5] See Moreau, *Faces of Inequality*, 65.

The account I am proposing would nevertheless allow that a gender-differentiated dress code for employees that took into account the preferences of customers and clients (and indeed recipients in general) would be legitimate provided it meets three criteria that relate to conditions (1) to (3): first, it does not pander to disrespectful attitudes and behaviour; second, it does not impose requirements on employees adherence to which would be inconsistent with norms that are integral to reasonable conceptions of how to live to which they are committed; third, it does not reinforce gender disadvantage or any other form of group disadvantage. So, for example, gender-differentiated appearance codes that require men but not women to wear a shirt and tie in a workplace may be legitimate, but not codes that require men to wear trousers and women skirts. The latter would go against some reasonable religious conceptions of how to live that are committed to ideas about what it is to dress modestly that exclude wearing skirts, so it would give too little weight to the interest in autonomous agency of some employees (and potential employees) who subscribe to these conceptions. Arguably such codes are also morally problematic because they reinforce gender-specific norms governing appearance that may exacerbate gender disadvantage.

Let me now move on to the key cases involving reaction qualifications that bring to the fore the relevance of the control that candidates may have over their appearance and the control that recipients may have over their responses to it. Consider *Facial Differences*. Suppose, to begin with, we assume that clients, judges, and jury members cannot help being repelled by the lawyer's facial scarring, to the point that they are unable to concentrate on court proceedings. In that case, counting a reaction qualification grounded in recipients' reactions would not seem to be illegitimate in virtue of condition (2) because not counting it would have such a large impact upon their interest in autonomous agency. But when their response to his facial scarring can be educated, without great cost or difficulty, giving due weight to the interests of those with facial differences would seem to require not counting a reaction qualification grounded in that response, rendering it illegitimate. There may be other reasons why, according to my account, this reaction qualification would be illegitimate, namely, that recipients' responses are potentially disrespectful, so counting a reaction qualification grounded in them would condone disrespectful behaviour. Furthermore, it is arguable that counting a reaction qualification grounded in such responses would exacerbate the unjust disadvantages that may be experienced by those with facial differences, either by contributing to an unjust distribution of benefits and burdens or by contributing to lowering their moral standing by stigmatizing them.

Now consider *Tattoo*, which is similar in one respect to *Facial Differences*: the recipients' responses to the facial tattoo are not motivated by reasons. Unlike *Facial Differences*, however, the person concerned chose to have the facial tattoo and did so in the light of a reasonable conception of how to live that regards body art as an important mode of self-expression. As a result, it would seem that giving due weight to his interests would require us not to count a reaction qualification grounded in recipients' responses, thus it is illegitimate. Their responses are non-rational but not debilitating to them. So their interest in autonomous agency is not threatened by counting a reaction qualification grounded in them, whereas counting it would threaten the interest in autonomous agency of candidates with facial tattoos.

We can, however, describe a variant of *Tattoo* that, according to my account, might permit a selector to give weight to a reaction qualification grounded in the recipients' responses: suppose that they don't have an instinctual negative reaction to the tattoo, but instead disapprove of it because they think it involves a kind of disrespect to one's body, perhaps for religious reasons. In that case, their response to it would be an expression of their autonomous agency, so a reaction qualification grounded in it would potentially be legitimate because giving due weight to the interests of candidates would not necessarily preclude us from counting it. So too, if an employer objects to tattoos on religious grounds, and wants his organization to express or reflect that judgement, weight can permissibly be given to his or her interest in autonomous agency, with the consequence that grounding a reaction qualification in his preference might be legitimate since it may be consistent with giving due weight to the candidates' interests.

Let us move on to *Dreadlocks*. The implications of my account for this case depend on whether we construe the beliefs of customers who disapprove of dreadlocks, or would prefer not to interact with those who have dreadlocks, as a prejudice or not. Are they rooted in some kind of racial prejudice?[6] If so, they might fall foul of condition (1) in virtue of expressing a disrespectful attitude. Are they based on unjustified beliefs about the cleanliness of those with dreadlocks? If so, they would struggle to ground a legitimate reaction qualification because they potentially fall foul of condition (2): counting such a qualification would fail to give due weight to the

---

[6] See Section 1.1.

interests of candidates with dreadlocks since doing so would not further the interests of the recipients in dealing with people with good hygiene. If the customers' disapproval is simply a non-rational response to what, for them, is an unconventional appearance, then it will also struggle to ground a legitimate reaction qualification. Although deliberative fairness permits selectors to give it some weight, in the case as specified this appearance feature is central to the candidate's identity, an identity he endorses, so it is crucial to his or her interest in autonomous agency. Giving that interest due weight would seem to require not counting a reaction qualification grounded in a non-rational response of this kind. Furthermore, the negative reaction his dreadlocks elicit doesn't seem to be the kind of non-rational response that would be costly or difficult for recipients to unlearn. Finally, counting a reaction qualification grounded in the customers' preferences would also be illegitimate according to condition (3) since it would tend to exacerbate the disadvantages that are experienced by Black and mixed-race people many of whom have afro-textured hair.

Consider the last of the cases, *Hijab*. The recipients object to the wearing of the hijab on the grounds that it is wrong or inappropriate to display overt religious symbols in public, not because they are prejudiced against Muslims. Since the recipients' preferences express their autonomous agency, counting a reaction qualification grounded in them would not be illegitimate in virtue of condition (2). But that reaction qualification might nevertheless be illegitimate in a society in which Muslims are denigrated because the recipients' behaviour might then convey a demeaning message even though recipients did not intend it to do so, thus falling foul of condition (1). Condition (3) may also, or instead, give us a reason to regard a reaction qualification rooted in such preferences to be illegitimate, even though they are a product of the recipients' reasonable conception of how to live and express their autonomous agency. If Muslims are unjustly disadvantaged as a result of living in a society afflicted by Islamophobia, then counting this reaction qualification would tend to exacerbate that disadvantage.

5.6 Lippert-Rasmussen's Account of Illegitimate Reaction Qualifications

Kasper Lippert-Rasmussen offers the most sophisticated alternative theory of when a reaction qualification is illegitimate, so it is instructive to compare my theory with his.[7] He maintains that 'a reaction qualification counts from the point of view of merit, that is, makes a difference to who is best qualified in the relevant sense, if, and only if, it is not rooted in non-individualized, antimeritocratic attitudes'. He adds that '[a]n attitude is antimeritocratic in a non-individualized way if, and only if, (a) its object is a group of people, and (b) it is such that if a selector decides between candidates influenced by it, the decision is not based solely on merit'.[8] According to his theory, when reaction qualifications are counted that are rooted in non-individualized, antimeritocratic attitudes, there is a strong prima facie reason for thinking that this unjustly disadvantages those who lack these qualifications, and therefore for regarding these qualifications as illegitimate. In contrast, when a reaction qualification is not rooted in such attitudes, there is no reason to think that any unjust disadvantage is created by counting it and therefore it should be regarded as legitimate.

Lippert-Rasmussen's account provides an initially plausible explanation of why we should think the reaction qualification involved in *Prejudiced Customers* is illegitimate. The preference not to be served by members of a particular racial group is rooted in negative attitudes towards that group, and towards individuals as members of that group, but considered independently of these attitudes, membership of the group has nothing to do with how well a person is able to perform the tasks that the position involves. According to Lippert-Rasmussen's account, giving weight to a reaction qualification grounded in this preference would therefore unfairly disadvantage members of the group.

In order to assess Lippert-Rasmussen's account, we need to probe further what it means to say that an attitude is non-individualized. His idea is that an attitude is non-individualized if its object is a group of people. But is it possible to respond negatively or positively to all possessors of a certain characteristic without having a non-individualized attitude to them? Lippert-Rasmussen seems to think so. For example, he allows that a person may respond positively to all those who are charming without having a non-individualized attitude towards them.[9] But consider a version of *Segregated Customers* in which the customers respond negatively to sales assistants who have a particular skin tone, but without holding any beliefs about people who share that skin tone or any other general attitudes towards

---

[7] See Lippert-Rasmussen, *Born Free and Equal?*, ch. 9.
[8] Lippert-Rasmussen, *Born Free and Equal?*, 245–6.
[9] Cf. Lippert-Rasmussen, *Born Free and Equal?*, 247–8.

them. In an unreflective way, they simply feel awkward or uncomfortable in the company of people with this skin tone because they have not come into direct contact with many of them before. The attitude that underlies the customers' responses seems to be individualized in the relevant sense since its object is not a group of people, and it is not a product of any beliefs about that group.

This might seem bizarre: how could a reaction to a person's skin tone be anything other than non-individualized? But a negative attitude or response to a person's skin tone may be no different in the relevant respects from a positive attitude or response to those who possess a characteristic, such as politeness or charm, which Lippert-Rasmussen allows may be an individualized attitude. Just as a person may respond positively to another's charm without any mediating beliefs or other attitudes concerning charming people in general, so too a person may respond negatively to a person's skin tone without any mediating beliefs or other attitudes concerning the racial group to which he or she belongs. In the variant of *Segregated Customers* under consideration, a person's skin tone provokes a negative reaction, in much the same way that charm may provoke a positive reaction. Even if the psychological explanation for this negative reaction makes reference to the experience of belonging to a different racial group, in particular to the way in which that group has been segregated from others, the reaction is not rooted in non-individualized attitudes in the relevant sense. So it would seem that Lippert-Rasmussen's account is implausibly committed to the view that giving weight to reaction qualifications rooted in people's negative responses to members of a racial group who share a particular skin tone, when those people do not hold any beliefs about that group as a whole or possess any other attitudes towards it, does not unfairly disadvantage members of this group and that these qualifications are therefore legitimate.

Could he avoid this problem by shifting his ground to the view that whenever a person responds negatively or positively to all possessors of a certain characteristic, whether charm or skin tone, then they must have a non-individualized attitude towards them? According to his account it would then follow that we have reason to regard reaction qualifications rooted in such responses as illegitimate if that characteristic has nothing to do with how well the person is able to perform the tasks involved in a job when considered independently of these responses. But it would be hard for him to shift his ground in this way without his account generating implausible conclusions. For example, it would then seem to imply that in *Normal Customers* we have reason to think that counting politeness as a reaction qualification would unfairly disadvantage the impolite and that it is therefore an illegitimate reaction qualification.

5.7 Counting Illegitimate Reaction Qualifications

I have left open the possibility that in some cases, even though a reaction qualification is illegitimate (that is, there is a weighty moral reason not to count it), counting it is nevertheless morally justified *all things considered*. Let me consider two cases to illustrate, which I shall call *Policing Preference* and *The Ironic Case*.

According to *Policing Preference*, those who live in a particular neighbourhood prefer to be policed by a member of their own ethnic group. They have been unfairly discriminated against and disadvantaged by another group. As a result, they distrust members of that other group and would cooperate less fully with a police officer who came from it. They have come to hold an unjustified belief that members of the other group are *incapable* of acting morally, and as a result they treat them as morally inferior.[10] According to my account, a reaction qualification grounded in such a preference would be illegitimate because it would violate condition (1), since counting it would condone disrespectful attitudes. But we might nevertheless think that under some circumstances it would be morally justified to count it all things considered: given the history of oppression experienced by this ethnic group, their preference is condonable, and counting the reaction qualification would be justified all things considered if it served to compensate some of those who would then be appointed as police officers for the past injustice they have experienced, and at the same time challenged the structures of injustice to which the group are subject by providing role models and undermining stereotypes.

The Ironic Case is another example where counting an illegitimate reaction qualification might be morally justified all things considered because it promotes greater justice.[11] In this case Black telephone sales assistants are hired because they tend to sound as if they are white, as a result of consciously trying to avoid sounding Black, because they know that if they sound Black they will sell less goods as a result of racial prejudice. White telephone sales assistants do not make the same effort, and as a result they

---

[10] I owe this particular twist in the case described to Shlomi Segall.
[11] It is discussed by Lippert-Rasmussen. See his *Born Free and Equal?*, 254.

are often mistaken for being Black, and consequently sell fewer goods. Here treating 'being a Black person', or 'sounding like a white person', as a reaction qualification seems illegitimate according to condition (1). The preference of white people to deal with other white people seems to be based on disrespectful attitudes that deny or disregard the equal standing of Black people, in which case counting 'sounding white' as a reaction qualification condones a disrespectful attitude. Despite this weighty potential reason for not counting 'sounding white' as a qualification, in some circumstances that might nevertheless be justified all things considered if it would significantly promote more just outcomes, for example, by reducing the unemployment levels of Black people and compensating a number of them for the injustice they have suffered in the past.

5.8 Concluding Remarks

The issue of when reaction qualifications are legitimate is pressing in the context of appearance discrimination, for there are often business-related reasons for employers to select people with particular appearance features or, at least, to select those with an appearance that doesn't provoke the disapproval of their clients or customers. In practice, however, drawing the distinction between legitimate and illegitimate reaction qualifications is fraught with difficulty. If the account that I have offered in this chapter is correct, in determining whether a reaction qualification is illegitimate, it matters whether it is grounded in disrespectful attitudes or behaviour; it matters whether counting it would give due weight to the interests of candidates; and it matters whether counting it would adversely affect the members of an unjustly disadvantaged group.

In particular cases the truth may be hard to establish, especially in determining whether counting a reaction qualification would give due weight to the interests of candidates. In forming this judgement, it can make a difference whether a reaction qualification is grounded in recipients' reasonable moral or aesthetic judgements or whether it is grounded in their non-rational responses. But the preferences of different recipients may have different bases. As a result, the legitimacy or illegitimacy of a reaction qualification in a given case may depend on the proportion of recipients whose preferences are rooted in non-rational responses (or indeed disrespectful attitudes), and the proportion whose preferences are rooted in reasonable moral or aesthetic judgements.

What role does the account I have given of when a reaction qualification is legitimate or illegitimate play within the overall theory of what makes discrimination wrong that this book is drawing upon? First, it contributes to that theory by analysing further the notion of deliberative fairness, delving more deeply into the issue of what it is to treat candidates' fairly in selection decisions, since condition (2), and the way I have elaborated it, provides more content to the idea of giving due weight to their interests. Second, by defending the idea that reaction qualifications are illegitimate when counting them would worsen the disadvantages experienced by members of unjustly disadvantaged groups, my account draws attention to the morally problematic role that counting reaction qualifications may play in contributing to the creation of unjust outcomes, including lowering the perceived moral status of those adversely affected, and reinforcing the power structures that create and sustain unjust disadvantages.

6
Appearance and Personal Relationships

People's looks have a profound effect on their opportunities to form personal relationships, particularly romantic partnerships, for appearance discrimination seems to be rife in this context. Employing the language of discrimination here might seem wrong-headed, but if, for the moment, we put to one side the issue of whether there is anything morally troubling about making choices of this kind on the basis of appearance, it seems clear there is nothing inappropriate about that language. According to the conceptualization that I have been employing, A discriminates against P whenever A treats P less favourably than Q because P has some property C that Q lacks. So understood, discrimination is not something that is confined to the public sphere. It occurs, for example, when one person avoids entering into a friendship or a romantic partnership with another because of his or her appearance.

How then does appearance discrimination affect the formation of personal relationships? A meta-analysis published in 1988 that drew upon seventeen studies of the link between physical attractiveness and romantic choices concluded that people prefer attractive partners when they form both long-term and short-term relationships, and that those with the same level of attractiveness tend to form relationships with each other.[1] A study of a sample of people who use the dating website 'Hot or Not' confirmed these findings.[2] This study found that the most attractive were likely to respond only to others who were also attractive, though men were more influenced by the attractiveness of potential partners than women. A large US study in which the mean age of the sample was 25 also found that appearance matters more to men than to women in romantic choices.[3]

---

[1] Feingold, 'Matching for Attractiveness in Romantic Partners and Same-Sex Friends', 226.
[2] Lee et al., 'If I'm Not Hot, Are You Hot or Not?'.
[3] Sprecher et al., 'Mate Selection Preferences'.

A Spanish study that involved interviewing a representative sample of almost two thousand people aged between 19 and 64 found that the majority of those who took part cited physical attractiveness as the most important characteristic in the choice of a new romantic partner, but that it was ranked only ninth out of twenty when people were presented with a list of potentially important features in a partner for a long-term relationship.[4] A relatively recent meta-analysis concluded that people attribute high value to physical attractiveness when entering romantic relationships but that the importance attached to appearance fluctuates during different stages of a relationship: 'When people initially consider someone as a potential romantic partner, attractiveness is very important, and the association between attractiveness and romantic evaluations drops once the relationship has been formed. Yet as two people remain together in a relationship, the association of attractiveness with romantic evaluations slowly begins to increase again.'[5]

People perceived as overweight, especially women, suffer considerable disadvantages when it comes to forming romantic partnerships. Many heterosexual men are not attracted to women they regard as overweight, whilst those for whom a potential partner's size or shape is not an issue are often ridiculed when they experience attraction for a woman with a larger body. As a result of internalizing appearance norms that are stigmatizing, women with a shape or size associated with a higher weight feel unappealing and put up barriers to forming relationships, yet at the same time they are the object of fetishes, which mean that they are often unsure about the intentions of those men who do express an interest in dating them. In this way, the negative effects of direct appearance discrimination on the basis of shape and size are reinforced by self-imposed constraints and epistemic challenges.[6]

It is clear that people discriminate on the basis of appearance in many of the fundamental choices they make about forming, cultivating, and sustaining romantic partnerships. But it is a further question whether and when doing so is morally wrong. It would be odd to suppose that decisions about

---

[4] Sangrador and Yela, '"What Is Beautiful Is Loved"'.
[5] Eastwick et al., 'The Predictive Validity of Ideal Partner Preferences', 633. 'Romantic evaluations' are positive or negative attitudes concerning a romantic partner or relationship.
[6] See A. Williams and M. Merten, 'Romantic Relationships among Women Experiencing Obesity: Self-Perception and Weight as Barriers to Intimacy', *Family and Consumer Sciences Research Journal* 41 (2021): 284–98; J. Gailey, 'Fat Shame to Fat Pride: Fat Women's Sexual and Dating Experiences', *Fat Studies* 1 (2012): 114–27.

what relationships to form should be made through an open competition in which there is some kind of application process that mimics fair procedures for making job appointments. But even if concerns about fairness in selection have no place here, some of the same reasons that explain why appearance discrimination is wrong (when it is) in the context of job appointments may also justify the conclusion that appearance discrimination is sometimes wrong in the context of the choices people make about forming, cultivating, or sustaining romantic partnerships.[7]

It is important to be clear that the issue of whether appearance discrimination can be wrong in this context is at least partially independent of the issue of whether it should be regulated by means of the law. It is also at least partially independent of the issue of whether a society, or groups within it, should promulgate social norms that frown upon such discrimination. Even if we were to conclude that appearance discrimination in romantic relationships is often morally wrong, it would not follow that we ought to legislate against it or even that we should seek to cultivate a social ethos that penalizes it by subjecting people's romantic choices to criticism and pressurizing them to make different choices.[8] Decisions about whether to enact legislation that opposes such discrimination, or whether to play one's part in seeking to cultivate social practices that counter it, would need to be made in the light of other relevant moral considerations, including what the consequences of doing so would be and whether there is a right to privacy with which these measures might come into conflict.[9]

In exploring these issues, I shall focus mainly on romantic partnerships, but in places I shall also consider friendships without a romantic character. In order to bring out more vividly the morally problematic character of some of the appearance discrimination that occurs in the context of these

---

[7] See H. Lazenby and P. Butterfield, 'Discrimination and the Personal Sphere', and Fourie, 'Wrongful Private Discrimination and the Egalitarian Ethos', in Lippert-Rasmussen (ed.), *The Routledge Handbook of the Ethics of Discrimination*, for attempts to apply general theories of what makes discrimination wrong, when it is wrong, to choices concerning personal relationships.

[8] This would amount to a practice of what Ellen Willis calls 'authoritarian moralism'. See E. Willis, 'Lustful Horizons: Is the Women's Movement Pro-Sex?', in E. Willis and Nona Willis Aronowitz (eds), *The Essential Ellen Willis* (Minneapolis, MN: University of Minnesota Press, 2014), 200–8, at 208. For relevant discussion, see also C. Fourie, 'Wrongful Private Discrimination and the Egalitarian Ethos', in K. Lippert-Rasmussen (ed.), *The Routledge Handbook of the Ethics of Discrimination* (London: Routledge, 2017); A. Srinivasan, *The Right to Sex* (London: Bloomsbury Publishing, 2021), especially 'The Right to Sex' and 'Coda: The Politics of Desire'.

[9] See Section 8.4.

types of personal relationships, I shall begin in Section 6.1 by considering the grounds for thinking that discriminating *on the basis of race* when forming or cultivating them is sometimes wrong, before examining in Sections 6.2 and 6.3 whether analogous reasons apply in cases of discrimination on the basis of appearance. I shall argue that there are powerful reasons for thinking that racial discrimination when forming or cultivating personal relationships is generally wrongful, and that at least some of these reasons transfer to appearance discrimination in this context. But even though there are strong grounds for thinking that discrimination in forming or cultivating personal relationships may be wrong for a variety of reasons, I shall argue in Section 6.4 that there is a moral prerogative that permits people to engage in both racial discrimination and appearance discrimination in the context of personal relationships when it would otherwise be impossible, or very difficult, for them to obtain to any great extent the goods that these relationships can provide. In the final part of the chapter, Section 6.5, I consider whether it is ever permissible for a person to discriminate on grounds of appearance when her friends or family would respond negatively to her forging a relationship with a romantic partner who they find visually unattractive, in part by considering the case, which may sometimes be analogous, of a person's family or friends disapproving of her embarking on a romantic relationship with a member of some particular racial group.

6.1 Disrespectful or Harmful Racial Discrimination in Personal Relationships

In the context of employment, discrimination may be wrong because it involves a failure to respect its victims. The choices that people make about whether to enter a personal relationship with another may also be disrespectful. This can be seen most clearly in cases of racial discrimination. If a man believes that the members of a racial group are untrustworthy because they do not possess the capacity to keep their word and as a result does not regard them as potential friends or lovers, then he is treating them with a lack of respect. He is failing to take due account of their moral standing by not giving due weight to their possession of the characteristics in virtue of which they have that standing.

It would also seem that the choices people make about what personal relationships to form are likely to send out a demeaning message when they involve discrimination against a marginalized or historically disadvantaged racial group, that is, these choices are likely to convey the message that people from this racial group are morally inferior.[10] Hellman disagrees. She argues that white people who prefer not to make friends with Black people do not in general demean those who as a result experience discrimination.[11] She maintains that, for the most part, when individuals do not occupy special institutional positions, they are not sufficiently powerful to demean the people with whom they avoid forming personal relationships. Like Carina Fourie, I am sceptical of this claim.[12] Through their place in a social hierarchy, white individuals who lack the kinds of power that are specific to particular social roles, such as that of employer or judge, may nevertheless put down people from disadvantaged racial minorities who they reject as potential friends or romantic partners, irrespective of their intentions. A person's power to demean is a function not only of the special institutional positions they occupy but also their place within social hierarchies.[13] This is not to deny that the impact of social hierarchies may be uneven when choices are made about personal relationships. When decisions about what friendships to cultivate or what romantic partnerships to form are made within a close-knit network in which the people who belong to it know each other well and have no reason to think that any racial bias is affecting each other's decisions on these matters, then an individual's rejection of a Black person as a potential friend or romantic partner may not carry the same social meaning that it would in a different social context where the connections between people are looser and racist attitudes are known to be common.

Even when people who belong to a privileged racial group choose a romantic or sexual partner *from* a marginalized racial group, this may send out a demeaning message. In the context of discussing 'yellow fever', particularly the preference of some heterosexual white men for Asian women, Robin Zheng argues that whatever the real motives of people from privileged racial groups who choose to form relationships with those from marginalized racial groups, 'they are still socially interpreted and *made sense of*

---

[10] See M. Mitchell and M. Wells, 'Race, Romantic Attraction, and Dating', *Ethical Theory and Moral Practice* 21 (2018): 945–61, at 953–7.

[11] D. Hellman, 'Discrimination and Social Meaning', in Lippert-Rasmussen (ed.), *The Routledge Handbook of the Ethics of Discrimination*, 103.

[12] See C. Fourie, 'Wrongful Private Discrimination and the Egalitarian Ethos', 426–7.

[13] See Mitchell and Wells, 'Race, Romantic Attraction, and Dating', 953–8. Moreau also points out that in order to determine whether someone's act puts another person down, we need to look at the social groups to which each belongs and their relative power, rather than primarily at their institutional roles: see Moreau, *Faces of Inequality*, 47.

in racially stereotypical ways'.[14] Furthermore, it is not just the choices of people who belong to privileged groups that have the power to demean. The choices made by people who belong to a disadvantaged racial group may also sometimes demean less powerful members of their own group. Charles Mills argues that whatever their motivation, when Black men marry white women then they 'will be *perceived* by other blacks as having married out of racial self-contempt... sending a message to the world that, once you have this option to choose: *black women just ain't good enough*'.[15]

The choices that people make about what personal relationships to form or cultivate can also play a role in generating unjust consequences, since their choices may contribute to creating an unjust distribution of benefits and burdens or to lowering the perceived moral standing of those they reject. When these choices reflect a widespread pattern of racial discrimination in forming personal relationships, the slight experienced by people who are rejected may be considerable in terms of its adverse impact on their self-respect, self-esteem, or self-confidence and its adverse effect on their perceived moral status. When members of a racial group are excluded as potential friends or lovers on grounds of their race, they are also deprived of the goods that they would otherwise realize through these relationships. Their access to these goods may be seriously compromised in a way that sets back their interest in autonomous agency and contributes to creating an unjust distribution of opportunities. There is ample evidence from dating sites that Black people (especially Black women) and Asian men are regularly rejected on grounds of their race.[16] When the members of a racial

---

[14] R. Zheng, 'Why Yellow Fever Isn't Flattering: A Case against Racial Fetishes', *Journal of the American Philosophical Association* 2 (2016): 400–19, at 412.

[15] C. Mills, 'Do Black Men Have a Moral Duty to Marry Black Women?', *Journal of Social Philosophy* 25 (1994): 131–53, at 149.

[16] Data from the dating website OKCupid reveals that Black men and women are rated as less attractive than the mean by members of all groups other than their own. On a scale of 1–5 stars, Black women are rated about three-quarters of a star lower than women from other ethnic groups: see C. Rudder, *Dataclysm: Who We Are (When We Think No One's Looking)* (London: Fourth Estate, 2014), 110–16. See also C. V. Curington, J. H. Lundquist, and K.-H. Lin, *The Dating Divide: Race and Desire in the Era of Online Romance* (Berkeley and Los Angeles: University of California Press, 2021); V. C. Phua and G. Kaufman, 'The Crossroads of Race and Sexuality: Date Selection among Men in Internet "Personal" Ads', *Journal of Family Issues* 24 (2003): 981–94; M. Herman and M. Campbell, 'I Wouldn't, But You Can: Attitudes toward Interracial Relationships', *Social Science Research* 41 (2012): 343–58; W. Huang, Wei-Chin, 'Who Are People Willing to Date? Ethnic and Gender Patterns in Online Dating', *Race and Social Problems* 5 (2013): 28–40; J. Bany, B. Robnett, and C. Feliciano, 'Gendered Black Exclusion: The Persistence of Racial Stereotypes among Daters', *Race and Social Problems* 6 (2012): 201–13; B. Robnett and C. Feliciano, 'Patterns of Racial-Ethnic Exclusion by Internet Daters', *Social Forces* 89 (2011): 807–28; G. Mendelsohn, L. Taylor, A. Fiore, and C. Cheshire,

group experience discrimination in other contexts, such as in employment, in a way that generates unjust consequences, then the discrimination that they suffer in the context of personal relationships will exacerbate that injustice.

Discrimination on grounds of race in the context of personal relationships may also damage its victims' interest in autonomous agency by impairing their deliberative freedom. As we saw in Section 3.3, Sophia Moreau argues that a person's deliberative freedom is impaired when 'normatively extraneous features', such as her skin colour or gender, impact upon her decisions concerning, for example, what jobs to seek, because she has to take into account the prejudices or negative attitudes that others have towards these features.[17] It would seem that a person's deliberative freedom is also impaired when she has to consider how features such as these will affect her opportunities to form personal relationships. At least, if we think this freedom is impaired when, in searching for jobs, victims of racial discrimination have to take into account the negative weight that selectors attach to their race or skin colour, then we need to be given a reason for thinking that it is *not* impaired when, in searching for friends or romantic partners, they have to take into account the negative weight that others attach to their race or skin colour.

It is important to my overall argument here that the distribution of a wide range of goods falls within the scope of justice, including friendship and love, and opportunities to form friendships and romantic partnerships, since I am claiming that racial discrimination in personal relationships may be wrong because of the injustice in the distribution of these goods and opportunities to acquire them that it creates or contributes to creating.[18] At one level this might seem straightforward and unproblematic. These goods are sizeable benefits, so any principles governing the just distribution of benefits and burdens must take them into account, regardless of whether these principles conceptualize benefits ultimately as ingredients of well-being, enhancements to capabilities, or as resources. At a deeper level, however, theories of distributive justice may have reasons for restricting the kind of benefits to which their principles apply.

'Black/White Dating Online: Interracial Courtship in the 21st Century', *Psychology of Popular Media Culture* 3 (2014): 2–18; J. White, S. Reisner, E. Dunham, and M. Mimiaga, 'Race-Based Sexual Preferences in a Sample of Online Profiles of Urban Men Seeking Sex with Men', *Journal of Urban Health* 91 (2014): 768–75.

[17] Moreau, 'What Is Discrimination?', 155.

[18] For relevant discussion, see S. Bedi, *Private Racism* (Cambridge: Cambridge University Press, 2019), especially ch. 1.

One potential reason for denying that friendship and romantic partnership, and opportunities to form them, come within the purview of justice is that they cannot be distributed by institutions, even though the goods these relationships make available have deep effects on our well-being. Indeed, it might be thought that Rawls's theory of justice places these goods outside of the sphere of justice for this very reason. For Rawls, the primary subject of justice is the basic structure of society, where that is understood as comprised of the institutions which have profound and pervasive effects on people's life chances.[19] He also thinks that even in 'ideal theory', adequate principles of justice must be realizable in the best of foreseeable conditions.[20] If the claim that the primary subject of justice is the basic structure of society is combined with the claim that principles of justice must be realistic in the sense described, then this might seem to imply that these principles must be such that they could be realized by some set of institutions, under the best of foreseeable conditions. This would rule out as inadequate any principle of justice that it would be impossible to institutionalize because, even in the best of foreseeable conditions, we would lack the power or knowledge required to do so.

According to such an approach, the adequacy of principles of justice is affected not only by limits on institutional design but also by limits on what goods could be distributed by institutions under the best of foreseeable conditions. The distribution of some goods cannot be brought under the control of institutions because of the contingent fact that we lack the power or knowledge or other means to do so, both now and in the best of foreseeable conditions, whereas the distribution of other goods cannot be brought under the control of institutions because of their very nature. Friendship and love are not things that can be distributed by institutions because they depend on appropriate feelings that cannot be commanded, whereas eyeballs are not something that can be distributed since the complexity of the optic nerve means that we lack the ability, now and in the foreseeable future, to transplant them.

But access to goods that cannot be directly distributed by institutions might be strongly affected by institutions and policies. For example,

---

[19] Rawls, *A Theory of Justice*, 6.
[20] See J. Rawls, *Political Liberalism*, paperback edition (New York: Columbia University Press, 1996), xix. Rawls sometimes characterizes the form of ideal theory he defends as 'realistically utopian': see, for example, J. Rawls, *Justice as Fairness: A Restatement* (Cambridge, MA: Harvard University Press, 2001), 4; J. Rawls, *The Law of Peoples* (Cambridge, MA: Harvard University Press, 1999), 4–6, 11–12.

institutions and policies cannot distribute health itself, but they can affect its distribution. Good and bad health is affected to a significant degree by institutions and policies, for example, by policies regulating the distribution of health care and governing aspects of the natural and social environment, such as housing and water quality, and by public information campaigns aimed at persuading people to change their lifestyles. With regard to friendship and love, institutions and policy may affect their distribution by promoting the conditions, including the psychological dispositions, required for opportunities to form friendships and romantic partnerships to arise, so principles of justice might govern these conditions without falling foul of the feasibility constraint that is being envisaged. Publicly funded educational institutions might have as one of their aims the cultivation of the abilities required to develop deep personal relationships, and justice may require us to devote resources to the cultivation of these abilities. So even on a narrow construal of the scope of justice, there are indirect ways in which friendship and love, and opportunities to acquire them, may come within its reach. But in any case, we should question whether the adequacy of principles of justice is constrained by what institutions can realistically deliver in terms of their outcomes. We might think instead that institutions are limited in their power to distribute some of the goods that nevertheless matter from the point of view of justice because of their vital contribution to our flourishing.[21]

6.2 Disrespectful Appearance Discrimination in Personal Relationships

I shall suggest that the reasons why racial discrimination is morally problematic in the context of personal relationships are relevant to our moral assessment of appearance discrimination in the same context. There may be some initial scepticism, however, concerning the existence, or at least the prevalence, of *disrespectful* appearance discrimination in the personal sphere. The most plausible candidates fall into three overlapping categories. First, when appearance discrimination interacts with an additional form of

---

[21] See A. Gheaus, 'How Much of What Matters Can We Distribute? Love, Justice, and Luck', *Hypatia* 24 (2009): 63–83; S. Bedi, 'Sexual Racism: Intimacy as a Matter of Justice', *The Journal of Politics* 77 (2015): 998–1011; T. O'Shea, 'Sexual Desire and Structural Injustice', *Journal of Social Philosophy*. 52 (2021): 587–600.

(direct or indirect) discrimination against members of a stigmatized group, such as racial discrimination itself or discrimination against those with physical disabilities, for example, when a potential friend or romantic partner is rejected because of their skin tone or because of their asymmetrical body. Second, when appearance discrimination is demeaning, or contributes to lowering the perceived moral status of its victims, because it relates to some particular feature of their appearance, such as their short height or heavier weight, the possession of which is stigmatized because in the public eye it is negatively associated with particular character traits or with being undesirable. Discrimination on the basis of these features in the context of forming or cultivating personal relationships may be disrespectful or convey a demeaning message, just as it does in the context of employment. Third, when an act of discrimination is disrespectful in virtue of *reducing* another to her appearance. By this, I mean treating her appearance as the only factor that matters in deciding whether to enter into a personal relationship with her, despite being in a position to know her other qualities.[22]

Let me focus on this third category of cases since it identifies a way in which appearance discrimination may be disrespectful that has not yet received attention. Of course, the appearance of another may deeply affect a person's decision about whether to form a romantic partnership with him or her without being treated as the only factor that matters. When appearance is one factor among several that influences someone's choices, a person who is rejected or accepted as a result of her appearance need not thereby be reduced to her appearance in a morally problematic way. But there may nevertheless be a significant range of cases in which prospective partners are reduced to their appearance in a manner that is morally troubling.[23]

Why should reducing a person to their appearance be thought to be disrespectful? Let me assume for the sake of argument that the moral standing of persons derives at least in part from their possession of a capacity for autonomous agency, that is, a capacity (at or above some threshold level) to set one's own ends and lead one's life in one's own way. When a man treats the appearance of others as the only factor that matters in deciding whether

---

[22] The kind of disrespect I have in mind here is not unique to appearance discrimination. For example, a person may reduce another to their race by treating their race as the only factor that matters in deciding whether to enter into a personal relationship with them.

[23] Søren Flinch Midtgaard defends the related thought that we have a duty of respect to 'look behind' appearance when we make dating choices: see S. F. Midtgaard, '"I'm Just Stating a Preference": Lookism in Online Dating Profiles', *Moral Philosophy and Politics* 10 (2023): 161–83.

to enter into a friendship or romantic partnership with them, he treats them with a lack of respect because he disregards the qualities they possess that have been shaped by their autonomous agency, and in this way does not take due account of their moral standing because he fails to give due weight to the capacity in virtue of which they have that standing. This is not to deny that aspects of a person's appearance may be a product of their choices, for example, body art is a way in which people express their identities, and even not modifying one's body, or not wearing makeup, may be a significant choice that reflects one's values and indeed one's political commitments.[24] When an appearance feature expresses a person's choices in this way, treating it as the only thing that matters in forming a romantic partnership with them may be a way of treating them with respect. In the remainder of this chapter, however, I shall focus on appearance discrimination that is based on those aspects of a person's appearance that are largely unchosen and, for convenience, when I refer to appearance, I shall mean the aspects of it that are to a considerable extent unchosen.

As we saw in Chapter 2, a person may fail to treat others with respect by disregarding the capacities that give them their moral standing without *denying* that they have these capacities.[25] For example, a surgeon who sterilizes a patient without her consent whilst performing an operation to which she has agreed for some other reason ignores her lack of consent in a way that fails to give due weight to her standing. My suggestion is that, in a different way, when a man decides not to form a personal relationship with a woman solely on grounds of her appearance, then he is disregarding the qualities she possesses that are, at least in part, a product of her choices and in that way fails to give due weight to her standing as a subject capable of autonomous agency.

Note that if a person disregards the capacities that give others their moral standing, and thereby treats them as if they lack those capacities, it does not follow that he or she would treat them in the same way if they really did lack those capacities. When a man sexually assaults a woman, he treats his victim as if she lacks the capacities in virtue of which she has her moral standing, but the pleasure he gets from exercising power over her in this way may depend upon the fact that she has these capacities, and is not, say, an

---

[24] See C. Chambers, *Intact: A Defence of the Unmodified Body* (London: Allan Lane, 2022), 5 and *passim*.
[25] See also R. Langton, *Sexual Solipsism: Philosophical Essays on Pornography and Objectification* (Oxford: Oxford University Press, 2009), 233.

automaton.[26] This means that a person may treat others as if they lack the capacities that give them their moral standing even though their possession of those capacities is crucial to how he or she treats them. In effect, a person may in one way treat others as if they lack moral standing whilst in another way treating them as if they possess it. Even if in one way a man takes into account others' possession of a capacity for autonomous agency because he would not be interested in trying to forge a relationship with, say, a robot or automaton, in other ways he may fail to give due weight to that capacity by disregarding the respects in which they have shaped themselves and their lives by their choices.

We might say that when a person is reduced to their appearance, they are *objectified*. But the notion of objectification is also complex. Martha Nussbaum argues that it is a cluster concept. She thinks that there is a range of different ways in which a person can be treated as a thing: someone can be treated as an instrument for realizing another's purposes; someone can be treated as lacking in autonomy and self-determination; someone can be treated as inert, that is, as lacking in agency and activity; someone can be treated as interchangeable with other things of the same type and/or with things of other types; someone can be treated as lacking in boundary-integrity, that is, as something it is permissible to break up, smash, or break into; someone can be treated as something that is owned by another that can, for example, be bought or sold; someone can be treated as if their experiences and feelings do not need to be taken into account.[27] To these different ways in which a person may be objectified that Nussbaum identifies, Rae Langton adds the further ideas that objectification occurs when someone is reduced to their body, that is, treated as identified with their body or body parts; when someone is reduced to their appearance, that is, treated primarily in terms of how they look or appear to the senses; and when someone is treated as silent, as lacking the capacity to speak.[28] It is the first two of these additional ways in which objectification may occur that have been central to my discussion.

As Nussbaum argues, objectification is not always wrong. But it is always wrong in one way when it involves disrespect. This is not in itself an illuminating observation, however, for someone is treated disrespectfully when

---

[26] See Langton, *Sexual Solipsism*, 234.
[27] See M. Nussbaum, 'Objectification', *Philosophy and Public Affairs* 24 (1995): 249–91, especially 257.
[28] Langton, *Sexual Solipsism*, 228–9.

there is a failure to take *due* account of their standing because the capacities in virtue of which they have that standing are not given *due* weight. So the notion of treating someone disrespectfully is itself moralized. The substantive issue for the question I am exploring is whether rejecting potential romantic partners solely on the basis of their appearance involves reducing them to their appearance in a way that fails to give due weight to their possession of the capacities in virtue of which they have their moral standing. On the view I am defending, it does.

In order to illustrate and provide further clarification of the idea of reducing a person to their appearance, consider four somewhat artificial models for understanding how individuals might make choices in relation to appearance in the context of personal relationships. First, a person might give weight *only* to the appearance of potential friends or romantic partners in deciding whether to form a relationship of one of these kinds with them. Second, she might give some weight to the appearance of others but be influenced by a range of other qualities they possess, such that these other qualities could in principle counterbalance a negative assessment of their appearance. Third, she might require that the appearance of others meet some threshold before she would consider entering into a personal relationship with them, but if that threshold is met other qualities enter the picture and influence her decision-making. Fourth, she might require others to possess particular qualities unrelated to appearance before she would consider entering into a personal relationship with them, but if that threshold is met, then her selection is determined solely by their appearance.

On the first model, not only those who are rejected, but also those who are chosen, are reduced to their appearance. In contrast, on the second model neither are reduced to their appearance. Nevertheless, depending on the weighting that a person gives to the appearance of others when making choices about whether to enter into a personal relationship with them, it may be that appearance *dominates* her decisions because she gives it very great weight relative to other considerations. Should we say that in these cases, there is also a lack of respect? There is room for reasonable disagreement about what it means to give due weight to the capacities in virtue of which people have their moral standing in the context of decisions about what personal relationships to form. When Langton says that a person is objectified when they are treated *primarily* in terms of how they look or appear to the senses, I take it that she is leaving open the possibility that a person may treat others disrespectfully when her decisions about whether to form personal relationships with them are dominated by her judgements about their appearance even when their appearance is not the only thing that matters to her. For the purposes of this chapter, I do not need to take a stand on the issue of how much weight needs to be given to those qualities of a person that are chosen or developed, compared to unchosen aspects of her appearance, in order for her to be treated respectfully, that is, without wrongful objectification. But so long as those qualities of a person that are responsive to her choices, such as her kindness, charm, or wit, are given significant weight, giving greater weight to features of appearance that are largely independent of choice, doesn't seem to involve any slight to her moral standing.

On the third model, the situation is mixed. Those above the threshold who are rejected as potential friends or romantic partners do not seem to be reduced to their appearance in a morally problematic objectifying way, even if their appearance is weighted heavily, so long as qualities that have been influenced by their choices (including, perhaps, some aspects of their appearance) are given significant weight. But importantly, those who are rejected because they are below the threshold do seem to have been reduced to their appearance in a way that has a morally problematic objectifying character. One might think that for many of us there is some such threshold that operates, at least when we are making choices about romantic partners, so this is potentially a significant way in which these choices may be disrespectful.

On the fourth model, neither those above the threshold nor those below it are reduced to their appearance. On this model, appearance plays a role in a person's choices about what personal relationships to form only when potential friends or romantic partners have a range of other desired qualities, including qualities that have been cultivated by them. Appearance thereby makes a difference but not one that involves disregarding the capacities in virtue of which others have their moral standing, provided that at least some of the desired qualities that are involved in specifying the threshold are cultivated through the exercise of autonomous agency.

Empirical research would be required to determine what proportion of people have each of these preference structures when making choices about personal relationships but, intuitively, it seems plausible to think that the third model is the dominant one for romantic partnerships, though there may be gender differences here. The use of an 'appearance threshold' is perhaps rarer in practice in the context of people's choices concerning friendship, and indeed it would seem that appearance in general is given less weight in this context. But such a threshold may still be employed, perhaps non-consciously, because of the way in which people may feel drawn to form friendships only with those whose looks are, in effect, above some level. Furthermore, it is worth noting that a person might operate with an appearance threshold with respect to his initial choice of romantic partners but disregard appearance entirely when making decisions concerning whether to sustain a romantic partnership or exit from it.

6.3 Harmful Appearance Discrimination in Personal Relationships

Appearance discrimination in the context of personal relationships may cause harm even when it is not disrespectful, just as racial discrimination does. Cumulatively, it may have a considerable effect on people's access to friendships and romantic partnerships, in a way that contributes to creating an unjust distribution of benefits and burdens.[29] Those who are deprived of friends or romantic partners as a result of appearance discrimination may experience a significant loss of well-being and indeed autonomy. Personal relationships of these kinds are ingredients of many people's conceptions of a life well lived. They may also be important for the acquisition of self-respect, self-esteem, and self-confidence, each of which may be vital for the realization of one's other plans.[30] Discrimination in the personal sphere poses an especially grave threat to people with particular appearance characteristics: to the well-being of people with facial differences, to the flourishing of those, especially women, who are regarded as over-weight, and to the flourishing of men who are short. These aspects of appearance are stigmatized as a result in part of the widespread internalization of norms

---

[29] There is evidence that attractive heterosexuals have more opposite sex friends: see G. White, 'Physical Attractiveness and Courtship Progress', *Journal of Personality and Social Psychology* 39 (1980): 660–8. Facial attractiveness for men is correlated with more short-term sexual partners, whilst facial attractiveness for women is correlated with more long-term sexual partners: see G. Rhodes, L. Simmons, and M. Peters, 'Attractiveness and Sexual Behaviour: Does Attractiveness Enhance Mating Success?', *Evolution and Human Behaviour* 26 (2005): 186–201.

[30] Being regarded as unattractive is correlated with loneliness, social anxiety, and overall dissatisfaction with one's life: see A. Feingold, 'Good-Looking People Are Not What We Think', *Psychological Bulletin* 111 (1992): 304–41; D. Umberson and M. Hughes, 'The Impact of Physical Attractiveness on Achievement and Psychological Well-Being', *Social Psychology Quarterly* 50 (1987): 227–36. On the importance of decent quality social connections for our well-being, see K. Brownlee, *Being Sure of Each Other: An Essay on Social Rights and Freedoms* (Oxford: Oxford University Press, 2020), especially chs 1 and 2.

that evaluate them negatively. Indeed, discrimination in the personal sphere against people with these appearance characteristics may form part of a pattern that undermines their perceived moral status.

To the extent that the third model described in the previous section, in which the looks of others have to be above a particular threshold for them to be regarded as potential friends or romantic partners, accurately reflects people's preference structures, when a person is below most people's thresholds of attractiveness then the harm caused when he or she is passed over is potentially serious in terms of its effect on his or her access to these relationships. So too when the second model is an accurate representation of a large number of people's preference structures, and they place great weight on the appearance of others in their decisions concerning what romantic partnerships to enter into, this may have a considerable impact on the flourishing of those who as a result end up finding it hard to form such relationships. Perhaps preference structures that conform to these models are less common with friendship—or, at least, perhaps the thresholds that people employ, or the weights they assign to appearance, are less restrictive with respect to this type of relationship. But they may still have a considerable effect on the access to friendship of those who, for instance, are regarded as obese or who have facial differences.

It is hard to avoid the conclusion that not only people who treat appearance as the sole basis for forming personal relationships, but also those who have a threshold of appearance below which they won't consider someone as a potential friend or romantic partner, or who give very great weight to appearance in making these decisions at the expense of other personal characteristics, are often acting wrongly. They may be acting wrongly either because they are acting disrespectfully or because of the way in which their decisions play a role in generating unjust consequences, in part through the damage these decisions cause to the interest in autonomous agency of the people they reject.

This is not to deny that people who discriminate on grounds of appearance when forming personal relationships may have a legitimate interest in the aesthetic dimension of these relationships. The appearance of others can be a considerable source of pleasure of various kinds, irrespective of whether their appearance expresses choices they make about how to present themselves or is largely unchosen. Furthermore, our own conceptions of the good may place considerable weight on the aesthetic value we find in the appearance of others. The harms caused to others who are the victims of appearance discrimination need to be balanced against these sizeable benefits that may arise from it. The judgements involved here, concerning whether appearance discrimination in the context of personal relationships plays a role in generating an unjust distribution of benefits and burdens, are sometimes complex. What conclusions we are entitled to reach will depend to some extent on the particular theory of distributive justice that is endorsed, for example, an egalitarian theory is likely to have more radical implications for our personal choices in the context of romantic partnerships than a sufficientarian theory. But there can be little doubt that appearance discrimination in personal relationships poses a particularly serious threat to distributive justice when it is shaped by appearance norms that are biased against groups that are unjustly disadvantaged in other contexts, such as employment: for example, when it is fuelled by norms that favour lighter skin tones, then this will compound the injustices experienced by some racial minorities in recruitment and promotion decisions.

6.4 A Worry about the Argument

It might be thought that the argument I have presented for why both racial discrimination and appearance discrimination may be wrong in the context of the choices people make about what personal relationships to form proves too much.[31] Doesn't it entail that heterosexuals act wrongfully when they discriminate on grounds *of gender or sex* when choosing romantic partners?[32]

Just as the preference of white people for partners of the same race threatens to be demeaning because of the message it conveys in a society in which Black people have been stigmatized and denigrated, so too it would seem that the preference of heterosexuals for romantic partners of the opposite (cis)gender is potentially demeaning because of the message it conveys in a society in which gay people and lesbians (and transgender people) have been stigmatized and denigrated. And just as Black people are potentially harmed as a result of a widely held preference for non-Black

---

[31] Cf. L. Thomas, 'Split-Level Equality: Mixing Love and Equality', in S. Babbitt and S. Campbell (eds), *Racism and Philosophy* (Ithaca, NY: Cornell University Press, 1999), 199; Zheng, 'Why Yellow Fever Isn't Flattering', 412–14.

[32] For a discussion that takes this possibility seriously, see I. Ayres and J. Brown, *Straightforward: How to Mobilize Heterosexual Support for Gay Rights* (Princeton, NJ: Princeton University Press, 2005), 30–7. They argue that discrimination on grounds of sex in sexual relationships is morally permissible only if it tends to undermine or challenge practices of subordination rather than perpetuate them.

romantic or sexual partners because it significantly reduces their opportunities for finding fulfilling romantic partnerships, it would seem that so too gay people and lesbians (and transgender people) are potentially harmed as a result of the preferences of heterosexuals for opposite (cis)gender partners. Since those who are willing to enter into a romantic partnership with someone of the same gender are much fewer in number, the options of those who do prefer same-gender partners are greatly reduced by the preferences of heterosexuals. It would therefore seem that such preferences may contribute to creating and maintaining an unjust distribution of benefits and burdens, in a way that is similar to how preferences not to form romantic partnerships with Black people may do so. The conclusion that heterosexuals act wrongly when they discriminate on grounds of sex or gender in deciding what romantic partnerships to form might seem deeply counterintuitive and to raise doubts about whether my argument could be sound.

Is there any morally relevant difference between white people discriminating on grounds of race in forming romantic partnerships and heterosexuals discriminating on grounds of gender in forming such partnerships? Carina Fourie argues that in terms of their potential to demean, there is a crucial disanalogy between the preferences of white people for same-race romantic partners and the preferences of heterosexuals for same-sex or same-gender partners. She points out that it is Black people—a disadvantaged group—who suffer discrimination as a result of white people's preferences for partners of the same race, whereas it is men in general who experience discrimination as a result of heterosexual men's preferences for women partners, but men are not a disadvantaged group.[33] If it is the case that only members of a disadvantaged group can be demeaned, then men cannot be demeaned by heterosexual men's preferences for women partners. Fourie seems correct that there is a disanalogy here. But the choice that heterosexual men are making is, in effect, a refusal to date those of the same sex or, perhaps, those of the same gender. Even though men are not a disadvantaged group, that refusal might send out a demeaning message about those who do date people of the same gender or same sex, and the latter might reasonably be regarded as members of a disadvantaged group. In other words, that message may not demean all of those who are subject to discrimination, but it nevertheless demeans some who experience it.

---

[33] See Fourie, 'Wrongful Private Discrimination and the Egalitarian Ethos', 428.

Robin Zheng arrives at the same conclusion as Fourie but via a different route. She argues that there is a crucial difference between romantic preferences based on race and romantic preferences based on sex or gender: 'The expressive meanings of such preferences are not the same. Insofar as the "rules of the game" are defined in terms of gender and sexual orientation, distinguishing potential partners on the basis of gender and sexual orientation does not mean that those others are submitted to any differential treatment.'[34] But it is hard to see what is supposed to be the significance of the fact that a person is choosing in accordance with the rules of the game when they choose to date someone of the opposite sex or gender. My claim is in effect that these rules, in combination with hierarchical social relations between heterosexuals and gay men or lesbians, convey a demeaning message, a message that is reinforced when people choose in accordance with them. Indeed, in a society in which Black people are marginalized where one of the rules of the game is that white people shouldn't choose a Black partner, then these rules are morally problematic precisely because they are degrading, and conforming to them is wrongful because of the way it reinforces them and sends out a message of inferiority. No doubt it simplifies too much to suppose that there is a single uniform message that is conveyed by the choices made by heterosexuals: more than one message may be conveyed, and what messages are conveyed will depend to some extent upon the immediate social environment in which these choices are made and the kind of relationships that are supported within it, for example, whether that environment is one in which gay relationships are respected and celebrated. But when homophobia is rife, the wider message conveyed by these choices is likely to be one that demeans those who act against the prevailing heterosexist norms.

Xiaofei Liu argues that there is a crucial difference between discrimination on the basis of race in forming romantic partnerships and discrimination on the basis of sex, on the grounds that 'sex as such is directly contributive to sexual appeal whereas race as such is not. It matters to sexual appeal how good looking one is, to which sex is indeed irrelevant; but what also matters to sexual appeal is, as a biological fact, one's sexual characteristics.'[35] But this seems question-begging. Race may, in some cases, directly contribute to sex appeal, for example, when a person finds the colour of another's skin or their hair texture attractive or unattractive, whereas, for some at

---

[34] Zheng, 'Why Yellow Fever Isn't Flattering', 413.
[35] X. Liu, '"No Fats, Femmes, or Asians"', *Moral Philosophy and Politics* 2 (2015): 255–76, at 271.

least, the sexual organs or gender of another person may be irrelevant to their sex appeal.

Liu would reply, in part, by arguing that the colour of a person's skin (or their hair texture) is correlated with their racial membership rather than being constitutive of it, since '[i]ndividuals in the same racial group can vary significantly in terms of skin color. East Africans and West Africans can have quite different skin colours; the same is true for Northern and Southern Europeans, Northern and Southern Chinese and so on.... To identify race with a specific skin color is both scientifically and sociologically ungrounded—it ignores a significant degree of variance.'[36] This point is forceful, but membership of particular racial groups generally depends on possession of some specific appearance features. When membership of a particular racial group does depend on a set of appearance features, even if none of these features is individually necessary for membership, one could not be a member of it if one lacked all of them. Even when membership of a racial group does not depend on the possession of any specific set of appearance features, the very same issue we are considering arises with respect to skin colour considered independently of racial membership: is there any morally relevant difference between discrimination on grounds of skin colour and discrimination on grounds of sex in the context of making choices about what romantic partnerships to form or sustain, when one finds the colour of some people's skin sexually unappealing? So far none has been found.

Lawrence Thomas argues that discrimination on grounds of gender in forming sexual relationships is different in kind from discrimination on grounds of race in forming these relationships.[37] He imagines a heterosexual woman, Naomi, saying that John is everything she ever wanted in a sexual partner whilst rejecting him because of his ethnicity, and maintains that this is relevantly different from Naomi saying that Leslie is everything she ever wanted in a sexual partner, whilst rejecting her because she is a woman. Thomas doubts whether the description of the second case is even coherent unless it means something like, 'I thought I was really attracted to one kind of gender, but my experience with Leslie has shown me otherwise'.

But Thomas's cases are under-described. Suppose that in the first case Naomi finds John sexually appealing, but rejects him because he is Black, whereas in the second case she simply does not find Leslie sexually

---

[36] Liu, '"No Fats, Femmes, or Asians"', 259.
[37] See Thomas, 'Split-Level Equality', 199–200.

appealing because Leslie is a woman. If that is the case, then indeed there is a difference between these two cases that seems morally relevant, even if we don't know the precise reason for her decision, for example, whether her preference not to have a Black partner is rooted in overt prejudice or implicit bias or has some other basis. But suppose instead that Naomi rejects John because, even though he is everything she ever wanted in a sexual partner, in that he is kind, intelligent, warm, and witty, has an attractive appearance, and possesses the same interests as her, she does not find him sexually appealing *because* he is Black. That seems analogous to Naomi saying that Leslie is everything she ever wanted in a sexual partner, in that Leslie is kind, intelligent, warm, and witty, has an attractive appearance, and possesses the same interests as her, but rejects her because she does not find her sexually appealing because she is a woman. This manner of describing the way in which relationships are formed may seem contrived—and indeed the evidence is that this is not the way in which people make decisions about whether to enter into romantic relationships[38]—but the point is that if the first description is coherent, then so too is the second. And if we assume that it is morally wrongful for Naomi to reject John simply because he is Black and she does not find Black men sexually appealing, then we would need a reason for not concluding that it is also wrongful for Naomi to reject Leslie simply because Leslie is a woman and she doesn't find women sexually appealing. It is hard to see what morally relevant difference there is between the two cases.

Could the origin of the respective desires make a difference to how we morally assess Thomas's cases? It clearly makes a difference whether or not these desires have their origins in prejudices. But suppose, for the sake of argument, it is the way in which Naomi is 'wired', that is, her physiological or biological constitution, that explains why she does not find Leslie sexually appealing, whereas her lack of sexual desire for John is a legacy of unjust institutions and practices, such as stigmatization, or informal practices of segregation that reduce the frequency of interactions between members of different racial groups and that are a product of an earlier era during which relationships between different racial groups were illegal or universally frowned upon. Would that make a moral difference to how we assess the

---

[38] Research on 'ideal partner preferences', that is, traits and attributes that people desire in their ideal romantic partners, suggests that these preferences are poor predictors of a person's evaluations of potential partners when he or she interacts with them face to face as opposed to reading descriptions of them. See Eastwick et al. 'The Predictive Validity of Ideal Partner Preferences', 642.

discrimination that is involved in these cases? It may make some difference, but it is hard to see why it should lead us to entirely different verdicts in the two cases, assuming that other things are equal, such as the strength of the relevant desires and their degree of responsiveness to attempts to change them.

These reflections may make some suspicious of the idea that the considerations that explain why discrimination is wrong (when it is wrong) in the context of, say, recruiting for jobs also apply to the choices that people make concerning what friendships or romantic partnerships to form. But those who are tempted to row back from that idea would need to explain what the relevant difference is between these two contexts, in light of the disrespect that may be involved in each and the potential there is in each for decisions to contribute to creating unjust consequences. A more plausible approach, in my view, is to acknowledge that moral considerations, relating to respect and to the potential role of one's choices in generating unjust consequences, are in play when reflecting on the decisions people make concerning what personal relationships to form, but that other moral considerations also enter the picture.

First, we need to acknowledge that people may make a smaller contribution to injustice by acting in accordance with their inclinations rather than against them. For a variety of legitimate reasons, some Black people may not want to form close personal relationships with white people, in which case white people may not have the chance of being in such relationships with them. When Black people suspect that a white person harbours negative attitudes towards them because of their race, or has an aesthetic preference for lighter skin tones, then they may be especially reluctant to enter into a personal relationship with him or her. But even when, say, a Black woman is willing to form a romantic partnership with a white man who is committed to working on changing his residual negative attitudes towards Black people or transforming his aesthetic tastes when these favour light skin tones, she may suffer harm as a result if he (or indeed she) underestimates the strength or depth of these attitudes or tastes. This may mean that when white people with these attitudes or tastes act in accordance with them by discriminating on grounds of race in forming personal relationships, they make a smaller contribution to injustice than they would otherwise do. In such cases, even though discrimination plays a role in generating unjust consequences, it is morally permissible because it makes less of a contribution than refraining from discriminating would do. As I proposed in Section 3.1, we act wrongly when we behave in a way that contributes to creating or sustaining an unjust distribution of benefits and burdens *only when* we can avoid behaving in these ways and can do so without creating, or contributing to creating, a greater injustice.

The idea that white people with negative attitudes towards Black people, or aesthetic tastes that favour lighter skin tones, may often cause less injustice by discriminating against Black people when making decisions about what personal relationships to form also receives some support from the argument that pursuing a friendship or a romantic partnership with a Black person under such circumstances is at worst disrespectful and at best insulting. Megan Mitchell and Mark Wells suggest that when a white person who is not attracted to Black people pursues a romantic partnership with a Black person in order to promote some end that she judges to be worthwhile, she treats the Black person as a means or tool towards her goals.[39] This argument has some force, but a white woman (say) might favour a relationship with a Black man even though it goes against her inclinations because she regards herself as being under an obligation to avoid contributing to an injustice, rather than having a reason to promote some worthwhile goal—or, indeed, being under an obligation to *promote* justice. It is not clear that under these circumstances she treats him as a means towards her goals. Furthermore, even if she were treating him as a means, she need not be treating him *merely* as a means—she might genuinely care about him and his interests and be taking them into account—and it is treating someone as a means only that is morally objectionable.[40] But is it nevertheless insulting for her to form a relationship with him, in part, because she wants to avoid violating a duty not to contribute to injustice? There is a genuine worry here. When her decision to pursue such a relationship goes against the grain of her negative attitudes towards Black people or her aesthetic judgements about his looks, and he knows that she has made that decision in part to comply with a duty to avoid contributing to injustice, then he might reasonably regard her behaviour as insulting.[41] This reinforces the case for holding that discriminating on racial grounds under such circumstances may minimize the injustice created even though it nevertheless contributes to it.

Second, we need to recognize that even when discriminating against someone in deciding, say, what romantic partnerships to enter into is demeaning or disrespectful, or makes a greater contribution to injustice

---

[39] See M. Mitchell and M. Wells, 'Race, Romantic Attraction, and Dating', 949.
[40] See R. De Bernardi, 'Dilemmas of Dating: The Case of Sexual Lookism' (unpublished paper).
[41] De Bernardi, 'Dilemmas of Dating'.

than refraining from discriminating would do, there is a moral prerogative that may permit a person to act in this way. As I suggested in Section 3.1, we act wrongly when we behave in a way that contributes to creating or maintaining an unjust distribution of benefits and burdens only if we are able to avoid doing so without incurring unreasonable costs. The same moral prerogative seems to apply even when we discriminate against potential friends or romantic partners in a way that is disrespectful or conveys a demeaning message.

To clarify, consider two kinds of case. First, when not discriminating would make it impossible for one person to form a friendship or a romantic partnership with another, given the nature of the feelings that are partially constitutive of these types of personal relationship. This would be the case with a prospective friendship if one person found the appearance of the other so off-putting that she did not enjoy spending time with them, since enjoying being in the company of a person seems to be a necessary condition of being in a friendship with them. When this is the case, there is a moral prerogative that permits a person to act in a way that would otherwise be wrongful. Second, when not discriminating in forming a friendship or romantic partnership would mean that a person could not realize, or could realize only to a very limited extent, the goods that are characteristically available through these types of relationship, then she is morally permitted to discriminate. This would be the case in a romantic partnership with a sexual character if one person felt little sexual attraction for the other because she did not like their skin tone. In this kind of case, a moral prerogative also kicks in and permits the person to discriminate. (We might think of the moral permission to discriminate in these two kinds of case as giving partial content to a right of free association in the context of forming, developing or sustaining personal relationships. In this context, the right of free association is grounded, at least in part, in the interest that each person has in forming sustainable close personal relationships.)

What justifies this moral prerogative in this context? The stakes can be very high when a person would struggle to realize the goods involved in friendships or romantic partnerships unless they discriminate on grounds of appearance. Given how hard it is to forge deep friendships or find fulfilling long-term romantic partnerships, and how important these are for most people's well-being, it is important for choices of these kinds to be unfettered in certain respects. In light of the potential importance for a person of goods related to sex in romantic partnerships with a sexual character, there is sometimes a moral permission to act on one's preferences when choosing romantic partners even when doing so plays a role in generating unjust consequences, and even when acting in this way is disrespectful or demeaning. Even if the injustice to which those who discriminate in this way contribute is considerable, for any individual act the contribution to injustice may be minimal. Those who are the potential victims of this type of discrimination are unlikely to forge fulfilling relationships, whether romantic partnerships or friendships, with a person who for one reason or another struggles to realize with them the goods that he or she is seeking in such a relationship, so they suffer limited direct harm when they are rejected.

People who exercise the moral prerogative I have described may nevertheless be under a duty to work to change their desires or feelings, as part of a duty to avoid demeaning behaviour and to avoid contributing to injustice.[42] Indeed, they may be morally required to fulfil this duty as a condition of justifiably exercising that prerogative. There is a danger, however, that attributing such a duty to people becomes part of an authoritarian moralism that involves pressurizing them into making choices that go against the grain of their deeply rooted desires in a way that means it is hard for them to flourish.[43] For this reason Amia Srinivasan seems reluctant to endorse a 'duty to transfigure, as best we can, our desires', even though she thinks that our desires can be morally problematic.[44] But the point of affirming such a duty need not be to berate those who fail to comply with it, or put pressure on them to comply with it, but merely to acknowledge the moral reasons each of us has to do so. In some cases, however, it may be impossible for people to 'reprogram' their sexual desires, for example, when they find those who belong to a different racial or ethnic group, or those of the same sex, or those whom they perceive as visually unattractive, sexually unappealing. And even when it is not impossible for a person over time to change the character of their sexual desires, it may be unreasonably demanding to require them to do so. In these cases, there is a further moral prerogative that kicks in that permits them to acquiesce in these desires.[45]

---

[42] For relevant discussion concerning how people might go about transforming their desires, see S. Irvin, 'Resisting Body Oppression: An Aesthetic Approach', *Feminist Philosophy Quarterly* 3.4 (2017): article 3; S. Irvin (ed.), *Body Aesthetics* (Oxford: Oxford University Press, 2016), especially the article by Eaton; Mitchell and Wells, 'Race, Romantic Attraction, and Dating', 950–1.

[43] Srinivasan, *The Right to Sex*, 83, 86. [44] See Srinivasan, *The Right to Sex*, 90.

[45] To say this is not to suggest that even in these cases the sexual desires are, in themselves, beyond moral reproach. We should raise questions not only about the moral appropriateness of those desires but also about the institutions and practices that shape them. For relevant discussion, see R. Robinson, 'Structural Dimensions of Romantic Preferences', *Fordham Law*

With friendship, a similar moral prerogative applies in cases (presumably rare in practice) when a person has an aversion to the colour of another's skin of a kind that makes it impossible for them to realize the goods that these relationships involve (or to realize them to any great extent), and complying with the duty would therefore preclude them from realizing these goods (or from realizing them to any great extent).[46] When they could change their feelings over time, without any great cost or difficulty, then they have a duty to do so. But if they could change them only at great cost to themselves, then it may be unreasonably demanding to require them to do so, in which case they have a moral prerogative that permits them to acquiesce in these feelings.

The moral prerogatives I have described leave intact the idea that it is morally wrongful to discriminate on grounds of race, sex, or appearance in the context of personal encounters or interactions that fall short of romantic partnership or friendship. And it leaves scope for the idea that it is morally impermissible to discriminate in forming a romantic partnership or friendship when people do not have the kind of feelings that would preclude such a relationship from being formed, or the goods that are characteristically available within it from being obtained in a reasonably full form. Indeed, it is an implication of this position that those for whom others must meet a threshold of attractiveness, before they will be considered as potential friends or romantic partners, discriminate wrongfully on grounds of appearance when they set this standard of attractiveness higher than that required for them to be able to realize to a significant extent, and without any great difficulty, the goods involved in these relationships.

Even with the moral prerogative in place that I have defended, doesn't my argument have deeply counterintuitive consequences? If there were a cheap pill available, with no side-effects, that could turn heterosexuals into bisexuals or pansexuals, wouldn't they be under a duty to take it? The idea that, in the context of societies with a history of racial discrimination that persists into the present, white people would be under a duty to take a similar pill to change the character of their desires if they found the dark skin tone of those who belong to another racial group sexually unappealing doesn't strike me as counterintuitive, at least when that preference doesn't rest upon racial prejudice or animus of a kind that would be better tackled in other

---

Review 76 (2008): 2787–819; Srinivasan, *The Right to Sex*, especially 'The Right to Sex' and 'Coda: The Politics of Desire'; Zheng, 'Why Yellow Fever Isn't Flattering', 415.

[46] Cf. Moreau, 'What Is Discrimination?', 161.

ways. The question is then: are there any morally relevant differences, in terms of their potential demeaningness or unjust effects, between the choices of white people living in a racist society who will not form romantic partnerships with Black people, and the choices of heterosexuals living in a homophobic society who will consider only those of the opposite gender (or sex) as potential romantic partners, that would justify the latter's refusal to take a desire-changing pill? It is hard to find such a difference. I have considered a number of potential candidates, but none of them seems to me to withstand critical scrutiny. With some reluctance perhaps, I follow the argument to its logical conclusion.

6.5 Appearance as a 'Reaction Qualification' in the Personal Sphere

Sometimes when people discriminate on grounds of race or ethnicity in making choices about what personal relationships to form, they do so because they worry about how a potential friend or partner will be received within their existing friendship group or by their family, rather than because of their own racial prejudices or biases. Much the same issue may arise with respect to appearance: those considering whether to develop a friendship or romantic partnership with someone who is obese or has facial differences may be put off not because they find his or her appearance unattractive, or regard it as by itself a decisive consideration against forming a relationship with him or her, but because they think that it will be regarded negatively by their existing friends or family members.[47] More generally, the choices that people make may be motivated, wholly or in part, by their desire for a 'high status' partner who will be valued or envied by others. When the members of a racial minority, or those with specific appearance features, are devalued in a society, people's choices about what romantic partnerships to form or develop may be influenced by these status hierarchies. Is it morally permissible to give weight to the preferences, judgements, or attitudes of others in these different ways when deciding what relationships to form? Here there

---

[47] Consider, for example, Virgie Tovar, who self-identifies as a fat woman and reports the reaction of 'Derek' to her suggestion that they meet in public rather than at her house: '"Listen," he says, "you are my absolute ideal body type, okay? I mean *absolute ideal*, but if I dated you then my friends would never let me hear the end of it." See Virgie Tovar, 'What It's Really Like to Date as a Fat Woman', https://www.goodhousekeeping.com/life/relationships/a35730257/plus-size-dating/, accessed 5 July 2022. I owe this reference to Rossella De Bernardi.

is a parallel issue to the one faced in employment decisions when one's colleagues, or one's customers or clients, have preferences not to deal with those who belong to a particular racial group, or preferences to deal with, or not to deal with, those who have a specific kind of appearance. We need to revisit the terrain of reaction qualifications.

As we saw in Chapter 5, some reaction qualifications are legitimate, others are illegitimate. The theory developed there in relation to employment decisions also seems relevant to decisions people make about what personal relationships to form when their friends and family, or members of the wider society in which they live, would respond positively or negatively to particular choices. It suggests that there are strong moral reasons not to give weight to these responses in at least two kinds of case. First, when giving weight to them would condone disrespectful attitudes or behaviour, that is, attitudes or behaviour that fail to take due account of the moral standing of others. Second, when giving weight to them would tend to exacerbate the disadvantages that are experienced by members of an unjustly disadvantaged group.

Consider the relevance of these points to cases of racial bias in the context of forming personal relationships. Suppose that a man's friends or family have internalized racial prejudices that fail to take due account of the moral standing of those who belong to a particular racial group, for example, they regard members of this group as untrustworthy on the grounds that they are incapable of acting morally. If these prejudices mean that they have a preference for him not to enter into a friendship or romantic partnership with a member of that group, then this preference would be disrespectful to people who belong to it, and for him to give weight to it would be to condone that lack of respect. So too if members of a racial group are devalued in a society, giving weight to this status hierarchy, because one wants a high-status romantic partner who is admired or envied by others, would be to condone disrespectful attitudes. Even if the reactions of a person's friends or family members are not disrespectful but are rooted instead in feelings of awkwardness that are the product of informal practices of segregation, giving weight to them might nevertheless harm members of this racial group in a way that contributes to creating an unjust distribution of benefits and burdens. Indeed, when this racial group is unjustly disadvantaged, giving weight to such reactions would tend to exacerbate the disadvantages that members of it have experienced.

Note, however, that even though there are generally powerful reasons not to take into account the racially biased reactions of one's friends or family in making decisions about what personal relationships to forge, these reasons might nevertheless be outweighed if entering into a relationship with a member of another racial group would lead to permanent and irrevocable estrangement from them, in which case the discrimination involved might be justified all things considered. This is partly analogous to the way in which it may be morally justified all things considered to count reaction qualifications even when they are illegitimate, for example, when counting them would minimize the injustice involved or promote greater justice (see Section 5.7). In the case I am envisaging, however, it is not that injustice would be minimized by refraining from entering into a relationship when doing so would lead to permanent estrangement from friends and family members; rather, there is a personal prerogative that permits a person to make that decision because it would be unreasonable to morally require him or her to bear such a burden.

Some parallel conclusions can be drawn in relation to appearance discrimination. Suppose that a person's friends or family have internalized prejudices about an appearance feature, for example, that those they regard as overweight are lacking in self-discipline, and these prejudices involve a failure to take due account of the standing of people who possess this feature, perhaps because these prejudices imply that people with this feature are unlikely to exercise appropriately the capacities in virtue of which they have their standing. In that case, preferences formed on the basis of these prejudices are disrespectful and giving weight to them would be to condone that disrespect. More generally, if a person takes into account the reactions of others, by seeking a friend or romantic partner whose appearance will be admired or envied by them, then he or she may condone disrespectful attitudes in a way that is morally objectionable because these attitudes may reflect status hierarchies concerning appearance. The most likely cases here involve taking into account negative attitudes concerning people regarded as overweight or as too short, or who have facial differences.

Furthermore, if taking into account the reactions of friends or family, or widely held attitudes concerning who has an attractive appearance, would harm potential friends and romantic partners in a way that contributes to creating an unjust distribution of benefits and burdens, then there is a powerful moral reason not to do so. People with facial differences, and indeed those regarded as obese or very short, may constitute unjustly disadvantaged groups, in which case taking into account the preferences of one's family and existing friends concerning the shape or size of one's potential friends or romantic partners, or their preferences for 'normal' faces, may exacerbate the unjust disadvantages experienced by members of these groups.

6.6 Concluding Remarks

Personal relationships are not a morality-free zone when it comes to the assessment of appearance discrimination. The decisions that people make concerning, for example, what romantic partnerships to form, develop, and sustain may reduce people to their appearance in a way that is wrong because it is disrespectful. As a result, appearance discrimination in this context may constitute a morally problematic form of objectification that fails to take due account of the standing of the victims. It may also be wrong because it contributes to generating an unjust distribution of benefits and burdens. But there is a personal prerogative that permits relatively extensive appearance discrimination in the context of personal relationships when people would otherwise struggle to realize to any great extent the goods that can be obtained in and through them, or indeed struggle to form sustainable relationships of these kinds without engaging in it.

7
Everyday Lookism

I have explored the morality of appearance discrimination in the context of decisions made about hiring and promotion, and in the context of choices made about what personal relationships to form, cultivate, or maintain. But appearance discrimination is also pervasive in our daily lives, especially on social media, in ordinary practices of commenting upon and judging people's looks, in ways that often include body-shaming.[1] This might seem to over-stretch the concept of discrimination—we don't immediately think of these practices as discriminatory—but they involve singling out individuals (sometimes as members of groups) and treating them unfavourably on the basis of their attributes, which counts as discrimination according to the definition I am using.[2] Indeed, these practices involve particularly concerning instances of appearance discrimination, for what has come to be known as 'everyday lookism'[3] seems to have contributed to fostering an epidemic of body anxiety, especially among teenagers and young adults, causing injuries to self-esteem and self-confidence.[4]

---

[1] It is somewhat misleading to refer to these practices as a *context* of discrimination in the way that I do because the treatment to which I am referring occurs in many different domains, for example, in the workplace when an employee ridicules the appearance of a colleague, or in a friendship when one person makes hurtful comments about the appearance of the other. This chapter draws upon my 'What's Wrong with Everyday Lookism?', *Politics, Philosophy and Economics* 20 (2021): 315–35.

[2] Although some of these acts count as microaggressions in Emily McTernan's sense, many of them don't, for those who perform them are often aware that they are making comments that will upset those at the receiving end. Furthermore, there is at least a prima facie case for saying that some of these acts are morally objectionable even when the victims of them are not part of a marginalized or disadvantaged group, for example, when a middle-aged heterosexual white man is ridiculed for wearing makeup. See E. McTernan, 'Microaggressions, Equality, and Social Practices', *Journal of Political Philosophy* 26 (2018): 261–81.

[3] For the notion of everyday lookism, see https://www.everydaylookism.com, accessed 1 May 2023.

[4] For relevant discussion, see S. Grogan, *Body Image: Understanding Body Dissatisfaction in Men, Women and Children*, 3rd edn (London: Routledge, 2016). For evidence of body dissatisfaction and its impact in the UK, see Government Equalities Office, 'Body Confidence: Findings from the British Social Attitudes Survey', 2014, available at https://www.gov.uk/government/publications/body-confidence-a-rapid-evidence-assessment-of-the-literature, accessed 5 July 2022. For evidence from the US, see M. Bucchianeri, A. Arikian, P. Hannan, M. Hannan, M. Eisenberg, and D. Neumark-Sztainer, 'Body Dissatisfaction from Adolescence

Heather Widdows maintains that a highly demanding conception of what it is to look beautiful has increasingly become dominant.[5] It is this ideal that seems to fuel everyday lookism.[6] She documents the way in which exacting norms relating to youthfulness, slimness, absence of body hair, skin texture, and firmness of flesh govern the appearance of women, and she illustrates the way in which increasingly men too are subject to norms governing muscularity and hair thickness that are comparable in terms of their demandingness.[7] In Widdows's view, these appearance norms have come to form an ethical ideal that has adverse effects. Translated into Rawlsian terms, her claim is that an ideal of beauty has become a partially comprehensive moral doctrine that exerts pressure on not only those who endorse it but also those who reject it. Even though this doctrine can be combined in a relatively harmonious way with a range of different conceptions of what gives value and meaning to our lives (for example, for the most part it is perfectly consistent with valuing artistic creativity or enjoying wilderness adventures), when a person endorses it, then it shapes and constrains her conception of how to live. Those who do not comply with the relevant norms, irrespective of whether they endorse them, are subject to disapproval of a kind that is not merely aesthetic but takes the form of ethical or moral criticism. Women especially are often subjected to criticism that is moral in tone for not making the best of themselves or letting themselves go, in a way that implies they have failed in their duty to themselves, and perhaps even to others, to take adequate care of their appearance. Furthermore, both men and women (and indeed boys and girls) are shamed for being overweight and are regarded as self-indulgent or lacking in self-control for failing to achieve what for them may be an unattainable body shape.

---

to Young Adulthood: Findings from a 10-Year Longitudinal Study', *Body Image* 10 (2013): 1–7. The Nuffield Council on Bioethics 2017 report *Cosmetic Procedures: Ethical Issues*, sections 1.6–1.11, provides a good summary of the empirical evidence on appearance dissatisfaction. Available at http://nuffieldbioethics.org/wp-content/uploads/Cosmetic-procedures-full-report.pdf, accessed 5 July 2022.

[5] H. Widdows, *Perfect Me. Beauty as an Ethical Ideal* (Princeton, NJ: Princeton University Press, 2018), especially ch. 1. She claims that this ideal now has global reach, though she allows that there may be some cultural variations, for example, with respect to how, exactly, the constituents are understood, or with respect to additional ingredients. Indeed, her claim is consistent with local variations in appearance norms, for example, different groups within a society or indeed a region may adopt different norms concerning how one should dress or adhere to different norms with respect to tattoos or piercings.

[6] Widdows, *Perfect Me*, 54–60.

[7] Widdows, *Perfect Me*, 236–43; see also Widdows, 'Structural Injustice and the Requirements of Beauty', especially 255–6.

Conceived in the way that I am proposing, everyday lookism can be morally objectionable because it involves acts of wrongful discrimination. These acts may be wrongful for the now familiar reason that they are demeaning. The appearance norms that fuel them, and the context in which they occur, may be such that they send out a message that those to whom these norms apply, or those who fail to comply with these norms, are morally inferior. The idea that the discrimination involved in everyday lookism may be demeaning in this way can be developed by drawing again upon Deborah Hellman's account of what makes discrimination wrong. In light of the power that men may possess over women, and the history of unjust treatment to which women have been subject, everyday lookism can be demeaning in virtue of conveying a message of inferiority, such as the message that women are *mere* objects of men's sexual desire. When men make comments to women about their appearance in a way that is sexualized, then this may be demeaning in a society in which women have been treated as mere objects for men's sexual use, for it may objectify women in a morally problematic way by reducing them to their bodies or body parts.[8] So too, women who are ridiculed for not removing body hair, and who are regarded as disgusting or dirty for letting it grow naturally, seem to be demeaned as a result of the attention it receives. More generally, everyday lookism fuelled by appearance norms that cast women as more superficial than men in virtue of the greater significance women are expected to attach to their appearance might be thought to treat women as having an inferior moral status.[9]

Irrespective of whether an instance of everyday lookism is demeaning, it may have harmful consequences in a way that contributes to creating an unjust distribution of benefits and burdens. As we saw in Chapter 4, the appearance norms that fuel it are often biased against disadvantaged groups. Appearance norms that value symmetrical faces and bodies are biased against some people with disabilities. Appearance norms that value straight hair rather than tight curls are biased against some Black and mixed-race people whose hair would require expensive or potentially harmful treatments to conform to these norms. Appearance norms that value ways of dressing that involve exposing one's arms and legs may be biased against people, especially women, who subscribe to a religion that is committed to a particular conception of modesty. More generally, appearance norms may

---

[8] See Section 6.2.
[9] See S. Bartky, 'Foucault, Femininity and the Modernization of Patriarchal Power', in D. Meyers (ed.), *Feminist Social Thought: A Reader* (London: Routledge, 1997), 102.

be naturally biased in a way that makes it costly or difficult, or even impossible, for people born with a propensity to acquire a particular body shape or size to comply with them. When everyday lookism is fuelled by biased norms, it may contribute to unjustly disadvantaging a group or lowering the perceived moral standing of its members, or it may reinforce the power structures that facilitate doing so.

But this is not the only way in which everyday lookism can have unjust consequences. In this chapter, I shall focus on another important way in which it can do so. I shall argue that the norms that fuel everyday lookism, and the costs of complying or failing to comply with these norms, may combine to make it oppressive in a way that is partially independent of whether these norms are demeaning or biased against disadvantaged groups. This is not peculiar to everyday lookism, since the costs of complying, or failing to comply with appearance norms may combine in a similar way in the two other contexts I have discussed. But examining everyday lookism and its effects provides me with an opportunity to explore in more depth the ways in which the significant but limited control that we have in relation to whether we comply with, or fail to comply with, a range of appearance norms may have a detrimental effect on our autonomy and well-being.

In developing my argument, I shall regard an appearance norm as an informal rule concerning how one should look that is generally endorsed or, at least, generally followed, within a society or a group.[10] I shall treat the costs of compliance with an appearance norm, such as the time, effort, and use of resources involved in doing so, and the costs of non-compliance, such as the disapproval or moral criticism to which people are subjected and the feelings of guilt or shame they experience, as extrinsic to the norm rather than constitutive of it.[11] By focusing on the way in which individual acts of commenting critically on the appearance of others, fuelled by appearance norms with which it is costly or difficult to comply, may

---

[10] I don't intend this characterization of an appearance norm to be a contribution to debates concerning the best way of understanding a social norm. It is formulated to leave open the possibility that an appearance norm might be sustained by a sizeable group of people complying with it even though they don't endorse it and indeed think it is bad for the society or group to which they belong, that is, to make space for what Cristina Bicchieri calls 'pluralistic ignorance': see C. Bicchieri, *Norms in the Wild: How to Diagnose, Measure, and Change Social Norms* (Oxford: Oxford University Press, 2017), 44. For a helpful discussion of the nature of norms to which I am indebted, see G. Brennan, L. Eriksson, R. Goodin, and N. Southwood, *Explaining Norms* (Oxford: Oxford University Press, 2013), especially part 1.

[11] This way of conceiving appearance norms has the plausible implication that the costs of complying and not complying with an appearance norm may change over time without affecting its identity.

combine to generate unjust consequences, I also hope to show how moral concerns about appearance discrimination may be integrated with concerns about structural injustices.

7.1 The Oppressiveness of Everyday Lookism

How could everyday lookism be oppressive without being demeaning or involving biased appearance norms? Doesn't the charge that it is oppressive reduce to claims about the demeaning character of the acts of discrimination it involves, or to the way in which acts of discrimination rooted in biased appearance norms may play a role in exacerbating the injustices suffered by disadvantaged groups? Suppose that everyday lookism was animated by appearance norms that applied uniformly to everyone, did not adversely affect disadvantaged groups in an unequal way, and did not treat anyone as morally inferior. How could it nevertheless be oppressive?

There are different theories of what it is for someone, or (more usually) some group, to be oppressed. But to say that a practice, such as everyday lookism, is oppressive is not the same as saying that those who are the victims of that discrimination are oppressed or members of an oppressed group. For example, it might coherently be claimed that everyday lookism rooted in appearance norms that require professional men to conform to rigid standards of dress and adornment that give little scope for creativity or self-expression is oppressive to them without supposing that they are an oppressed group.[12] To avoid becoming mired in a debate about what is the best way of interpreting the claim that a practice is oppressive, I shall simply stipulate that a practice is oppressive if and only if it impairs the capacity of those who are the victims of it to be the authors of their own lives, that is, a practice is oppressive if and only if it *impairs the personal autonomy* of its victims. And I shall also stipulate that a practice impairs a person's autonomy if and only if it adversely affects their autonomy in such a way that it gives us at least a reason for regarding it as wrongful in virtue of imposing an unjust burden on them. A practice could in principle be oppressive in this sense even if it involved no direct or indirect discrimination against

---

[12] More generally, it might coherently be thought that men and boys can experience wrongful sex discrimination even if they are not an oppressed group. See D. Benatar, *The Second Sexism: Discrimination against Men and Boys* (Oxford: Wiley-Blackwell, 2012).

members of a group that is unjustly disadvantaged independently, and even if it did not treat anyone as inferior in terms of their moral status.

I propose to explore the issue of how practices in general may impair autonomy to cast light on the way in which everyday lookism in particular may do so.[13] In order to illustrate the potential oppressiveness of practices, consider a society that has a strong work ethic. It operates with a norm compliance with which requires its members to work no less than twelve hours a day, take no more than a day off a week, and no more than a week's holiday a year. As a result, its members work long hours and have little leisure time, even though they would not be dismissed if they worked seven-hour days, took two days off a week, and had a month's holiday a year. Compliance with the norm is burdensome not only in terms of the effort of will required to comply with it but also in terms of the opportunities for leisure, self-development outside of the work environment, and participation in family life that are foregone as a result. But *non*-compliance with the norm is burdensome too. Other members of society act disapprovingly towards those who take more time off than the norm permits, sometimes shunning them completely, openly criticizing their behaviour, and more generally regarding them as failing in their obligation to make a full contribution to society.

Members of this society internalize the norm through a process of socialization and habituation. As children, they are encouraged to devote most of the hours they are awake to schoolwork as a preparation for their working lives. When they become young adults, they are praised when they comply with the norm and criticized when they fail to do so. As a result of internalizing the norm, they gain pleasure from complying with it and feel guilty if they take more time off than it permits.[14] For some, the norm even becomes

[13] Both Clare Chambers and Heather Widdows have argued that assumptions are often made about the way in which choosing an outcome makes it just (or about the way in which choosing to participate in a practice renders the burdens involved in doing so just) that make it hard to see how appearance norms of the kind I have been discussing could wrongfully impair individual freedom. Like them, I reject the idea that 'choice', considered independently of the social context in which it is made, is sufficient for an outcome to be just, or that choice considered in this way has a morally transformative effect in relation to outcomes in the sense that outcomes that would otherwise be regarded as unjust are automatically rendered just by it. See C. Chambers, *Sex, Culture and Justice: The Limits of Choice* (University Park, PA: Penn State University Press, 2008), especially ch. 4; Widdows, *Perfect Me*, especially ch. 9.

[14] For his seminal discussion of the way in which power operates through the internalization of social norms, see M. Foucault, *Discipline and Punish: The Birth of the Prison* (Harmondsworth, Middlesex: Penguin, 1991). Foucault's insights have been developed by a number of feminist writers: see especially Bartky, 'Foucault, Femininity and the Modernization of Patriarchal Power'; Chambers, *Sex, Culture, and Justice*, ch. 1.

part of their identity.[15] Many of those who internalize the norm endorse it. They may think that it is good that society is governed by it. They may think that they have a moral duty to others to comply with it, perhaps even an unconditional obligation to do so, that is, a duty to comply with it regardless of how others behave. They may think that a life of hard work is the only way of achieving personal fulfilment. They may experience feelings of pleasure when they comply with it and suffer feelings of guilt when they fail to do so, as a result in part of endorsing the norm. Others who internalize the norm may nevertheless reject it because they regard it as bad for their society or for them, but they may still gain pleasure from complying with it, and feel guilty when they take time off, as a residual effect of the process of socialization and habituation that they have undergone.

The practice in which this norm is embedded seems oppressive, at least if we assume it is not a justifiable moral norm even though many in the society I have described treat it as if it were.[16] It seems oppressive even though the norm is not enforced by employers, and even though those who are subject to it are not physically prevented from taking more time off, and indeed would not be dismissed from their jobs if they did so. Furthermore, the practice seems oppressive even for people who endorse the norm and criticize others for failing to live up to it. Let me explain why this practice threatens the autonomy of the people involved in it, in a way that supplies a moral reason for objecting to it in virtue of the unjust burden it imposes on them.

The processes of socialization and habituation through which a norm is internalized may undermine (or contribute to undermining) an agent's capacity adequately to reflect upon that norm and decide whether she should seek to comply with it; for example, these processes may result in her being unable to stand back from the norm and question it, or they may involve shielding her from relevant information concerning the risks involved in complying with it. Even when they do not undermine (or contribute to undermining) her capacity to stand back from a norm and

---

[15] Compare N. Hirschmann, *The Subject of Liberty: Toward a Feminist Theory of Freedom* (Princeton, NJ: Princeton University Press, 2003), 79; Chambers, *Sex, Culture and Justice*, 90.

[16] If it were a justifiable moral norm, then the practice would not impair personal autonomy in my sense even when the costs of complying with the norm, and the costs of not complying with it, were high, because it would not adversely affect autonomy in a way that gives us a reason to regard it as wrongful. Compliance with the norm might be morally required in circumstances where, for example, the worst off were below the level at which they could lead decent lives and adherence to it was necessary in order to bring them up to that level. But I shall assume that these are not the circumstances that obtain in the case I have described.

subject it adequately to critical scrutiny, the practice in which it is embedded may nevertheless impact upon her autonomy in other ways. When the costs of both complying and not complying with a norm are high, the practice may negatively affect her exercise or development of autonomy in one or more respects.

First, if she endorses the norm because she mistakenly regards it as a correct moral norm that spells out what she owes to others, then it may adversely affect her capacity to pursue her own projects effectively, perhaps by reducing the time and energy that she has available to do so after complying with it, or by limiting her opportunities for creativity and self-expression. So even though acting in accordance with the norm may be regarded as an exercise of her autonomy, at the same time her pursuit of her own conception of how to live is inhibited in a way that adversely affects her autonomy.

Second, even if she endorses the norm as part of her conception of how to live conceived independently of what she owes to others (for instance, she believes that personal fulfilment comes only through hard work), the practices in which it is embedded might seriously inhibit her capacity to pursue a revised conception in the future should she change her mind. She may face high costs associated with rejecting the norm, for example, anger from friends or family who might even regard her rejection of it as a betrayal of them and ostracize her as a result. More generally, the high costs of non-compliance with it may set back her interest in being able to pursue a revised conception of how to live should she decide that she wants to do so.

Third, when she does not endorse the norm, it may be very costly for her not to comply with it, and in some cases she may be forced to abide by a conception of how to live that she rejects: the norm may express that conception and the costs of non-compliance with it may be so great that she has no reasonable choice but to comply with it.

Whether the costs of compliance and non-compliance with a norm impair a person's autonomy in my sense depends on whether the extent and nature of these costs adversely affect her capacity to pursue her own conception of how to live in such a way that there is a moral reason for objecting to that norm, and the practice in which it is embedded, in virtue of the unjust burdens it imposes on her. These costs can be divided into those that are in some sense *external* to her, for example, the opportunities of which she is deprived, and those that are *internal* to her, that is, burdensome mental states such as painful experiences or feelings of guilt. It would seem that external costs of non-compliance are generally relevant for determining whether a social practice involving a norm impairs the autonomy of those subject to it. But what about the internal costs of non-compliance, such as the guilt that would be felt as a result of non-compliance, and indeed the internal costs of compliance, such as the exhaustion experienced as a result of the physical exertion that is needed for compliance? When can internal costs such as these legitimately be taken into account when judging whether a practice is oppressive?

There is a clear case for holding that when an agent *rejects* or, at least, does not endorse a social norm (that is, she regards it either as an objectionable norm or as simply 'one of the rules of the game'), but she nevertheless experiences feelings of shame and guilt when she doesn't comply with it, and she cannot get rid of these feelings or can do so only with great difficulty, then these internal costs should count in determining whether her autonomy is impaired. When these feelings are the product of the processes of socialization and habituation that she has experienced, and persist even though she rejects the norm, then they potentially contribute to making the practice in which that norm is embedded oppressive for her.

But what about the internal costs that may result from her *endorsing* the norm, for example, from regarding it as a good or justifiable norm because she thinks it is beneficial in some way or expresses a moral requirement? Suppose for, example, that non-compliance is accompanied by feelings of guilt that arise only because she thinks that she ought to comply with it. It would seem that these costs cannot legitimately be taken into account when making judgements about whether a practice impairs her autonomy, that is, in making judgements about whether her autonomy is adversely affected in a way that gives us a moral reason to object to it. Indeed, to take them into account is to fail to give due weight to her status of as an agent with a capacity to make her own judgements about what she should do, including whether she should endorse, and comply with, a social norm that applies to her, and experience the appropriate feelings that would flow from doing so. In effect, we should hold a person responsible for exercising her capacity to reflect upon the norm and determine whether she should comply with it, by not taking into account the internal costs of failing to comply with it when these are solely a product of her endorsing it, in judging whether the practice in which that norm is embedded impairs her autonomy, that is, whether the practice is oppressive for her.

Partly because the internal costs of non-compliance with a norm count in determining whether a practice in which that norm is embedded is oppressive for a person only if they are not solely a product of her endorsing that norm, there is in one sense an irreducibly subjective aspect to judgements concerning whether a practice is oppressive: a practice might be oppressive for some of those whose behaviour it governs but not for others. These judgements are also subjective in part because the costs of compliance with a norm, both internal and external, may vary between people since less exertion or fewer resources may be required for some to comply with it compared to others. Furthermore, the costs of non-compliance, both internal and external, may vary from one person to another, depending on their psychological dispositions, and on whether their family, friends, and acquaintances are inclined to criticize them for non-compliance with it.

What are the implications for everyday lookism of this analysis of how norms may be oppressive? My analysis provides the basis for a powerful argument that everyday lookism impairs the autonomy of many people, especially women and young adults. In some extreme cases, everyday lookism may contribute to undermining a person's capacity to reflect upon the norms that fuel it. Even when it does not do so, the costs of complying with these norms, together with the costs imposed on non-compliers, are often very high. At least, that seems true when we consider the full set of appearance norms that spell out an ideal of what it is to look beautiful, even though it may be less plausible in relation to particular appearance norms.

What conclusions we are entitled to draw here will depend in part on the precise role that is given to our interest in autonomy within a theory of justice, an issue that I have left unresolved. If personal autonomy is of such importance that it merits protection by a lexically prior principle of justice, so that, in effect, damage to it cannot be outweighed by other types of benefit, or if our interest in it is so weighty that we are warranted in endorsing a right to autonomy, then it will be easier to justify the conclusion that everyday lookism, and the appearance norms that fuel it, are oppressive for a wide range of people, including many men. On the other hand, if autonomy should be treated simply as one important good among several, to be given great weight by principles of justice but such that a person can be compensated for damages to their autonomy by sufficient other advantages, then it may be the case that everyday lookism is oppressive only for members of groups that are unjustly disadvantaged independently and who are subject to appearance norms that are biased against them.

Whichever particular theory of justice is endorsed, there is ample evidence for the way in which appearance norms, and the practices in which they are embedded, burden and constrain the choices of many people. First, as documented by Widdows and others, some appearance norms are particularly demanding because the costs of complying with them are high. As the bar is raised for the 'routine' beauty treatments that are required to meet minimum standards for an acceptable appearance, the range of measures that women, and sometimes men, need to take in order to do so expands.[17] Some of these treatments, such as extreme dieting and cosmetic surgery, may involve taking high risks with respect to one's health and future well-being, whether in the short term or the long term.

Second, there are high costs involved in failing to comply with appearance norms. The costs imposed by everyday lookism, such as the body shaming experienced not only by women but also by men, can be very burdensome. For example, people regarded as overweight are accused of lacking self-discipline; women who fail to remove body hair are regarded as disgusting or unhygienic; women who are regarded as making insufficient effort with respect to their appearance are portrayed as letting themselves go, as failing in their duty to themselves, and sometimes in their duty to others, to be aesthetically appealing objects; men who paint their nails or wear makeup suffer ridicule and homophobic abuse. As a result, non-compliers may experience debilitating appearance anxiety, low self-esteem, and low self-confidence which, even when they endorse the relevant norm, do not arise solely from their endorsement of it. A failure to comply with an appearance norm may even threaten a person's status within a group or indeed a society. Being badly dressed according to the prevailing norms, for example wearing worn-out clothes because one cannot afford new ones, may lead to being devalued by others in one's society.[18] Merely being unfashionably dressed may within some groups lead to a loss of status, that is, to being judged as less valuable than other members. Even when the costs of non-compliance with an appearance norm are not actually very high, they may sometimes reasonably be believed to be high, for example, media images may convey the message to young women that they ought to be very thin rather than merely not overweight. In these cases, we might regard the perceived costs as contributing to making everyday lookism oppressive.

Third, the external costs of compliance and non-compliance sometimes work together to create a double bind, especially for women. People may

---

[17] Widdows, *Perfect Me*, 107–19; Widdows, 'Structural Injustice and the Requirements of Beauty', 252–3.
[18] See T. Scanlon, *Why Does Inequality Matter?* (Oxford: Oxford University Press, 2018), 30–1.

face a situation where if they comply with appearance norms that govern their group or economic class, they face ridicule or shaming from those outside it, but if they do not comply with these norms, then they will be taunted and treated as if they do not belong to it. For example, young women who dress in short skirts and apply makeup liberally in order to conform to the appearance norms in their group may be victims of 'slut shaming' by outsiders, but if they dress more conservatively than the others in it, then they may be accused of being prudes. Working class women who adopt the dress, makeup, and hair styles characteristic of their economic class may be subject to ridicule or be taken less seriously in professional contexts that are governed by different appearance norms, but if they change their appearance in order to fit in, they may then be accused by others with the same class origins as acting if they were superior. In cases such as these, a person suffers a cost to their well-being and experiences a negative effect on their capacity to shape their lives, whatever they do.[19]

It is true that sometimes the costs of non-compliance with an appearance norm are avoidable. In light of the aesthetic interest that we may have in commenting on the appearance of others, it might be argued that when people who are at the receiving end of these comments can develop a thicker skin so that they would avoid experiencing any negative effects, or would experience only minor annoyance, then the costs of non-compliance cannot justifiably be regarded as contributing to the impairment of their autonomy, that is, as restricting their autonomy in a way that provides us with a reason for thinking that an unjust burden has been placed on them. Indeed, it might seem that, for many people, even those who do not endorse the relevant appearance norms, the psychological costs of non-compliance, such as body anxiety, and the low self-confidence and self-esteem that may result from everyday lookism, should not be included within an assessment of whether it is oppressive for them, because they have the capacity to develop thicker skins to avoid being psychologically damaged.

But here we need to distinguish at least three different types of case. (In each, I shall assume that the people concerned possess an adequate capacity for critical reflection.) First, cases where the cost borne by people as a result of non-compliance with appearance norms is such that they had no control

---

[19] For a seminal discussion of double binds in the context of gendered norms, see M. Frye, 'Oppression', in *The Politics of Reality: Essays in Feminist Theory* (New York: Crossing Press, 1983), 1–16. Sukaina Hirji argues that what is distinctive about double binds is that whatever the agent does, she is to some extent complicit in her own oppression: see S. Hirji, 'Oppressive Double Binds', *Ethics* 131 (2021): 643–69.

over incurring it: it was not a result of any decisions they made, and they could not have taken any steps to avoid incurring this cost, for example, they could not have cultivated greater resilience in the face of the body shaming they experience. Second, cases where people have some control over the cost borne by them, for example, they could take steps to become more resilient in response to negative comments about their appearance, but we cannot reasonably expect them to do so, because it would be very burdensome for them, for example, great effort and will-power would be required. Third, cases where people could avoid incurring the cost, or take steps to avoid incurring it, and it would not be unreasonable to expect them to do so, perhaps because the effort involved would be minimal. It is plausible to think that only in cases of the first and second type should the cost incurred be included in an assessment of whether the overall costs of compliance and non-compliance with appearance norms makes everyday lookism oppressive for a person. When the costs involved are 'reasonably avoidable', they should be discounted.

In practice, cases may be hard to classify. It is clear that children and adolescents who experience fat-shaming are generally unable to avoid the anxiety and other adverse psychological effects it creates for them, or if they could do so, it would be unreasonable at their level of maturity to expect them to cultivate greater resilience to the taunts they suffer. Furthermore, they may not yet have developed to any great extent the capacities required to reflect critically on the practice of fat-shaming. But what about mature adults? When adults experience a serious loss of self-confidence or suffer severe anxiety as a result of casual comments such as 'you've put on a bit of weight recently' or 'you need to be more careful with what you eat', then even if we are confident that they could have developed a thicker skin, it is often unclear whether it is reasonable to expect them to do so. As a result, it is hard to know whether cases such as these fall into the second category or the third category. Context may make a significant difference here: for example, it is reasonable to expect people to develop thicker skins when they are floored by negative remarks about them in the context of supportive friendships, but not necessarily when such remarks are made on social media by acquaintances with malicious intent.

To sum up: when everyday lookism is oppressive for people, it is objectionable, at root, because it adversely affects their personal autonomy in a way that contributes to placing an unjust burden on them. It can do so by negatively affecting their capacity to reflect upon the appearance norms in which it is rooted and decide whether to comply with them; or by compromising their ability effectively to pursue their current conceptions of how to live or to pursue a different one in the future should they change their minds; or by forcing them to abide by a conception of how to live that they do not endorse. Compliance with these norms may reduce their appearance-related opportunities for creativity or self-expression or reduce the time and energy that they have to pursue their own conceptions of how to live, whereas non-compliance with the norms may negatively affect their confidence in their ability to do so successfully as a result of feeling unattractive. These costs may also combine to force them to pursue a partially comprehensive moral doctrine (which is what 'the beauty ideal' amounts to) that they do not endorse, and indeed from which they may feel alienated. In judging whether the costs of complying and not complying with the appearance norms that fuel everyday lookism work together to make it oppressive for a person, we should bracket any costs that he or she might reasonably be expected to avoid incurring or that are due solely to his or her endorsement of these norms.

Of course, if we focus on everyday lookism in isolation we will not get a full picture of the way in which appearance norms fuel oppressive practices. Appearance norms play a key role in the other two contexts that I have been exploring, in such a way that the costs of non-compliance with them can be very great. For those who fail to comply with appearance norms, opportunities for jobs and other advantaged social positions may be greatly reduced, and opportunities to form personal relationships, including romantic partnerships may be scarce as a result. In general, practices of appearance discrimination, not merely everyday lookism considered on its own, impose large burdens for non-compliance on those who find it difficult, costly, or impossible to comply with the prevailing appearance norms that fuel these practices, making them oppressive for many, and creating a structure of injustice from which it is hard to escape.

7.2 Harm, Avoidability, and Injustice

Irrespective of whether everyday lookism is oppressive for a person, it can cause, or contribute to causing, physical or psychological harm to him or her. Consider again the society with the strong work ethic that I described earlier. Members of this society may suffer from illnesses as a result of work-related stress when they strive to comply with the norm. Similarly, the cosmetic procedures that some women undergo in seeking to make themselves more beautiful when judged against these norms may lead to health problems in the short or long term, even when there is no negligence on the part of the practitioners who perform these procedures.[20] Those who don't comply with the work ethic may experience anxiety about their failure to do so, and feelings of guilt that they are not working as hard as others expect and think they should. Similarly, people who do not comply with appearance norms may suffer from anxiety about their appearance as a result of everyday lookism, and they may be debilitated by lack of confidence and low self-esteem. But when does the physical or psychological harm that a person suffers as a result of seeking to comply with an appearance norm, or believing that their appearance falls short when judged against that norm, count as a wrong that is done to them by the acts of discrimination that constitute everyday lookism, or as an unjust burden that is imposed on them by these acts?

Assuming that people are capable of critically reflecting on the norms that fuel everyday lookism, it seems to me that there are two conditions that need to be met for harms that they suffer, either as a result of attempting to comply with these norms or as a result of failing to comply with them, to count as wrongs that are done to them by everyday lookism (or, more precisely, by the acts of discrimination that constitute it). First, the harms that they suffer must not be due to costs they incur that are a result solely of endorsing the norms. So, for example, costs that arise due to body shaming by others are relevant, but not the feelings of guilt that a person experiences solely as a result of endorsing a norm with which he or she fails to comply. Second, the harms that they suffer must not have been reasonably avoidable. In making judgements about what is reasonably avoidable for a person, we should again put to one side any costs that are solely a product of his or her endorsement of the norms.

To be clear, I am not here defending the view that when the harms people suffer are not wrongs done to them, then they can be required to deal with these harms without any support being morally required from others. The position I am defending is consistent with supposing that whether it is just to expect a person to bear the costs of mitigating the reasonably avoidable harm he or she suffers will depend, in part, on the magnitude of those costs. For example, we might think that it would be unjust to require people with modest means who suffer severe but reasonably avoidable harm as a result

---

[20] So too there are health risks associated with cosmetics and the use of drugs as aids for dieting. See Rhode, *The Beauty Bias*, 35–40.

of cosmetic surgery that has gone wrong to pay the full costs of putting things right, even when they were fully aware of the risks, and the surgery was done competently.

The defence of the two conditions that I am claiming need to be met for a harm that is done to a person by everyday lookism to count as a wrong suffered by them has in effect already been provided. In the same way that internal costs that arise solely from the endorsement of a norm should not be counted in making judgements about whether everyday lookism is oppressive to a person, because to count them would be to fail to respect his or her capacity for choice, so too these costs should not be counted in judging whether a harm that a person suffers as a result of everyday lookism is a wrong that is done to him or her by it. In the same way that costs that were reasonably avoidable should not count in determining whether everyday lookism is oppressive to a person, because counting them would fail to respect his or her capacity for choice and involve giving too little weight to the aesthetic interest some may have in commenting on the appearance of others, so too these costs should not count when determining whether a harm that a person suffers is a wrong that is done to him or her by it. As a result, the same conditions that need to be met for everyday lookism to count as oppressive for a person will need to be met for a harm that he or she suffers in consequence of it to count as a wrong done to him or her by the acts of discrimination that it involves.

As I suggested earlier, in practice it may be hard to tell whether a cost was reasonably avoidable. But we can at least describe clear cases where it is, even though there may be doubts about how often they occur in reality. Suppose, for example, that a woman makes a decision to have a buttock enhancement, not because she is anxious about her body, or subject to taunts, but because one of her ambitions is to make herself more beautiful when judged against appearance norms that she endorses, and she ends up with health problems as a result of the risks she has consciously taken, without any negligence on the part of the surgeons who operated on her.

Clare Chambers holds the view that if a significant harm is caused by complying with an appearance norm, then that harm is an injustice whenever the only benefits derived from complying with the norm are a consequence of the norm's being endorsed by the agent or by other members of his or her society.[21] She builds her case through a discussion of breast

---

[21] Chambers, *Sex, Culture and Justice*, 175–6, 195–7.

implants. She points out that the damage caused to women's health and well-being by this surgery, in both the short and longer term, are potentially high, and the benefits of complying with the relevant norms concerning breast size or shape are solely the product of widespread endorsement of these norms.[22] Her account therefore yields the conclusion that the harms suffered by women as a result of breast augmentation surgery are an injustice to them. But Chambers' general view seems to me to have counterintuitive consequences.

Consider a variant of the society with the work ethic, in which the productivity of workers decreases to such an extent that after a certain point there is no benefit in terms of increased productivity for the additional hours worked. Suppose again that in this society there is a high risk to one's health from compliance with the social norm that the ethic involves. Those who comply with the norm by working additional hours receive no extra pay, and indeed the only benefits they obtain from doing so are the result of the norm being endorsed by them and by others, for example, feelings of intense satisfaction at being perceived to have contributed to society by working hard or thinking that they have complied with their moral obligation to do so. Widespread endorsement of the norm is a product of being socialized to accept it and habituated to comply with it from an early age, though members of society also acquire and retain the ability critically to reflect upon the norm and its role in their society. But the costs of non-compliance are very low: although employers and managers may sometimes raise their eyebrows when employees leave early, and make the occasional negative comment to them privately, there is little or no public criticism or shaming of those who fail to comply with the norm, it does not affect their career prospects, and they merely experience mild feelings of anxiety and guilt as a result of their non-compliance. It is not clear that under these circumstances those who do comply with the norm, and develop stress-related health problems as a result, are the victims of an injustice or wronged in any way, for the harm they suffer is solely a product of their endorsing the norm and the harm is reasonably avoidable.

To say this is not to deny that the society would be better without such a strong work ethic. It is merely to insist that if people have the capacity to reflect on a norm adequately, then they are harmed by compliance with it (or by attempting to comply with it) in a way that is wrongful only if the

---

[22] Chambers, *Sex, Culture and Justice*, 187–91.

harm they suffer is not solely due to their endorsement of it and that harm is not reasonably avoidable, for otherwise they have no reasonable complaint. (And again, this is not to deny that justice may require that society pay some or all of the cost of any health care they require even when they are not wrongly harmed.) Even if it would be feasible for a society to adopt a less demanding norm, compliance with which would be easier for everyone, and those who comply with it or attempt to do so would not suffer any harm as a result, it would not follow that, by adopting the more demanding norm, people who suffer harm as a result of complying with it or seeking to do so have been treated wrongfully.

My approach to assessing the justice or injustice of harms caused by breast implants is correspondingly different from that of Chambers, though how far my conclusions diverge from hers in practice will depend on empirical facts that are not readily accessible. Perhaps for some individual women who seek this surgery, the combined internal and external costs of *not* acting on the relevant norms concerning breast size and shape would be relatively low. According to my view, in these cases, provided the women concerned are aware of the risks and have an adequate capacity to reflect upon the norm, even if they give less weight to these risks than they should, there is no wrong suffered by them if they are harmed as a result of this surgery.[23] But for many women who seek breast augmentation surgery—perhaps the vast majority—the costs of not complying with the relevant norms would be high, for example, some suffer from serious anxiety or a debilitating lack of self-confidence because of body shaming practices and because they believe that their breasts are too small or the wrong shape when judged against that norm. In these cases, there is good reason to suppose that the victims are wronged by the harms they suffer as a result of opting for surgery because these harms were neither reasonably avoidable nor solely a product of their endorsement of these norms.

7.3 Concluding Remarks

I have argued that the acts of discrimination involved in everyday lookism can be non-contingently wrong because they are demeaning. Furthermore,

---

[23] There might nevertheless be good reasons for regulating, or even prohibiting breast enlargement surgery, even for those who are not unjustly harmed by it. I return to these issues in Chapter 9.

these acts may be contingently wrong because they contribute to worsening the position of disadvantaged groups as a result of being fuelled by biased appearance norms. The bulk of this chapter, however, has focused on a particular way in which everyday lookism can have unjust effects. When we examine the costs of complying and not complying with the appearance norms that fuel everyday lookism, and the processes of socialization that lead to these norms being internalized, we can see that the acts of discrimination it involves may have an oppressive character in virtue of impairing the autonomy of those adversely affected. Everyday lookism is implicated in various harms, such as mental health problems that are rooted in body anxiety, and physical harms that result from trying to improve one's appearance, including the side-effects of undertaking risky cosmetic procedures. Its oppressive character means that many of these harms can justifiably be viewed as moral wrongs.

People may have an aesthetic or other interest in commenting upon the appearance of others, and depending upon the context and the manner in which it is done, there may be nothing morally problematic about it. Even when it is morally objectionable, the outcomes generated by those striving to comply with the norms that are embedded in everyday lookism may not all be bad. Widdows points out that the pleasure that people may gain from their attempts to do so, together with the creativity that may be involved, and the feelings of solidarity they may enjoy from sharing their experiences with others, can have significant value.[24] But the good that comes about in this way does not seem to outweigh the injustices that are often produced in and through the practices these norms govern and by which they are sustained.

---

[24] Widdows, *Perfect Me*, 151–6, 185–91; Widdows, 'Structural Injustice and the Requirements of Beauty', 254–5.

PART III
RESPONDING TO APPEARANCE DISCRIMINATION

8
Prevention

When appearance discrimination is morally wrong, how should we respond to it? This book has examined three contexts in which wrongful appearance discrimination takes place: in the sphere of employment when employers and selectors decide who to hire or promote; in the personal sphere when individuals make decisions about what personal relationships to form, cultivate, or sustain; and the everyday practices in which people judge and comment upon the appearance of others. Should we aim in any of these contexts to prevent wrongful appearance discrimination? Should existing anti-discrimination legislation be extended to prohibit morally objectionable appearance discrimination in some (or all) of them? In this chapter, I address these questions.[1]

8.1 Prevention versus Compensating for Disadvantages Experienced

There are a number of responses that we might give collectively, via state institutions, to wrongful appearance discrimination. Consider two of the main possibilities. First, we might seek to *prevent* it from occurring, for example, by prohibiting it through the criminal law or penalizing it through the civil law. Second, we might adopt policies that aim to *compensate* victims for its adverse effects on them when it occurs, that is, policies that aim to provide either some recompense to those who have experienced appearance discrimination or some remedy for the disadvantages they face as a result of it. Of course, these two approaches might be employed in tandem, for example, the civil law might be used both to try to prevent its occurrence and to provide compensation for it when it nevertheless does

---

[1] In Sections 8.2 and 8.3, I draw upon an article I co-authored with Francesca Minerva. I would like to thank her for permission to use this material here. See A. Mason and F. Minerva, 'Should the Equality Act 2010 Be Extended to Prohibit Appearance Discrimination?', *Political Studies* 70 (2022): 425–42.

occur. I shall focus on the use of compensation in the next chapter, but in the current section of this chapter I shall explore the reasons why seeking to prevent wrongful appearance discrimination from occurring, primarily by enacting legislation to prohibit it, may be part of the best response to it, rather than (say) adopting an approach that seeks only to compensate those adversely affected by it.[2]

When appearance discrimination is wrong because a selector acts disrespectfully, or treats some candidates unfairly in a selection process, then compensation seems a less good response when prevention is a feasible alternative. But does it seem a worse response because in these cases it is impossible even in principle to compensate for its wrongness or inappropriate to attempt to do so for some reason, or merely because in practice it is more effective or more efficient to enact legislation to prevent it from occurring?

It might seem that in principle compensation is possible: even though discrimination is non-contingently wrong when it is disrespectful or involves unfair treatment, just as its wrongness could in principle be outweighed if the outcomes that resulted from acting disrespectfully or unfairly were sufficiently good, so too compensation that is sufficiently large could in principle redress the wrong that is involved in treating a person disrespectfully or unfairly. But this seems to me to misunderstand the nature of our moral concern about disrespectful behaviour or unfair treatment. At the fundamental level, we should care about avoiding acting disrespectfully or unfairly, rather than merely caring about acting in a way that produces the best consequences or acting in a way that minimizes the number of disrespectful or unfair acts that occur.[3] Compensation rather than prevention seems appropriate when it is a response to the badness of the outcomes that an act of discrimination brings about, but not when it is a response to the failure of the agent who performs it to treat others fairly or respectfully. These failures can lead to harmful consequences for which compensation might be an appropriate response, but compensation doesn't seem to redress the wrongfulness of the unfairness or disrespect itself. Acts of discrimination

---

[2] Since I'm focusing on preventing wrongful appearance discrimination, I don't consider the possibility that those who discriminate wrongly should be punished simply because they are wrong doers, even if this were to have no deterrence effect. On some theories of punishment, criminal justice is important primarily because it provides a process through which wrong doers can come to see that they have acted wrongly and experience remorse. See R. A. Duff, *Punishment, Communication, and Community* (Oxford: Oxford University Press, 2001).

[3] See Section 3.3.

that are disrespectful or unfair are *pro tanto* wrong, that is, unconditionally wrong in one way, not merely conditionally wrong. So even if compensation is provided for them, it doesn't extinguish the wrongness involved. That remains true even if victims of discrimination who have been treated disrespectfully or unfairly feel that were they to be given a sufficiently large benefit of some kind, then they would have no remaining complaint against the perpetrator, or they would be indifferent between the act's not having taken place and its having taken place but with them being compensated for it. Since the wrongness involved in these types of case is not extinguished by compensation, in one way prevention is better, assuming that it can be done successfully.

The inadequacy of compensation as a response to appearance discrimination that involves disrespectful or unfair treatment is what makes prevention a better approach, in one way at least. When appearance discrimination is not itself disrespectful, if it contributes to lowering the perceived moral status of its victims, that is, to creating a society in which they are widely regarded and treated as inferior, then compensation also seems an inappropriate response, for the disrespectful treatment that occurs in such a society is also unconditionally wrong in one way. But when appearance discrimination is wrong only because it harms its victims in a manner that contributes to an unjust distribution of benefits and burdens, without treating them disrespectfully or unfairly in selection decisions, and without contributing to lowering their perceived moral status, then it might be thought that the most effective and most efficient response is to compensate them for the discrimination they have suffered rather than to seek to prevent it from occurring in the first place. Indeed, when discrimination is wrong solely because of its contribution to creating an unjust distribution of benefits and burdens, it is only conditionally wrong precisely because it is possible in principle to compensate fully those who are adversely affected by that unjust distribution. For much the same reasons we might think that we should compensate people for not getting employment opportunities as a result of lack of natural talent when the best-qualified candidates are appointed, so too we might think that we should compensate people for not getting employment opportunities as a result of their perceived unattractiveness, whether by lower taxes or by providing some other kind of good.

But some of these harms are potentially severe, including serious damage to the victims' interest in autonomous agency, and potentially preventable through a combination of legislation and self-limiting behaviour. The benefits to others of allowing appearance discrimination that causes such harms are, in general, relatively small, compared to the damage caused to the victims' interest in autonomous agency, and indeed compared to the benefits potentially created by other forms of discrimination that we allow and regard as justifiable, such as selecting for jobs and other advantaged social positions on the basis of qualifications. The latter may in one way damage the interests in autonomous agency of people with lower levels of marketable talents and abilities, but it can provide weighty benefits for all, including those with talents in less demand, at least when there is fair access to qualifications and redistributive schemes are in place. When there is fair access to qualifications, and the best-qualified or the better-qualified are appointed to jobs, then the goods and services we obtain as customers and clients are likely to be of a higher quality. The benefits to customers and clients of allowing appearance discrimination are much less weighty, at least when the appearance characteristics on which it is based are not legitimate qualifications of some kind. As a result, preventing at least some harmful appearance discrimination in the sphere of employment by legislative means, rather than providing compensation for the disadvantages it creates when it has taken place, seems preferable and potentially justifiable.

8.2 How Should Appearance Discrimination in Employment Be Prevented?

Different strategies might be used to prevent wrongful appearance discrimination from taking place in recruitment for jobs. Legislation might be enacted to forbid employers from requiring applicants to provide a CV with a photograph on it, unless appearance is a legitimate qualification for the post that is being filled. But if this were the only constraint imposed on the recruitment process to prevent the occurrence of appearance discrimination, then it would be unlikely to have any great success. It would not prevent employers from searching the internet for images of candidates, and appearance discrimination might still take place in the context of interviews. It might be combined, however, with prohibiting employers from holding face to face interviews or video calls with applicants as part of the selection process, except when a case can be made that appearance is a legitimate qualification for a job. If this more radical measure were adopted, some 'in-person' interviews might still be permitted even when appearance was not a legitimate qualification, for example, if the interviewees were placed behind a screen.

Even though this strategy is worthy of serious consideration, it has its limits. For some jobs, it is important to observe how the candidates interact with an audience who they can see. If a job requires addressing groups, or working together in a group, how candidates engage with others, including how they pick up on visual cues, may matter. To some extent that might be replicated by having screens that allowed candidates to see who they were addressing without themselves being seen, but that is imperfect because it is unlikely to provide selectors with the evidence they need when what matters is how the candidates operate within a group that is involved in a cooperative activity. It would seem that strategies such as these would need to be supplemented, at least, by legislation forbidding appearance discrimination.

The arguments for forbidding at least some appearance discrimination in the context of employment are especially powerful in countries that already have legislation in place to prohibit other kinds of discrimination that occur in this context. But very few countries have gone down the path of prohibiting appearance discrimination. In Europe, only Belgium, France, and Serbia explicitly prohibit it.[4] In the US, appearance is not a protected characteristic under Federal law, but some jurisdictions have prohibited forms of appearance discrimination as part of their civil rights law. Michigan included height and weight as protected characteristics in the 1975 Elliot-Larsen Civil Rights Act, and the District of Columbia prohibited appearance discrimination as part of the 1982 DC Human Rights Act. Howard County's Human Rights Law, the Urbana Human Rights Ordinance, and the City of Madison prohibit discrimination on the basis of appearance, albeit with some exceptions, whereas Santa Cruz's Ordinance No. 2017-09 prohibits discrimination on grounds of involuntary physical characteristics, and Article 33 of the San Francisco Police Code prohibits discrimination on grounds of height and weight. In Australia, the State of Victoria prohibits appearance discrimination through its 1995 Equal Opportunity Act. The

---

[4] In Belgium, the Anti-Discrimination Law (10 May 2007) prohibits discrimination on the basis of 'physical or genetic characteristics'. In Serbia, Article 2(1) of the Act on the Prohibition of Discrimination forbids discrimination on grounds of appearance. Article L 122–45 of the French Labour Code specifies that 'no person may be excluded from a recruitment procedure or an internship or a training program; no employee may be sanctioned, dismissed, or be subject to a direct or indirect discriminatory measure, in particular as regards compensation, training, relocation, assignment, qualification, classification, professional promotion, transfer, or contract renewal, as well as measures of profit-sharing and allocation of shares based on his/her...physical appearance.'

Act explicitly forbids discrimination on the basis of characteristics such as height, weight, size, shape, facial features, hair, and birthmarks.

Even though very few jurisdictions have explicitly prohibited appearance discrimination, existing legislation may forbid it when it is a form of indirect discrimination relating to some other characteristic, such as race, sex, religion, sexual orientation, or disability.[5] Appearance codes compliance with which is made a condition of employment often have a worse impact on racial minorities, women, or religious minorities. Employers' appearance codes that forbid hairstyles such as dreadlocks or hair braids have a worse impact on black or mixed-race men and women whose hair is naturally suited to such styles. Employers' appearance codes that require women to wear dresses, high-heeled shoes, and full-face makeup, but merely require men to wear a jacket, tie, and shoes, have a worse impact on women in several respects, namely, the time and energy required to comply with them, the financial cost of doing so, and in the case of high-heeled shoes their effects on health. Employers' appearance codes that forbid women from wearing headscarves or men from wearing turbans, or require women to wear skirts rather than trousers, may have a worse impact on Muslim women or Sikh men. In many countries, existing anti-discrimination legislation may already provide a weapon against indirect discrimination of these kinds, even though the role that appearance codes play in their occurrence may not be explicitly acknowledged or appreciated.[6]

Although there is little legislation in existence that targets direct appearance discrimination, the moral case against it in employment developed in Chapters 4 and 5, together with the reasons given in the previous section for why prevention is often a better strategy than compensation on its own,

---

[5] Even when it is not a *disadvantaged* group that is worse affected by a form of appearance discrimination, the protected characteristics enshrined in anti-discrimination legislation may prohibit it when it is a form of indirect discrimination against those with such a characteristic. For example, the UK Equality Act might be thought to protect men from being discriminated against on grounds of their baldness, in virtue of the worse effects discriminating on grounds of lack of hair has on men compared to women. For a partly relevant case, see https://www.theguardian.com/world/2022/may/13/calling-a-man-bald-is-sexual-harassment-employment-tribunal-rules, accessed 5 July 2022; https://assets.publishing.service.gov.uk/media/627a4d19d3bf7f1c38d58caa/Mr_A_Finn_v_The_British_Bung_Manufacturing_Company_Ltd_-Reserved_1803764.2021.pdf, especially paras 227ff., accessed 5 July 2022.

[6] When existing anti-discrimination legislation does not prohibit appearance codes that indirectly discriminate against protected disadvantaged groups or that are a mask for direct discrimination against them, it may be relatively easy to persuade legislatures to extend it. There is a growing movement in the US to provide greater protection against racial discrimination by prohibiting discrimination on the basis of hairstyles or hair texture, with California the first state to do so under the Crown Act (SB188), signed into law in July 2019.

provides the basis of a powerful argument for prohibiting at least some forms of it. But there are different ways in which this might be done in practice. First, legislation might be enacted that targets appearance discrimination specifically by making a new provision, for example, when a legislative framework protects people from discrimination on the basis of one or more of a list of characteristics, appearance, or particular appearance features, might be added to that list. Second, appearance discrimination might be targeted by legislation that already prohibits another form of discrimination to which it is connected, for example, an existing protected characteristic might be re-thought, or broadened, in such a way that it can be used as a basis for prohibiting appearance discrimination, or at least, for prohibiting the kinds of appearance discrimination that are especially objectionable. I favour the first strategy. But the second strategy is worth exploring, in particular, whether re-thinking or broadening the notion of *disability* might provide adequate protection for those vulnerable to wrongful appearance discrimination.

A number of legal theorists have discussed the merits of prohibiting appearance discrimination through legislation against discrimination on the basis of disability.[7] There are deep philosophical difficulties in defining what is to count as a disability.[8] But if we put these difficulties to one side, and work with some widely held views about the nature of disability, it is not implausible to think that some appearance characteristics might be understood as disabilities. For example, what used to be referred to medically as morbid obesity might plausibly be regarded as a disabling impairment.[9] But it is not clear how many other appearance-related characteristics can be brought within this approach.

The UK 2010 Equality Act treats severe disfigurement as a disability. It regards people as disabled if they have a mental or physical impairment that has a substantial and long-term adverse impact on their ability to carry out their normal day-to-day activities, and stipulates that a severe disfigurement is to be treated as such an impairment.[10] Treating severe disfigurement in

---

[7] Note, 'Facial Discrimination: Extending Handicap Law to Employment Discrimination on the Basis of Physical Appearance', *Harvard Law Review* 100 (1987): 2035–52, at 2042–8; H. Fleener, 'Looks Sell, but Are They Worth the Cost: How Tolerating Looks-Based Discrimination Leads to Intolerable Discrimination', *Washington University Law Quarterly* 83 (2005): 1295–1330, at 1328; Hamermesh, *Beauty Pays*, 150–1.
[8] See E. Barnes, *The Minority Body. A Theory of Disability* (Oxford: Oxford University Press, 2016), ch. 1.
[9] See Wang, 'Weight Discrimination', 1921–3.
[10] UK Equality Act 2010, Schedule 1, Article 3.

this way requires us to adopt what is often called a social model of disability, according to which a disability consists in a cognitive or physical impairment that is rooted wholly or in part in the social environment inhabited, for in so far as severe disfigurement does place an obstacle in the way of carrying out one's day-to-day activities, it is generally because of the reactions of others, including the stigmatizing effect of these reactions and their debilitating impact on one's mental health. But does regarding severe disfigurement as a disability, and the consequent adoption of the social model of disability, open up the possibility of treating 'being regarded as unattractive' as a form of disability?

It is clear that being regarded as unattractive would not count as a severe disfigurement under the Act in the way that it is currently interpreted. Although the Act doesn't define the term 'disfigurement', the guidance given by the Office for Disability Issues provides some clarification, and significantly narrows down what can reasonably be considered as a severe disfigurement under the Act: '[e]xamples of disfigurements include scars, birthmarks, limb or postural deformation (including restricted bodily development), or diseases of the skin. Assessing severity will be mainly a matter of the degree of the disfigurement which may involve taking into account factors such as the nature, size, and prominence of the disfigurement. However, it may be necessary to take account of where the disfigurement in question is (e.g. on the back as opposed to the face)'.[11] But these criteria for determining the severity of a disfigurement do not seem to track what ultimately matters from the point of view of the Act, namely, whether a disfigurement can be seen as constituting, or forming the basis of, a mental or physical impairment that has a substantial and long-term adverse impact on a person's ability to carry out their normal day-to-day activities. As Hannah Saunders points out, people with what this guidance would regard as minor disfigurements may experience worse psychological side-effects as a result of appearance discrimination than those with more severe disfigurements.[12]

Nevertheless, even when people do not have severe disfigurements according to the criteria provided by the Office for Disability Issues, their appearance could in principle be regarded as a disability under the Act when the reactions of others to it produces a psychological effect that

---

[11] Office for Disability Issues, 2010: B25.
[12] H. Saunders, 'The Invisible Law of Visible Difference: Disfigurement in the Workplace', *Industrial Law Journal* 48 (2019): 487–514.

adversely affects their ability to carry out their normal daily activities in a substantial way over an extended period of time. As we saw in Chapter 7, it is well documented that being regarded as unattractive, whether because of facial features or height or weight, can have severe effects on one's self-confidence, self-esteem, and general well-being, especially in a society beset by everyday lookism, and this in turn may affect one's ability to carry out those activities. The Act in principle allows that an aspect of one's appearance might justifiably be regarded as a disability in virtue of the way others respond to it, so it could take into account the severely debilitating effects of body-shaming practices such as 'fat shaming', or the stigmatizing impact of prejudices about aspects of appearance.[13]

But I think that, all things considered, regarding forms of unattractiveness as potential disabilities is not the best strategy for protecting people vulnerable to appearance discrimination, for at least two reasons. First, it will protect only those whose appearance is such that negative reactions to it affect in a substantial way their ability to carry out their normal day-to-day activities over an extended period of time. It does not protect people who are subject to appearance discrimination in the labour market because they are regarded as unattractive when this does not adversely affect their ability to carry out their normal daily activities. Nor would it protect people who suffer discrimination in the labour market as a result of their unconventional looks, such as tattoos, piercings, or brightly coloured hair. Second, in many cases, recourse to the legislation would require making the argument in court that being regarded as unattractive has made one unable to carry out one's daily activities as a result of the severe mental health problems it has caused. This would be potentially humiliating.[14] It would require admitting in public that one has severe mental health problems as a result of the reactions of others to one's appearance.

Discrimination against the unattractive is not the same as discrimination against the disabled, and unattractiveness is not necessarily a form of disability, even if we endorse the social model of disability. (This is not to deny that these two forms of discrimination are sometimes entwined: people may be regarded as visually unattractive because of some particular physical disability. And in some cases, people may be discriminated against both on

---

[13] T. Hervey and P. Rostant, '"All About That Bass"? Is Non-Ideal-Weight Discrimination Unlawful in the UK?', *Modern Law Review* 79 (2016): 248–82.
[14] Saunders, 'The Invisible Law of Visible Difference'; J. Wolff, 'Fairness, Respect, and the Egalitarian Ethos', *Philosophy & Public Affairs* 27 (1998): 97–122; J. Wolff, 'Fairness, Respect and the Egalitarian Ethos Revisited', *Journal of Ethics* 14 (2010): 335–50.

grounds of their appearance and on grounds of their disability, whether directly or indirectly.) In order to counter morally objectionable appearance discrimination, it seems preferable to extend existing legislation against discrimination specifically to include appearance. This could protect not only people with disfigurements but also people considered unattractive according to widely accepted beauty norms and those with unconventional appearances. By extending a legislative framework in this way, it would be better able to provide redress to those who are the victims of wrongful appearance discrimination. If a legislative framework were extended in this way, severe disfigurement would no longer need to be included as a form of disability.

In the context of recruitment and promotion decisions, the most defensible strategy for targeting direct appearance discrimination would include prohibiting selectors' decisions from being influenced by appearance characteristics when no plausible argument can be made that these characteristics constitute qualifications for the post being filled. This would serve to protect candidates not only from discrimination rooted in selectors' own biases or personal moral or aesthetic judgements concerning appearance features but also from appearance discrimination that an employer attempts to justify by claiming that it promotes the moral or aesthetic vision of his company or organization, when there is no good reason for thinking that he or she has such a vision for it or that selecting on this basis would promote this vision. Such an approach would therefore serve to rule out many instances of direct appearance discrimination in which it is unfair, and indeed a significant number of cases in which it is demeaning or especially harmful, since in the context of selection it is rare for an act of direct discrimination to be demeaning, or harmful in a way that contributes to an unjust distribution, without it also involving unfair treatment.

Guidance, however, would need to be given for determining when appearance can plausibly be regarded as a qualification for a job (including when it can be plausibly regarded as a reaction qualification). This guidance would need to provide some basis for determining when selecting on the basis of a particular appearance feature could justifiably be seen as expressing or promoting a company's reasonable moral or aesthetic vision. Here it seems to me that the onus should be placed on the employer to demonstrate that his or her company has a moral or aesthetic vision, that expressing or promoting this vision requires making an appearance feature a qualification for jobs in it, and that its vision is reasonable in the minimal sense that it is not based on any prejudices concerning those who lack this feature and that it is not disrespectful in failing to give due weight to the moral status of those who lack it.

Can the account developed in Chapter 5, concerning what makes a reaction qualification *illegitimate*, help to specify further criteria that might be used legislatively for prohibiting additional instances of direct appearance discrimination that are particularly morally troubling? The way in which deliberative fairness involves balancing the interests of candidates and recipients does mean that one element of the account I have defended could not straightforwardly be encoded in anti-discrimination legislation. How are we to tell in practice whether customers' or clients' preferences concerning appearance are based on reasonable aesthetic or moral judgements, in a way that means their interest in autonomous agency is engaged, or whether they are based on prejudices or rooted in relatively mild non-rational reactions, where their interest in autonomous agency would not be under threat to the same extent were we to exclude reaction qualifications rooted in them?

The practical challenges here might seem to be too great. Even when recipients' preferences converge, they may have different bases. Some of these preferences may be a product of their conceptions of how to live, whilst others are rooted in prejudices or non-rational reactions. How much weight a selector is morally justified in giving to a reaction qualification will depend on the preponderance of reactions that are grounded in aesthetic preferences or reasonable moral judgements in a way that engages the recipients' interest in autonomous agency, which will be hard to discern in practice. Furthermore, the sensitivity my account displays towards whether a candidate's appearance is part of his or her commitment to a reasonable moral vision would create a serious moral hazard if it were to be translated as it stands into legislation: candidates could pretend that their appearance was an integral part of their conception of how to live (including their view of how they should present themselves to others) so as to avoid having to change it in order to acquire a reaction qualification for a job.

Nevertheless, when appearance discrimination occurs on the basis of reaction qualifications that are rooted in widely held prejudices at least, such as prejudices about people who are regarded as overweight, or men who are short, or those who have prominent tattoos, it seems to me that it should be made illegal to count them. Again, the onus should be placed on employers in these cases to provide evidence, first, that their customers or clients really do have a preference not to deal with people who possess that characteristic, and, second, that this preference is not based on such a prejudice. For example, if employers claim that their clientele would prefer to deal with slim, attractive employees, they need to provide evidence that their clientele genuinely do have this preference (rather than it being a matter of indifference to them) and that their clientele's preference isn't based on prejudices about overweight people.

Should employers also be legally required to provide evidence that customers' preferences concerning appearance characteristics are not rooted in their non-rational reactions before they are permitted to count reaction qualifications based on these preferences? That seems harder to justify. Where there are widespread prejudices about appearance characteristics, such as weight or height, this provides some justification for a presumption that customers' preferences not to deal with those who possess such characteristics are based on these prejudices, and this in turn justifies placing the onus on employers to provide evidence to the contrary. But there is no comparable empirical basis for making the presumption that when these preferences are not based on prejudices, they are grounded in their non-rational reactions rather than their conceptions of how to live. It is therefore harder to justify requiring an employer to demonstrate that they are not grounded in customers' non-rational reactions before he or she is legally permitted to count reaction qualifications rooted in these characteristics.

8.3 Objections to Legislating against Appearance Discrimination in Employment

There are several objections, however, to prohibiting appearance discrimination in employment decisions. I shall consider a number of challenges, some relating to the alleged unimportance of appearance discrimination, some relating to practical difficulties of designing legislation to prohibit it, and others having to do with the potentially bad effects of enacting such legislation.

First, it might be argued that there is no need for such legislation, on the grounds that the most serious forms of appearance discrimination occur when it constitutes indirect discrimination on some other basis, such as race, sex, religion, or disability, and that in practice direct appearance discrimination is much less widespread and much less damaging. Since many legislative frameworks already prohibit appearance discrimination when it is a form of indirect discrimination of these kinds, additional legislation against appearance discrimination might seem unnecessary or unjustifiable in light of the cost of trying to enforce it. But the idea that appearance discrimination is a serious problem in practice when, and only when, it constitutes indirect discrimination on some other basis fails to recognize that direct appearance discrimination in the context of employment is both systematic and consequential.[15] If, as seems to be the case, people regarded as unattractive experience comparable economic disadvantages to those experienced by members of already protected groups, then this gives us a strong reason for providing them with comparable protection against discrimination in the context of job appointments and promotions.

Second, even though appearance discrimination is, in general, of serious moral concern, it might be argued that legislation against it in the sphere of employment will end up prohibiting trivial forms of it, leading to an explosion of court cases, with all the attendant burdens that this would place on the legal system.[16] In other words, we cannot ban the egregious cases of appearance discrimination without also banning the trivial cases. But this seems to me to be an unfounded worry. The legislation I am proposing is limited in its ambitions. It aims to prohibit two broad types of appearance discrimination, namely, discrimination that is rooted in employers' or selectors' preferences concerning an appearance feature where no plausible case can be made that this feature is a qualification for the job in question; and discrimination that is based on reaction qualifications rooted in customers' and clients' prejudices concerning appearance. Even when the discrimination that is prohibited is based on aspects of appearance, such as hair colour or tattoos, that may seem trivial, the effects of such discrimination in terms of its adverse impact on people's interest in self-expression may be considerable.

Third, it might be argued that if legislation against appearance discrimination is going to include a prohibition on selectors choosing more attractive over less attractive candidates when no plausible case can be made for regarding attractiveness as a qualification, then we need criteria for distinguishing the more attractive from the less attractive, and since this is a subjective matter, we are unable to do so in a way that would be justifiable.[17] With characteristics such as sex, race, disability, and religion, it might be argued that there are objective criteria for determining whether an

---

[15] See Section 4.2, for some of the evidence.   [16] Rhode, *The Beauty Bias*, 111.
[17] See L. Tietje and S. Cresap, 'Is Lookism Unjust? The Ethics of Aesthetics and Public Policy Implications', *Journal of Libertarian Studies* 19 (2006): 31–50. See also Hamermesh, *Beauty Pays*, 156.

individual 'possesses' them that we lack with respect to the unattractive or the less attractive.

But regardless of whether there are objective criteria for determining a person's sex, race, and religion, and whether or not they are disabled, we do not need objective criteria for classifying people as attractive or unattractive for legislation against appearance discrimination to work. What matters is whether a person's appearance is treated as a basis for favouring or disfavouring them when no plausible case can be made that their appearance is a qualification for the job without relying on the prejudices of customers or clients. For the purpose of enforcing the legislation, at least, it does not matter whether there are objective, or even inter-subjectively shared, criteria for classifying people as attractive or unattractive. Of course, in order to motivate the idea that someone has been the victim of discrimination on the basis of their appearance when applying for a job or promotion, it may be relevant to point to inter-subjective assessments of their looks compared to similarly qualified but successful candidates. And it would be prima facie implausible to think that someone with the looks of Angelina Jolie or Brad Pitt has been discriminated against for a position because of their unattractiveness. But inter-subjective agreement in relation to whether someone is attractive or unattractive is not a condition of being a victim of appearance discrimination, and indeed it is possible in principle for someone to suffer appearance discrimination because they are regarded as *too* attractive even though that does not affect their ability to do the job.

Still, it might be argued that even if we do not need objective criteria for judging whether one person is more or less attractive than another to determine whether appearance discrimination has taken place, we need criteria of this kind to establish that it is systematically disadvantaging some people in order to justify extending a legislative framework that governs discrimination to cover it. But even if we lack objectively justified criteria for determining whether a person is unattractive or less attractive, there is nevertheless widespread inter-subjective agreement: studies show that people's judgements concerning who is attractive and unattractive are consistent across ethnic groups and geographical areas.[18]

Fourth, it might be claimed that it is unfeasible to use legislative means to prevent appearance discrimination on the grounds that the appearance preferences that fuel discrimination are hard-wired: we prefer symmetrical

---

[18] Hamermesh, *Beauty Pays*, 24–8.

faces, for example, because of the way our brains have come to be constituted, perhaps as a result of evolutionary processes.[19] But even if this were so, it would not morally justify the discrimination, and indeed legislation against appearance discrimination will provide reasons for people not to act on their hard-wired preferences. Even if preferences are hard-wired, it is implausible to claim that employers or selectors cannot help acting upon them in the workplace or the wider society. Here it is worth noting that we would not accept an analogous argument against legislating to forbid discrimination on grounds of race. Even if there was evidence that many of us have hard-wired preferences to deal with members of our own racial groups, we would not think that this was a sufficient reason to refrain from legislating against racial discrimination.

Fifth, it might be argued that legislation against appearance discrimination would be unlikely to be effective because many victims of such discrimination would not make use of the legislation, either because they are unaware that they are victims of it or because it would require admitting publicly that they have suffered discrimination because they are regarded as unattractive. Even if such an admission was followed by monetary compensation for being a victim of discrimination, it is likely that many people will be reluctant to make use of the legislation. Indeed, as noted by Deborah Rhode, if we look at the amount of litigation related to appearance discrimination in regions where it is prohibited, it is clear that people are not keen to resort to enforcement of the law: 'jurisdictions that have such laws report relatively few complaints. Cities and counties average between zero and nine cases a year, and Michigan averages about thirty.'[20] But even if only a small number of people ended up successfully prosecuting an employer for appearance discrimination, providing protection against it would help promote awareness of the issue and deter some employers who are inclined to engage in it. The effectiveness of the legislation could also be enhanced by giving a public body (such as the Equality and Human Rights Commission in the UK) the power and resources to take measures to enforce it, particularly in cases that might have some strategic pay off in bringing home to employers the importance of abiding by it.

Sixth, as Hamermesh points out, given the limited resources available, extending the legislative framework to cover appearance discrimination might take up resources that could otherwise be used to prosecute

---

[19] N. Etcoff, *Survival of the Prettiest: The Science of Beauty* (New York: Anchor, 2011).
[20] Rhode, *The Beauty Bias*, 113.

employers who discriminate on other grounds, such as race or disability.[21] So it might be objected that legislative frameworks shouldn't be extended to cover appearance discrimination because this would have a detrimental effect. This is a serious concern, but if it is true that the economic disadvantages that result from appearance discrimination are comparable to those experienced by the victims of discrimination on grounds of race or disability, then it would be justifiable to make available additional resources, or redistribute resources so as to reduce the impact of wrongful appearance discrimination even if on some occasions doing so would be detrimental to the protection of other groups.

8.4 Legislating against Appearance Discrimination in Other Contexts

There is a powerful argument for extending anti-discrimination legislation to cover appearance discrimination in the context of decisions about who to hire and promote, but is there also a case for extending it to apply to appearance discrimination in the context of decisions about what personal relationships to form, cultivate, or sustain, or in the context of everyday lookism?

Laws against wrongful appearance discrimination in the context of forming personal relationships would be hard, if not impossible, to enforce because of the difficulty of identifying when it has occurred.[22] Whether a person discriminates wrongfully on the basis of appearance in the context of forming or cultivating personal relationships depends, in part, on whether she has exercised a moral prerogative that permits her to discriminate, and that will depend on the character and malleability of her desires and preferences. It would be incredibly difficult, practically impossible I think, to devise legislation that is both appropriately sensitive to that moral prerogative and publicly checkable, that is, to formulate a law which tracks the prerogative but is such that there are clear criteria for determining whether it or not it has been broken that can be applied in the light of evidence that is available to others.[23]

---

[21] Hamermesh, *Beauty Pays*, 165.   [22] See Moreau, *Faces of Inequality*, 237.
[23] See Andrew Williams's discussion of publicity in his 'Incentives, Inequality, and Publicity', *Philosophy and Public Affairs* 27 (1998): 225–47.

In response it might be argued that even if it is unfeasible to devise and enforce a law against appearance discrimination in the context of personal relationships in a way that meets the requirements of publicity and captures precisely those cases in which it is morally objectionable, it might nevertheless be desirable to have a law against it on the statutes, on the grounds that this would serve both to highlight the moral issues appearance discrimination raises in this context and publicly condemn some forms of it.[24] Although this argument has some force, it applies equally to, for example, discrimination on the basis of race or disability in the context of personal relationships, which could potentially lead to a raft of legislation that was very difficult to enforce. There is the danger that anti-discrimination laws in general would be brought into disrepute if the complexity of legislation in the context of personal relationships, and the difficulty of gathering publicly checkable evidence in relation to whether the relevant laws had been broken, meant that there were no successful prosecutions on the basis of it.

It might be supposed that there are deeper reasons for thinking that it would be undesirable for there to be such legislation. If there is a right of free association, then it might be thought to protect from coercive interference the decisions people make concerning with whom to form (or not to form) close personal relationships, even if they act wrongly, that is, the right of free association might be regarded as a claim right that provides protection against intervention in such decisions. But just as with decisions that employers make about who to hire, the importance of the interests at stake here should make us wary of simply asserting the existence of such a right. In Chapter 6 I suggested that we think of a right of free association as providing us with a limited moral prerogative to discriminate on grounds of appearance in a range of decisions we make about what personal relationships to form when doing so is disrespectful or demeaning, or contributes to creating unjust consequences, including in cases when unless we discriminate we would be unable to realize the goods that these relationships provide or, at least, would be unable to realize these goods to any great extent. If this also defines the limits of a claim right to discriminate in personal relationships, then it would not entail that it is impermissible to legislate against wrongful appearance discrimination that falls outside these bounds.

---

[24] According to some theories of criminal justice, it may be important to criminalize wrongful discrimination in order to publicly condemn it, even if doing so makes no contribution to preventing it, and even if no wrong-doers are brought to trial or punished.

Would legislation against appearance discrimination in the personal sphere violate a right to privacy of some sort? There is a legitimate public interest in knowing when wrongful appearance discrimination in the personal sphere has taken place and countering it, given the disrespect that may be involved and the harm that may be caused by it. But many people would resent having their reasons for forming (or not forming) particular personal relationships scrutinized, and might experience it as humiliating to have to reveal the inner workings of their minds concerning these decisions. Might we have a right not to have our reasons examined in this context, including not being asked about them? Even if there is no such right, should we be permitted to refuse to disclose these reasons without that being regarded as casting doubt on our motives? Might we have a right that forbids others, without our consent, from collecting evidence that bears upon these motives? These are complex questions that cannot be answered confidently without a full analysis of the right to privacy. But it is plausible to think that there are some such rights, even if their precise contours are hard to determine.[25] Even if whether we have a moral right not to have our motives examined, or evidence collected about them, turns in part on whether we have acted wrongly, in practice that right would be violated unless all of us are given legal rights not to be questioned about our motives or inquiries made about them. As a result, it seems to me that the fundamental problem with legislating against morally objectionable appearance discrimination in personal relationships is that it is unfeasible to prohibit it in a way that would make its enforcement publicly checkable and respect defendants' right to privacy.

In the previous chapter, I argued that the acts of discrimination that constitute everyday lookism are often wrong: they may be demeaning, or contribute in various ways to creating an unjust distribution of benefits and burdens, or to lowering the standing of members of a group. Is there a case here for legislating to prevent some or all of these acts? Again, the argument for legislating against these acts seems weak, especially since they are acts of expression and as such may merit special protection, at least when they do not fall into the category of hate crimes. In the final section of the next

---

[25] According to the account defended by Andrei Marmor, our right to privacy is grounded in our interest 'in having a reasonable measure of control over ways in which we present ourselves to others and the ability to present different aspects of ourselves, and what is ours, to different people' (A. Marmor, 'What Is the Right to Privacy?', *Philosophy and Public Affairs* 43 (2015): 3–26, at 7). Understood in this way, it is plausible to think that some of the rights I have mentioned could be justified as part of a broader right to privacy.

chapter, however, I shall suggest that there is a case for greater regulation of some of the spaces in which everyday lookism is prevalent, such as social media, and for pursuing an agenda that involves seeking to make appearance norms less demanding and more inclusive, and seeking to reduce the importance attached to appearance in order to counteract its oppressiveness.

8.5 Concluding Remarks

In this chapter, I have considered the case for prohibiting some forms of appearance discrimination. This case is strong in relation to the appearance discrimination that occurs in decisions that are made about who to hire and who to promote. In this context, discrimination that is rooted in selectors' or employers' preferences concerning appearance features should be prohibited when these features have nothing to do with a candidate's ability to perform the job and do not reflect a company's genuine aesthetic or moral vision. So too appearance discrimination that occurs on the basis of reaction qualifications that are rooted in the widely held prejudices of customers or clients should be prohibited. If an employer (or selector acting on her behalf) gives weight to an appearance characteristic by counting a reaction qualification that responds to it, then the onus should be on her to provide evidence that her customers or clients really do prefer to deal with employees who possess that characteristic and that their preference is not based on any widely held prejudices. The case for prohibiting wrongful appearance discrimination is much less strong in relation to the other two contexts I have been considering in this book, namely, the choices that people make about what personal relationships to form, cultivate, or sustain and the ordinary practices in which people comment upon and judge the appearance of others.

9
Compensation and Beyond

Even though many individual acts of appearance discrimination are harmful only in a minor way, they may combine to cause considerable harm, making some much worse off than others; for example, cumulatively these acts may place serious limits on some people's access to advantaged social positions or lead some to develop severe body anxiety. Different theories of distributive justice may guide us to different conclusions concerning inequalities that are a cumulative effect of practices involving appearance discrimination. In this chapter, however, I shall assume that there is a strong case for regarding these inequalities as unjust when they are large and generated by features of appearance over which people lack control, especially when some are unable to lead flourishing lives as a result.

Some of the individual acts of appearance discrimination that contribute to creating an unjust distribution of benefits and burdens may be morally permissible. When people make choices about what romantic partnerships to form, they may be exercising a moral prerogative that permits them to reject people solely because they find them unattractive. As a result, without anyone acting wrongly, the choices people make can play a role in seriously limiting the romantic opportunities of those who, through no fault of their own, are widely regarded as unattractive, in a way that contributes to fostering an unjust distribution of these opportunities. In many cases, however, the acts that contribute to creating an unjust distribution of opportunities of one kind or another will be morally impermissible in virtue of doing so. As we saw in the previous chapter, legislation to prevent these acts from occurring might nevertheless be unfeasible, undesirable, or morally objectionable for some reason, or they may occur because even though there is legislation in place, it does not succeed in preventing them. How should we respond to the unjust disadvantages created by acts of appearance discrimination, either when these acts are morally permissible or when they are morally impermissible?

In the previous chapter, I argued that compensation cannot fully redress the wrong involved in appearance discrimination when it is demeaning, or when it is deliberatively unfair, or when it has the effect of contributing to lowering the perceived moral status of its victims. In contrast, when appearance discrimination is morally permissible but contributes to creating an unjust distribution, or when it is wrongful only because it does so, then compensation may in principle provide full redress for the unjust disadvantages that are experienced. Indeed, when the wrongness of appearance discrimination consists solely in the unjust distribution of benefits and burdens to which it contributes, then it is only *conditionally* morally impermissible, for in principle at least the victims might be fully compensated by benefits of one kind or another. In these circumstances, when there is a scheme of compensation in place, such as a system of redistributive taxation that counteracts what would otherwise be an unjust distribution, then appearance discrimination is not wrongful at all. It is morally permissible as long as the scheme remains in operation.

Some, however, will be deeply opposed to giving a role to compensation in responding to appearance discrimination. Indeed, there is a potential divide here between relational (or social) egalitarians, many of whom will think that compensation is the wrong path to go down in addressing appearance discrimination, and theorists of distributive justice, many of whom will think that compensating those who suffer from such discrimination is often appropriate and warranted. The theoretical perspective that has informed this book is sympathetic to some of the central ideas defended by relational egalitarians, for example, it gives a key role to the notion of respect and the idea that we are morally required to regard and treat others as our moral equals in various spheres, including civil society and the sphere of personal relationships. But it also gives a key role to ideas about distributive justice that cannot straightforwardly be derived from the commitments of relational egalitarians and that express, at least in part, what it is for the state to show equal concern for each person's well-being or interest in leading a flourishing life.[1] I shall suggest that these ideas justify giving a significant role to compensation in its broadest sense, despite various practical and theoretical difficulties with identifying who should receive compensation, what form it should take, and who should bear the costs of it. However, in a way that resonates with relational egalitarian themes, I shall in the final section draw attention to some of the limitations of a combined

---

[1] This is not to deny that there are sophisticated forms of relational egalitarianism that seek to identify not only instrumental but also non-instrumental reasons why the unequal distribution of resources matters. See, for example, C. Schemmel, *Justice and Egalitarian Relations* (New York: Oxford University Press, 2021), ch. 8.

strategy of seeking to prevent wrongful discrimination (when it is feasible, permissible, and desirable to do so) and compensating those who are unjustly disadvantaged by appearance discrimination when it occurs.

9.1 A Hypothetical Insurance Approach

Appearance discrimination often creates, or contributes to creating, unjust consequences. When it cannot be prevented, or it is undesirable to prevent it, or it occurs despite measures being taken to prevent it, we seem to be faced with a choice between, on the one hand, simply living with these consequences and, on the other hand, providing at least some compensation to those who are disadvantaged as a result. Here by 'compensation', I mean any measure that provides some recompense to people who experience unjust disadvantages or that provides some remedy for such disadvantages. Compensation in this broad sense and 'living with the consequences' are each compatible with acting individually and collectively to prevent these injustices from occurring in the future or to reduce the risk of them occurring. Faced with such a choice, compensation combined with working towards better prevention or reducing the risk of future occurrences, when that is feasible and desirable, seems the morally preferable response.

When morally permissible appearance discrimination has unjust consequences, there is a strong argument, both in principle and in practice, for sharing between the members of a society the costs of adequately compensating people who are adversely affected. No one acted wrongly, and there seems insufficient reason to require those who are merely *causally* responsible for these adverse effects to bear the costs of the compensation that is due, or even a greater share of those costs than others, simply in virtue of being causally responsible. An approach that involves sharing the costs among all members of society seems more defensible (though that leaves open precisely how these costs should be shared, including whether they should be shared equally, an issue to which I shall return later in the chapter).

In contrast, in the case of those who are adversely affected by *wrongful* appearance discrimination, we might think that in principle the wrong-doers should be required to bear the costs of compensation. (Indeed, when there are good reasons for prohibiting wrongful appearance discrimination because it contributes to creating an unjust distribution, the civil law might be used to force wrong-doers to pay those costs.) But even here there is room for considerable doubt about whether a targeted approach is justifiable, at least if we are employing Gibbard's objective sense of 'wrong', for many of those who act wrongly in this sense by contributing to the creation of an unjust distribution will not be culpable for doing so. Surely, if we are going to target a specific group of people to bear the costs of compensation, it should be those who are blameworthy for acting in this way, not those who acted wrongly but blamelessly.

Targeting those who are blameworthy might seem to be the right response in principle. In practice, however, identifying the blameworthy, in a publicly checkable manner, seems unfeasible. There are difficulties in doing so that arise from the complexities involved in giving appropriate weight to the way in which social factors influence culpability: for instance, ignorance of the effects of one's actions or their social meaning may be less blameworthy among people with lower levels of education. Even if we put to one side these complexities, before we can assess whether someone has acted wrongly in a way that is blameworthy, in virtue of culpably contributing to an unjust distribution, we have to determine whether he or she really has acted wrongly, and that may be fraught with difficulty. Indeed, this is one of the reasons I gave in Chapter 8 for why prohibition is unjustifiable in response to harmful discrimination in the sphere of personal relationships that contributes to creating or maintaining an unjust distribution. How do we tell whether someone is exercising a moral prerogative in discriminating on the basis of appearance, or whether he or she is acting wrongly in discriminating on that basis? Distinguishing between the two requires a reasonably precise understanding of the boundaries of the moral prerogative, one that is hard to acquire, together with knowledge of his or her psychological makeup. As a result, justifying the claim that someone has wrongfully discriminated, for example, in choosing a romantic partner, in virtue of the unjust consequences to which he or she has contributed, would be unfeasible to do in a publicly checkable way.[2] This is a wider problem because it is wrong to behave in ways that contribute to creating or maintaining an unjust distribution only if two conditions are met:[3] first, it is possible to avoid behaving in these ways without incurring unreasonable costs; and second, it is possible to avoid behaving in these ways without creating, or contributing to creating, a greater injustice. Determining in a publicly checkable way whether these two conditions have been met is surely often unfeasible.

---

[2] For the importance of publicity, and the difficulties that moral prerogatives can create for it, see Williams, 'Incentives, Inequality, and Publicity'.

[3] See Section 1.4.

We might think that, as a second best, compensation should be paid by the *beneficiaries* of the wrong-doing or, at least, that the beneficiaries should pay a greater share of the costs of compensation.[4] But even if we grant that, in principle, this would be the second-best solution, in practice there will still be considerable difficulties in identifying the beneficiaries in a way that allows for public checks, partly because, again, doing so requires identifying acts of wrongful discrimination in the first place. We cannot identify someone as a beneficiary of wrongful appearance discrimination that consists in contributing to an unjust distribution unless we are able to identify acts of appearance discrimination that are wrongful in virtue of doing so, and identifying these acts in a publicly checkable way seems unfeasible for the reasons already given.

These practical difficulties might be regarded as sufficient reason to abandon compensation as a strategy, to live with the consequences of the wrongful appearance discrimination that has already occurred and that continues to occur, but to work towards better prevention and to implement other measures for reducing the risk of it occurring in the future. But I think this would be premature. Despite the practical difficulties in identifying the beneficiaries of wrongful discrimination, we have strong evidence that people regarded as attractive benefit from their perceived attractiveness in various ways, including as a result of wrongful appearance discrimination against those who are regarded as unattractive. One possible response, imperfect in various respects, is that we might use a hypothetical insurance approach to mitigate in an ongoing way the unjust disadvantages suffered by people who are disadvantaged by their appearance not only as a result of discrimination that is conditionally wrong in virtue of contributing to an unjust distribution but also as a result of discrimination that is morally permissible.[5]

Such an approach could guide us in practice in reaching answers to questions about the level of compensation required, the form it should take, and how the costs of it should be distributed. In the context of employment decisions, we could treat being regarded as attractive in the same way that Ronald Dworkin treats marketable talents. We could ask how much the average person, with equal but limited purchasing power, would be willing

---

[4] For relevant discussion, see D. Butt, 'On Benefiting from Injustice', *Canadian Journal of Philosophy* 37 (2007): 129–52; R. Goodin and C. Barry, 'Benefiting from the Wrongdoing of Others', *Journal of Applied Philosophy* 31 (2014): 363–76.

[5] For the idea of hypothetical insurance, see Dworkin, *Sovereign Virtue*, especially chs 2, 8, and 9.

to insure against being regarded as unattractive in ways that are beyond their control if they know their ambitions but not how others will regard their looks, and they are aware of how being regarded as unattractive would impact upon their ambitions as a result of appearance discrimination that takes place in decisions about hiring and promotion. The outcome of such a scheme—what insurance the average person would buy to protect themselves against being regarded as unattractive in the context of employment decisions—could be used to devise and fund policies that we can then regard as sharing fairly the costs of morally impermissible appearance discrimination in this context when it is merely conditionally wrong, as well as the costs of morally permissible appearance discrimination. We could think of the adoption of the policies yielded by this approach as compensating for the wrongness of appearance discrimination in the context of employment decisions when its wrongness consists solely in the way in which it would otherwise contribute to creating an unjust distribution of benefits and burdens.

Making use of a hypothetical insurance model in this way would not require us to adopt Dworkin's entire theory of equality of resources. For example, we would not need to use the envy test to determine whether one person is disadvantaged relative to another; instead, we might favour employing a theory of welfare, such as an objective list theory of well-being. This might seem odd or incoherent: if we were to endorse a welfarist theory of what makes people's lives go better, why wouldn't we use that theory in determining how much compensation is due to those who are disadvantaged through no fault of their own as a result of appearance discrimination? If, say, well-being is what really matters, understood in terms of a list of objectively valuable ingredients of a flourishing life, it might be thought that the kind of subjective assessments involved in hypothetical insurance choices won't necessarily track these ingredients, and the value that people attribute to their appearance and how it is regarded by others may be too great, even taking into account what we know to be true about its potential importance for flourishing in societies, such as ours, that elevate its worth.

This worry resonates with a general challenge to the use of hypothetical insurance models. Tom Parr asks us to imagine the case of Jennifer Eccles who, unlike in the song, has only very small freckles on her arm, and is very upset about them even though they are imperceptible to the naked eye.[6]

---

[6] T. Parr, 'How to Identify Disadvantage: Taking the Envy Test Seriously', *Political Studies* 66 (2018): 306–22, at 317.

He describes this case in the context of considering, and partly rebutting, an objection to the envy test, which he calls the mistakes objection, namely, that the test 'allows the judgement that an individual is disadvantaged to be held hostage by mistaken judgements concerning the value of an opportunity'.[7] It might be thought that much the same objection arises in relation to hypothetical insurance choices, for some might buy expensive coverage to insure against what are minor imperfections to their appearance that others would not even notice, and they would prefer to purchase that insurance rather than coverage against the potential loss of genuinely valuable opportunities.

In response, it might be pointed out that a hypothetical insurance approach guides policy by reference to what choices would be made by the *average* person, and the average person will not be like Jennifer Eccles. But that response seems unsatisfying. Young people with body dysmorphia do get hung up on what are at most only minor flaws in their appearance. In an imaginary society where the average person was similarly afflicted, public policies modelled on their hypothetical choices could involve providing expensive state-funded treatments for minor imperceptible imperfections in appearance. This is a potentially powerful objection to a hypothetical insurance approach when that approach is thought to *determine* what constitutes a just mitigation of the disadvantages faced by people as a result of morally permissible appearance discrimination, in a way that allows no possibility of error. But I don't think it undermines such an approach when it is understood as a practical device that can be used as a *guide* to just mitigation, even by those who endorse an objective list theory of well-being. Provided that egregious mistakes about the intrinsic importance of (features of) appearance, such as the one made by Jennifer Eccles, are relatively rare, a hypothetical insurance approach can provide insight.

But is it a problem for this approach that the general importance we attach to appearance, and the contexts and ways in which people are disposed to give weight to appearance, both consciously and non-consciously, are a product of the particular societies and cultures in which we live? I think not. I shall return to this issue in the final section of the chapter, but note for the moment that hypothetical insurance is being proposed as, in part, an answer to the question: how should we compensate for harmful appearance discrimination in societies, like ours, in which appearance is

---

[7] Parr, 'How to Identify Disadvantage', 314.

given great weight and affects the realization of our ambitions, including the ambitions we have to find fulfilling or well-paid jobs? There may be good reason to think that our societies would be better in various ways if much less weight was given to appearance in them, but the weight it is given forms the background against which we should consider hypothetical choices in order to guide decisions about just compensation.

Even if the outcome of a properly constructed hypothetical insurance market does not determine in a constitutive way what counts as a just mitigation of inequality, modelling public policy on the hypothetical choices that individuals would make seems to provide us with a fair method for reaching practical conclusions on this matter that gives weight to people's existing preferences. Of course, different hypothetical insurers will reach different conclusions: for some, given their ambitions, it will be extremely important for them to be regarded as attractive, whereas for others, that may not be so important. But the vast majority of people will regard their appearance as of considerable instrumental importance, at least, in the light of its role in contributing to flourishing in a variety of spheres of life, and many will regard a beautiful appearance as non-instrumentally valuable. That is why our question should be, 'what insurance would the average person, relevantly situated, purchase against being regarded as unattractive by others (or indeed by herself) in ways that are beyond her control, in the light of the disadvantages she may then experience as a result of appearance discrimination that it is unfeasible to prohibit or that there are good reasons not to prohibit?'

Some object to the use of hypothetical insurance choices to assess levels of just compensation on the grounds that these choices have no relevance to determining what citizens owe to each other. Elizabeth Anderson points out that '[s]ince these choices were not, in fact, made, the failure to reflect them in state allocations violates no one's actual autonomous choices'.[8] The conclusion that a person would have insured themselves against a risk does not mean that she should receive the benefit she would have been due had she actually done so; conversely, the conclusion that a person would not have insured themselves against a risk does not mean that she can be held responsible for not doing so. But thinking of hypothetical insurance choices as quasi-agreements misunderstands their purpose. The underlying idea is that hypothetical insurances choices cast light on what would constitute just

---

[8] E. Anderson, 'What Is the Point of Equality?', *Ethics* 109 (1999): 287–337, at 309.

mitigation for unchosen inequalities, for these choices seem to provide a fair basis in practice for determining the level of compensation that should be provided.

9.2 Kinds of Compensation

What kinds of compensation would a hypothetical insurance approach justify in order to redress the systematic disadvantages people experience as a result of suffering discrimination on the basis of appearance features over which they lack control? In the sphere of employment, hypothetical insurers might elect to purchase policies that in effect provide financial compensation for what would otherwise be unjust disadvantages that arise as a result of morally permissible appearance discrimination, or morally impermissible appearance discrimination that there are good reasons not to make illegal. But if states provided monetary compensation in accordance with such policies, would that send out a demeaning or insulting message? Elizabeth Anderson suggests that it would because it involves the state attaching 'an official stamp of recognition' to negative private judgements that particular citizens make about their own attractiveness.[9] But compensation here could take the form of benefits supplied through a system of progressive taxation modelled on the basis of hypothetical insurance decisions. In effect, hypothetical insurers would treat being regarded as unattractive as akin to having talents that are not in demand in the market. Nevertheless, it might be thought that in order to obtain any compensation that would be available, citizens would need to engage in what Jonathan Wolff calls 'shameful revelation', that is, to make humiliating disclosures that are similar in kind to those he thinks claimants are required to make in order to access resources through conditional welfare benefit schemes.[10] But in institutionalizing a scheme of compensation for lack of marketable talent, and treating 'being regarded as unattractive' as a lack of such a talent, a state need not require claimants to demonstrate that they have not found employment, or are in less well-paid jobs, because they are untalented in general, or unattractive in particular. It might merely require them to demonstrate that they have tried to find work (or more highly paid work) but been unsuccessful.

---

[9] Anderson, 'What Is the Point of Equality', 305.
[10] See J. Wolff, 'Fairness, Respect, and the Egalitarian Ethos', 115.

Compensation of this sort wouldn't mitigate the unjust effects of morally wrongful or morally permissible discrimination in the personal sphere. In this context, there would be something deeply inappropriate about offering monetary compensation. We could nevertheless ask hypothetical insurers, unaware of how attractive they will be perceived to be, but knowing what impact being perceived as unattractive will have on their opportunities to form personal relationships of different kinds, what policies they would purchase to protect themselves against being deprived of these opportunities or having a reduced set of them. Hypothetic insurers are not restricted to purchasing policies that would provide monetary compensation. In so far as they regard compensation in this form as inappropriate, it is open to them to elect to pay for policies that would compensate for particular disadvantages by supplying specific goods or services.[11] For example, they might decide to fund state provision of cosmetic surgery for features of appearance that are regarded by others as deeply unappealing and that can be improved by it, such as some facial differences, in the way that many public health care systems in developed countries already do. Hypothetical insurers would know that some facial features, such as large birthmarks or extensive burns, may place a significant burden on people who possess them, partly by placing an obstacle in the way of forming romantic partnerships and other personal relationships, and partly because of the unwanted comments and attention their looks receive when they are in public spaces.

There is scope, however, for reasonable disagreement among hypothetical insurers concerning what cover, if any, they would purchase. Acquainted with the testimonies of people with facial differences, and mindful of the fact that cosmetic surgery is limited in what it can achieve and may involve repeated interventions with long and painful recovery times, some hypothetical insurers might decide not to insure against facial differences.[12] They might reason that if they do turn out to have facial differences, they would prefer to live with these differences and use non-surgical means to gain the acceptance of others, such as devising ways of taking the initiative in social

---

[11] As Andrew Walton argues, if there are reasons why people would not want monetary compensation, and would prefer goods in kind, these reasons can figure in the deliberations of hypothetical insurers. See A. Walton, 'Resources In-Kind, Considering the Case of Housing' (unpublished paper).
[12] See Partridge, *Face It*, especially ch. 11 and 108–9, for a sense of what cosmetic surgery may involve, its limits, and the complexities encountered by surgeons in offering advice on when to pursue it and by patients in deciding when to call an end to it. See also L. Grealy, *In the Mind's Eye. An Autobiography of a Face* (London: Arrow Books, 1995); T. Sorell, 'The Ethics of Saving a Face: The Case of Lucy Grealy' (unpublished paper).

encounters that enable them to defuse the negative forms of behaviour to which they are vulnerable.[13] Hypothetical insurance, in the way that I am utilizing it, is merely a practical guide, so where reasonable disagreement is possible, we have to make a judgement about what the average hypothetical insurer would favour. There is good reason to think that the average hypothetic insurer would be risk averse in relation to facial differences. They would insure against having them, so that they would possess the option of publicly funded cosmetic surgery to change their looks to make their faces as presentable as possible, in the light of existing norms and the predictable responses of others in the societies in which they live, even if they did not choose to avail themselves of it.

It might seem, however, that the worry about shameful revelation has greater force when cosmetic surgery is the benefit to be provided. For example, if state-funded cosmetic surgery for facial differences is available, then it might seem that in order to obtain it an individual will have to make a case that his opportunities are being restricted because others find his facial features repellent. But there is no necessity here. Mindful of the potential demeaningness of having to demonstrate that others find one's facial features unappealing, state-funded providers of cosmetic surgery might adopt a policy of applying widely accepted appearance norms to determine who is eligible for treatment. Furthermore, the state need not endorse the judgements that people seeking cosmetic surgery make about their own appearance, or the judgements made about it in the wider society to which they belong. The state can instead respond solely to citizens' own judgements about their appearance and its effects on their lives, made in the light of their ambitions, their knowledge of the significance that others in society attach to it, and the appearance norms to which they are subject.

But there are limits to what compensation in the form of providing goods and services can do to redress the unjust disadvantages created by both permissible and impermissible appearance discrimination, especially beyond the sphere of employment. Some will no doubt continue to experience difficulty in finding friends or romantic partners because of their looks. What more might be done? Opportunities to form such relationships cannot be distributed directly by institutions, for the obvious reason that they depend on appropriate feelings that cannot be commanded, but the distribution of these opportunities might nevertheless be influenced by policies. Compare

---

[13] See Partridge, *Face It*, 157.

health in this respect. Institutions cannot distribute health itself, but they can affect its distribution, for example, by investing in public health care and by discouraging lifestyles that negatively affect health. So too, institutions and policy may influence the distribution of opportunities for forming friendships and romantic partnerships, and foster the conditions that make available a greater range of these opportunities. Hypothetical insurers might therefore choose to fund policies that do so. For example, they might elect to provide financial support to clubs and activities in civil society that afford opportunities for forging new personal relationships, or to support educational initiatives in schools that are designed to cultivate the social skills and psychological dispositions that facilitate forming friendships and romantic partnerships.

It might be argued that in addition to shaping opportunities for forming friendships and romantic partnerships, the state could compensate those who are disadvantaged by the morally permissible weightings or significance that people attach to the appearance of others in forming personal relationships, by providing them with opportunities to obtain various 'surrogate' goods. For example, knowing the effect that being perceived as unattractive may have on their prospects for forming friendships and romantic partnerships, and the consequent impact of that on their wellbeing, hypothetical insurers might elect to pay for a policy that would provide them with greater opportunities for social contact or companionship. Again, in practice this might take the form of providing subsidies for public venues and spaces, and for organizations and activities in civil society.[14]

It would be naïve, however, to think the measures I have outlined could fully address the injustices suffered by people who lose out on advantaged social positions, or friendships or romantic partnerships, as a result of their looks. It may be tempting to reply here that we shouldn't regard all these disappointments as injustices. And obviously that's true. But my focus has been on the disappointments that *can* legitimately be regarded as injustices because they are, at least in part, a product of a pattern in the distribution of opportunities to occupy advantaged social positions, or to form friendships and romantic partnerships, that is unjust. Of course, what we regard as a pattern of unjust distribution will depend upon the particular theory of justice that we bring to bear in making that judgement. Some theories of distributive justice, such as sufficientarianism, will allow that luck can play a

---

[14] See Brownlee, *Being Sure of Each Other*, 140–1.

large role in the allocation of these opportunities without raising any issue of injustice; other theories, such as luck egalitarianism, will think that luck can play only a very limited role in generating just inequalities in these opportunities. But any plausible theory should acknowledge *some* scope for luck to influence just outcomes, and indeed should recognize that there are considerable limits in practice concerning the extent to which unjust inequalities in the distribution of opportunities to occupy advantaged social positions, or to form friendships and romantic partnerships, can be countered, whether by prevention or compensation.

9.3 Beyond Compensation and Prevention

The limits of a policy of providing money, goods, and services, and improving people's access to these things, as compensation for the unjust disadvantages faced by those who experience appearance discrimination might be regarded as indicative of deeper difficulties with the approach I have been defending. Do these limits reveal problems with hypothetical insurance models and, more broadly, with the two-fold strategy of seeking to prevent the occurrence of appearance discrimination in its most morally pernicious forms (when that is feasible and can be done without causing a greater injustice), and then compensating people who continue to be disadvantaged by their appearance when the disadvantages they experience contribute to creating an unjust distribution of benefits and burdens? It might be argued that instead our fundamental goal should be to *reduce* the importance attached to appearance in our society, and to *transform* the demanding and exclusionary norms that currently govern our appearance in order to make them less demanding and more inclusive, so that the need to prevent appearance discrimination from occurring, or to provide compensation for it when it does occur, either dissipates or becomes less morally urgent.

Consider, for example, my claim that hypothetical insurers would purchase cover against facial differences so they would be provided with the opportunity for publicly funded cosmetic surgery if it turns out that they have them. Rather than offering people with facial differences publicly funded cosmetic surgery, shouldn't we instead seek to change appearance norms so that their looks would no longer count against them, and so that they would not be stigmatized or experience unwanted attention in public places? Clare Chambers defends 'the principle of the unmodified body', that is, the principle that our bodies are alright, and indeed have value, just as they are, as a baseline with moral and political significance that can be used to provide protection against the social pressures we experience to modify our bodies.[15] But the public provision of cosmetic surgery, and the hypothetical insurance approach that I have used to justify it, is compatible with Chambers's principle, and indeed she is insistent that she doesn't want that principle to be used to deny people publicly funded procedures that they genuinely want or need.[16] Viewing these issues through the lens my theory provides, it is clear that there is no necessary incompatibility between, on the one hand, seeking to prevent appearance discrimination from occurring and to compensate those who are disadvantaged by their appearance, and on the other hand, aiming to reduce the weight that is given to appearance in our society, to transform the demanding and exclusionary appearance norms that govern it, and to reduce the pressure on people to modify their bodies, so that no one feels they are under an obligation to do so. The key question is whether the latter should be our long-term public goals. In order to answer that question adequately, we need to be clear about what would be involved in reducing the importance that people attach to appearance and in making appearance norms less demanding and more inclusive.

Consider the first of these goals. When people attach importance to appearance or, more precisely, to the possession or absence of various appearance features, then they value these features either for instrumental reasons, because they think these features will further other goals that they have, or for non-instrumental reasons, because they think that these features are valuable for their own sake, perhaps because they regard them as morally required or as aesthetically appealing. When the members of a society or group attach high value to some set of appearance features, then a range of decisions they make may be influenced by the presence or absence of these features. A reduction in the importance that the members of a society attach to an appearance feature might involve (or lead to) a reduction in the number of jobs for which that feature is a qualification, including the number of jobs for which it is a reaction qualification in particular. It may involve (or lead to) a reduction in the weight that people attach to that feature when making choices about what personal relationships to form and cultivate. And it may involve (or lead to) a reduction in either the incidence of everyday lookism or its oppressiveness. Even if there remains a practice of commenting upon, and judging, the appearance of others, attributing less

---

[15] See Chambers, *Intact*, especially Introduction and chs 7–9.
[16] Chambers, *Intact*, 259.

significance to various appearance features may have the effect of reducing the oppressiveness of this practice, for reducing the importance people attach to these features would be likely to lead to a reduction in the costs of non-compliance with an appearance norm that prizes them.

Making appearance norms more inclusive is a different matter, however, for these norms might be made more inclusive without reducing the importance that people assign to appearance. In order for appearance norms to be *fully* inclusive, compliance would have to be equally feasible for everyone, that is, it would have to be possible for each person to comply with the norm and it would have to be equally burdensome for them to do so. A dress code, such as a school uniform policy, might be fully inclusive in this way if the clothes required to comply with it were available in the full range of shapes and sizes required to fit diverse bodies and were inexpensive to buy. Even when an appearance norm was not fully inclusive in this way, it might be partially inclusive. It might be the case that everyone could comply with it, but there was some variation in the costs that would need to be incurred by different people in order to do so, for example, a dress code that each person could comply with, but where the costs of obtaining the clothes required to comply with it were moderately high, thereby placing a greater burden on those who were worse off. Or there might be an appearance norm with which most people could comply, where those who are able to comply with it incurred equal but low costs in doing so, for example, a dress code with which only those with a particular shape and size could comply, but where the costs of doing so were low for each of them. In this way, appearance norms might display varying degrees and kinds of inclusivity.

With dress codes, it is often easy to see how they might be made more inclusive. It is generally less clear with appearance norms that relate to our bodies. In some cases, these norms might become more inclusive as a result of changes in our aesthetic sensibilities. If aesthetic judgements are regarded as attempts to respond appropriately to aesthetically relevant properties, the process of making appearance norms more inclusive might involve cultivating new ways of looking at the appearance of others that bring into focus aesthetically valuable features of it that are neglected or given insufficient weight, for example, taking pleasure in a person's curves rather than regarding him or her as unattractively fat.[17] In a rather different vision of inclusivity in which no comparative judgements are made about the relative

---

[17] For relevant discussion, see Irvin, 'Resisting Body Oppression'.

attractiveness of different faces, James Partridge imagines a world of 'face equality' in which 'all human faces are celebrated in all their glorious uniqueness.... In place of the narrowing cultural norms that prize "perfect faces", societies across the world would savour and delight in everyone's face, making no judgement that one is better than another. Signs of uniqueness such as each individual's facial colouring, anatomical features, wrinkles and eye bags—now so scorned—would be interesting, indeed fascinating'.[18]

Appearance norms might also be regarded as more inclusive when people have a range of choices in relation to what particular norms would govern their appearance. We can imagine a society containing various groups that people could elect to join that are governed by different appearance norms, with each person in effect having to be a member of at least one. When there are diverse groups of this kind, the net result might be to provide each member of a society with access to a valued appearance, just as Robert Nozick argued that a diverse society in which different activities are valued by different people could provide everyone with access to a source of self-esteem because each person is likely to possess the skills to be successful in at least one such activity.[19] In a society of this sort, however, appearance might still be given great weight.

Even if appearance norms were made fully inclusive, they might nevertheless be very demanding. For example, we can imagine an appearance code requiring each of us to be immaculately groomed compliance with which was equally feasible for all, but where considerable time and energy was required to satisfy it. Although there may be a correlation in practice between the demandingness of an appearance code, and the importance that the members of a society or a group attach to people's appearance, in principle the acceptance of a demanding appearance code might not even be indicative of high value or importance being placed on people's appearance. The members of the society governed by such a code might not think particularly badly of those who didn't devote the required time or effort to complying with the code. Compare, for example, demanding norms governing the way in which people eat at a dinner table that are universally accepted but which many fail to comply with without attracting any great attention from fellow diners, because they don't care very much about table manners.

---

[18] Partridge, *Face It*, 248.
[19] R. Nozick, *Anarchy, State, and Utopia* (Oxford: Blackwell, 1974), 241–6.

Having clarified what it would mean to reduce the importance attached to appearance in a society or group, and to make the appearance norms that govern it more inclusive and less demanding, it is worth noting that there is no straightforward inference from the argument that I have developed in this book to the radical conclusion that justice requires us to work towards a society in which appearance is given little or no weight, and in which any appearance norms that persist are undemanding and fully inclusive. It seems that, in principle, even if a society were successfully to eradicate wrongful appearance discrimination, its members might continue to regard appearance as very important, and they might continue to endorse and comply with appearance norms that are demanding and that are less than fully inclusive in various ways.

Nevertheless, my argument supports the conclusion that we are under an obligation, collectively, to eradicate, or at least reduce, the occurrence of demeaning appearance discrimination, to eradicate or reduce the incidence of deliberative unfairness in selection decisions when the appearance of candidates is given undue weight, and to counteract the unjust consequences that flow from patterns of appearance discrimination. In practice, this will require pushing back against some appearance norms, including appearance norms that are demeaning, and appearance norms that are non-inclusive because they are biased in ways that exacerbate the injustices suffered by groups that are disadvantaged independently. And it may involve acting individually and collectively to make the practices that are fuelled by appearance norms less oppressive, for example, by seeking to reduce the costs imposed on those who don't comply with these norms, which might be best achieved by reducing the value that people attach to the possession of an attractive appearance or to the possession of specific appearance features. Perhaps the most effective approach here would be part of an integrated strategy that targeted other kinds of discrimination. To the extent that racially biased appearance norms are sustained to a significant extent by racial prejudice, then acting to reduce racial prejudice may help to transform these norms and make them more inclusive. So too with appearance norms that are biased against a particular gender, or against transgender people, or against those with particular disabilities, or against the elderly, or against those who follow a minority religion. This might seem to take us in a different direction to a hypothetical insurance approach that focuses on compensating those disadvantaged by their appearance by providing them with money, goods, and services of various kinds, and on funding policies that give improved access to these.

Indeed, it might be thought that the limitations of offering money, goods, and services and funding policies that are likely to improve people's access to these things, as compensation for the disadvantages that people experience as a result of their appearance, reveal a deep problem with a hypothetical insurance approach, for it might seem ill-equipped to identify the measures that would be needed to address the structural forms of injustice that are sustained by appearance discrimination. But although a hypothetical insurance approach starts from where we are now, living in societies that place great value on appearance and where judgements of attractiveness are shaped by demanding and non-inclusive appearance norms, it need not be limited to providing access to money, goods, and services in order to compensate for the disadvantages that flow from appearance discrimination. In the absence of knowing how their looks will be regarded by others, hypothetical insurers might concur with the judgement that it would be preferable if the society of which they are part gave less weight to appearance and was governed by less demanding and more inclusive appearance norms. They might, therefore, elect to fund policies with the goals of reducing the weight attached to appearance and making appearance norms less demanding and more inclusive, provided that the available policies were not too expensive and offered some reasonable prospect of success. For example, they might choose to fund educational initiatives within schools that attempt to change the weight that young people attach to appearance and to transform the norms that are biased against marginalized groups. They might elect to fund social movements that campaign against organizations and companies that are complicit in elevating the importance of appearance and promoting compliance with biased appearance norms. More generally, they might decide to fund policies that take a holistic approach to tackling wrongful discrimination because they recognize the way in which different forms of discrimination interact to reinforce the marginalization of various groups. In this way, hypothetical insurers might fund policies that go beyond compensation and in effect address structural forms of injustice.

But it is true that there are likely to be limits to what state policies can achieve here, especially when members of society—as opposed to fully informed hypothetical insurers—are not particularly concerned about the weight given to appearance and about the exclusionary or demanding character of appearance norms. The best strategy for transforming appearance norms to make them more inclusive and less demanding will be determined, at least in part, by what sustains them. People's reasons for conforming to a norm will make a difference to which strategies stand a chance of being effective in transforming it or the practices that it fuels. Might the situation with respect to some demanding or non-inclusive appearance norms be one of what Cristina Bicchieri calls 'pluralistic ignorance', with all or most pretending to endorse these norms but none or few liking them?[20] That seems improbable, but it may nevertheless be the case that *many* people conform to these norms either because they want to avoid the sanctions that non-compliance attracts (which, after all, often involve unpleasant forms of ridicule, shaming, or moral criticism, and may even include social exclusion of various kinds) or because they want the advantages that compliance with these norms brings with it, including various opportunities, and the approval and attraction of others. If that were the case, then non-coercive public policy initiatives that bring into question the appropriateness of these forms of cajoling and moral criticism, and draw attention to the damage they cause, could reasonably be expected to have some efficacy. This is especially so when these initiatives are accompanied by a degree of individual and collective resistance to them within social media and civil society.

It is not part of my purpose to allocate duties to work to transform appearance norms, or duties to change the weight that people attach to appearance, to individual or collective agents beyond the state, but there are grounds for thinking that the allocation of such duties and the strength we attribute to them should to some extent track an agent's ability to make a difference to the achievement of these goals. Some individuals and groups are much better positioned to bring about change. When high-profile individuals, such as celebrities and social media influencers, act against appearance norms, this sets an example which may start a trend. Collective resistance may also be particularly effective when it takes the form of acting on informal conditional agreements reached on social media or in civil society not to comply with an appearance norm if others refuse to do so too.

It seems probable that appearance norms that are demanding or non-inclusive, and the oppressive practices in which they are embedded, are sustained by a variety of different feelings, dispositions, and beliefs, as well as the formal and informal rules that govern the behaviour of individuals in institutions and practices. Some people will conform to these norms, and criticize those who fail to do so, mainly because they want to fit in or, at

---

[20] See Bicchieri, *Norms in the Wild*, 44.

least, do not want to 'stand out'. Some will conform to these norms mainly because they fear the sanctions they will attract if they diverge from them, including ridicule, moral condemnation, exclusion from social groups, and being blocked for promotion. Some will conform to these norms mainly because they want the advantages that doing so brings with it, including the approval of others, and jobs and personal relationships that might not otherwise be available. Some will conform to these norms mainly because they know they will suffer from anxiety or feel bad about themselves and their bodies if they do not, even if their considered view is that these norms or the practices in which they are embedded are harmful or oppressive. Others will wholeheartedly endorse these norms, even those that are deeply biased against disadvantaged groups, strive to comply with them, and express their disapproval of others who do not do so. Some appearance norms may also be sustained, in part, by evolutionary processes. For example, perhaps people have 'hard-wired' preferences for their sexual partners to possess smooth and unblemished skin—sometimes at least, a symptom of good health—and their preferences may underpin a norm that prizes skin with this appearance.[21]

More empirical research would be required to identify the different factors involved in sustaining appearance norms and practices, and their relative significance. If it is the case that most people conform to appearance norms not merely because of fear of sanctions or feelings of guilt when they transgress them, but also because they believe that compliance with them achieves something valuable in its own right that could not be achieved in any other way (for example, an appearance that is genuinely beautiful, or the satisfaction of a religious requirement concerned with modesty), then these norms are likely to be resistant to change, especially if there are also dispositions in play in the background that are the product of evolutionary processes or deeply entrenched prejudices against a disadvantaged group.

If appearance norms turn out to be highly resilient, or we cannot be sure how malleable they are, hypothetical insurers might decide that the best response to them involves trying to limit the damage they cause, and reduce the costs of non-compliance with them, through a mixture of education, regulation, and coercive measures. In addition to the kind of measures I have already discussed, including those targeted at preventing wrongful appearance discrimination and compensating for the unjust disadvantages

[21] See Etcoff, *Survival of the Prettiest*.

it creates, hypothetical insurers might seek to reduce the costs imposed on those who do not comply with demanding or non-inclusive appearance norms by funding policies that oppose appearance-related abuse and bullying. Such policies might involve greater regulation of social media, or encouraging more robust self-regulation, to counter the nastiest forms of body shaming. These measures could be combined with policies that seek to cultivate better compliance with norms of civility online. Hypothetical insurers might also fund greater regulation of advertising for beauty products, and of 'the beauty industry' in general, in order to protect those who seek to improve their appearance, including increased regulation of private cosmetic surgery, such as breast enlargement surgery, and risky non-invasive interventions, such as Botox injections.[22] Perhaps they would also favour prohibiting some cosmetic procedures that carry with them a particularly high risk of harm, for example, buttock implants, even if there was reason to think that the norms and practices that encourage these procedures are not oppressive for very many people, in order to protect from unjust harm those for whom they are oppressive.

9.4 Concluding Remarks

Compensation may be appropriate for the disadvantages that people suffer as a result of appearance discrimination. A Dworkinian hypothetical insurance model can guide us in determining the levels and kinds of compensation that are justifiable. When people are disadvantaged by appearance discrimination in the context of choices about who to hire and promote, then hypothetical insurers would treat it as they do lack of marketable talent or ability and insure themselves against being too badly affected by being perceived as unattractive. In the case of discrimination on the basis of appearance in personal relationships or civil society, hypothetical insurers might want to purchase protection against facial differences and other aspects of appearance that are regarded by others as deeply unappealing, which would justify the provision of state-funded cosmetic surgery. They might also want to purchase insurance that would provide them with better

---

[22] See the recommendations of the *Review of the Regulation of Cosmetic Interventions*, an independent report in the UK chaired by Bruce Keogh, available at https://www.gov.uk/government/publications/review-of-the-regulation-of-cosmetic-interventions, accessed 6 July 2022. These are endorsed by the Nuffield Council on Bioethics report *Cosmetic Procedures: Ethical Issues*, with further recommendations; see especially chs 4 and 8.

opportunities for meeting people, or opportunities to obtain various surrogate goods, such as companionship or social contact, and this might justify state funding for organizations and activities that provide opportunities for socializing. But there are limits to the compensation that it is feasible to provide in practice, whether for the disadvantages faced in the job market or the disadvantages faced in the dating market. In practice, the best way of combatting wrongful appearance discrimination, and mitigating the unjust consequences of morally permissible appearance discrimination, will include measures to reduce the importance that is attached to appearance and to make appearance norms more inclusive, especially when these norms are biased against groups that are unjustly disadvantaged in other ways. This is likely to require an integrated strategy that involves at the same time addressing other kinds of discrimination.

Bibliography

Agerström, J. and D. Rooth, 'The Role of Automatic Obesity Stereotypes in Real Hiring Discrimination', *Journal of Applied Psychology* 96 (2011): 790–805.

Albright, L., D. Kenny, and T. Malloy, 'Consensus in Personality Judgements at Zero Acquaintance', *Journal of Personality and Social Psychology* 55 (1988): 387–95.

Alcoff, L., *Visible Identities: Race, Gender, and the Self* (Oxford: Oxford University Press, 2006).

Alexander, L., 'What Makes Wrongful Discrimination Wrong? Biases, Preferences, Stereotypes, and Proxies', *University of Pennsylvania Law Review* 141 (1992): 149–219.

Andreasen, R., 'A New Perspective on the Race Debate', *British Journal for the Philosophy of Science* 49 (1998): 199–225.

Anderson, E., 'What Is the Point of Equality?', *Ethics* 109 (1999): 287–337.

Anderson, E., *The Imperative of Integration* (Princeton, NJ: Princeton University Press, 2010).

Aragon, C. and A. Jaggar, 'Agency, Complicity, and the Responsibility to Resist Structural Injustice', *Journal of Social Philosophy* 49 (2018): 439–60.

Arneson, R., 'Discrimination, Disparate Impact, and Theories of Justice', in D. Hellman and S. Moreau (eds), *Philosophical Foundations of Discrimination Law* (Oxford: Oxford University Press, 2013).

Ayres, I. and J. Brown, *Straightforward: How to Mobilize Heterosexual Support for Gay Rights*. (Princeton, NJ: Princeton University Press, 2011).

Banducci, S., J. Karp, M. Thrasher, and C. Rallings, 'Ballot Photographs as Cues in Low-Information Elections', *Political Psychology* 29 (2008): 903–17.

Bany, J., B. Robnett, and C. Feliciano, 'Gendered Black Exclusion: The Persistence of Racial Stereotypes among Daters', *Race and Social Problems* 6 (2012): 201–13.

Barnes, E., *The Minority Body. A Theory of Disability* (Oxford: Oxford University Press, 2016).

Barro, R., 'So You Want to Hire the Beautiful, Well, Why Not?', *Business Week*, 16 March 1998, available at https://scholar.harvard.edu/files/barro/files/98_0316_hire_bw.pdf.

Bartky, S., 'Foucault, Femininity and the Modernization of Patriarchal Power', in D. Meyers (ed.), *Feminist Social Thought: A Reader* (London: Routledge, 2014).

Bedi, S., 'Sexual Racism: Intimacy as a Matter of Justice', *Journal of Politics* 77 (2015): 998–1011.

Bedi, S., *Private Racism* (Cambridge: Cambridge University Press, 2019).

Beeghly, E., 'Discrimination and Disrespect', in K. Lippert-Rasmussen (ed.), *The Routledge Handbook of the Ethics of Discrimination* (London: Routledge, 2017).

Benatar, D., *The Second Sexism: Discrimination against Men and Boys* (Oxford: Wiley-Blackwell, 2012).

Berggren, N., H. Jordahl, and P. Poutvaara, 'The Looks of a Winner: Beauty and Electoral Success', *Journal of Public Economics* 94 (2010): 8–15.

Bicchieri, C., *Norms in the Wild: How to Diagnose, Measure, and Change Social Norms* (Oxford: Oxford University Press, 2016).

Biddle, J. and D. Hamermesh, 'Beauty, Productivity, and Discrimination: Lawyers' Looks and Lucre', *Journal of Labor Economics* 16 (1998): 172–201.

Blum, L., 'Racial and Other Asymmetries: A Problem for the Protected Categories Framework for Anti-Discrimination Thought', in D. Hellman and S. Moreau (eds), *Philosophical Foundations of Discrimination Law* (Oxford: Oxford University Press, 2013).

Blum, L., 'Racialized Groups: The Sociohistorical Consensus', *The Monist* 93 (2010): 298–320.

Bóo, F. L., M. Rossi, and S. Urzúa, 'The Labor Market Return to an Attractive Face: Evidence from a Field Experiment', *Economics Letters* 118 (2013): 170–2.

Borkenau, P. and A. Liebler, 'Trait Inferences: Sources of Validity at Zero Acquaintance', *Journal of Personality and Social Psychology* 62 (1992): 645–57.

Brennan, G., L. Eriksson, R. Goodin, and N. Southwood, *Explaining Norms* (Oxford: Oxford University Press, 2013).

Brighouse, H., *School Choice and Social Justice* (Oxford: Oxford University Press, 2002).

Brighouse, H. and A. Swift, *Family Values: The Ethics of Parent-Child Relationships* (Princeton, NJ: Princeton University Press, 2014).

Brownlee, K., *Being Sure of Each Other: An Essay on Social Rights and Freedoms* (Oxford: Oxford University Press, 2020).

Brunello, G. and B. d'Hombres, 'Does Body Weight Affect Wages? Evidence from Europe', *Economics & Human Biology* 5 (2007): 1–19.

Bucchianeri, M., A. Arikian, P. Hannan, M. Eisenberg, and D. Neumark-Sztainer, 'Body Dissatisfaction from Adolescence to Young Adulthood: Findings from a 10-Year Longitudinal Study', *Body Image* 10 (2013): 1–7.

Butt, D., 'On Benefiting from Injustice', *Canadian Journal of Philosophy* 37 (2007): 129–52.

Caney, S., 'Climate Change', in S. Olsaretti (ed.), *The Oxford Handbook of Distributive Justice* (Oxford: Oxford University Press, 2018).

Carastathis, A., 'The Concept of Intersectionality in Feminist Theory', *Philosophy Compass* 9 (2014): 304–14.

Cavalli-Sforza, L., *Genes, Peoples, and Languages* (Berkeley and Los Angeles: University of California Press, 2001).

Chambers, C., *Sex, Culture, and Justice: The Limits of Choice* (University Park, PA: Pennsylvania State University Press, 2008).

Chambers, C., *Intact: A Defence of the Unmodified Body* (London: Allan Lane, 2022).

Clayton, M. and A. Williams, 'Egalitarian Justice and Interpersonal Comparison', *European Journal of Political Research* 35 (1999): 445–64.

Clucas, B., K. McHugh, and T. Caro, 'Flagship Species on Covers of US Conservation and Nature Magazines', *Biodiversity and Conservation* 17 (2008): 1517.

Cohen, G. A., 'Expensive Taste Rides Again', in J. Burley (ed.), *Dworkin and His Critics* (Malden, MA: Blackwell, 2004), 3–29.

Cohen, G. A., *On the Currency of Egalitarian Justice, and Other Essays in Political Philosophy* (Princeton, NJ: Princeton University Press, 2011).
Crenshaw, K., 'Demarginalizing the Intersection of Race and Sex: A Black Feminist Critique of Antidiscrimination Doctrine, Feminist Theory and Antiracist Politics', *University of Chicago Legal Forum* 1 (1989): 139–67.
Curington, C., J. Lundquist, and K.-H. Lin, *The Dating Divide: Race and Desire in the Era of Online Romance* (Berkeley and Los Angeles: University of California Press, 2021).
Dabiri, E., *Don't Touch My Hair* (London: Allen Lane, 2019).
Dancy, J., *Ethics without Principles* (Oxford: Oxford University Press, 2004).
Darby, B., and D. Jeffers, 'The Effects of Defendant and Juror Attractiveness on Simulated Courtroom Trial Decisions', *Social Behavior and Personality: An International Journal* 16 (1988): 39–50.
Darwall, S., 'Two Kinds of Respect', *Ethics* 88 (1977): 36–49.
Dion, K., E. Berscheid, and E. Walster, 'What Is Beautiful Is Good', *Journal of Personality and Social Psychology* 24 (1972): 285.
Dobos, N., 'The Duty to Hire on Merit: Mapping the Terrain', *Journal of Value Inquiry* 50 (2016): 353–68.
Duff, R., *Punishment, Communication, and Community* (Oxford: Oxford University Press, 2001).
Dusek, J. B. and G. Joseph, 'The Bases of Teacher Expectancies: A Meta-Analysis', *Journal of Educational Psychology* 75 (1983): 327–46.
Dworkin, R., *Sovereign Virtue: The Theory and Practice of Equality* (Cambridge, MA: Harvard University Press, 2002).
Eagly, A., R. Ashmore, M. Makhijani, and L. Longo, 'What Is Beautiful Is Good, but…: A Meta-Analytic Review of Research on the Physical Attractiveness Stereotype', *Psychological Bulletin* 110 (1991): 109.
Eastwick, P., L. Luchies, E. Finkel, and L. Hunt, 'The Predictive Validity of Ideal Partner Preferences: A Review and Meta-Analysis', *Psychological Bulletin* 140 (2014): 623–65.
Efran, M., and E. Patterson, 'Voters Vote Beautiful: The Effect of Physical Appearance on a National Election', *Canadian Journal of Behavioural Science/Revue Canadienne des Sciences du Comportement* 6 (1974): 352–6.
Eidelson, B., *Discrimination and Disrespect* (Oxford: Oxford University Press, 2015).
Elford, G., 'Survey Article: Relational Equality and Distribution', *Journal of Political Philosophy* 25 (2017): 80–99.
Etcoff, N., *Survival of the Prettiest: The Science of Beauty* (New York: Anchor, 2011).
Feingold, A., 'Matching for Attractiveness in Romantic Partners and Same-Sex Friends: A Meta-Analysis and Theoretical Critique', *Psychological Bulletin* 104 (1988): 226–35.
Feingold, A., 'Good-Looking People Are Not What We Think', *Psychological Bulletin* 111 (1992): 304–41.
Fleener, H., 'Looks Sell, but Are They Worth the Cost: How Tolerating Looks-Based Discrimination Leads to Intolerable Discrimination', *Washington University Law Quarterly* 83 (2005): 1295–1330.
Foucault, M., *Discipline and Punish: The Birth of the Prison* (Harmondsworth, Middlesex: Penguin, 1991).

Fourie, C., 'Wrongful Private Discrimination and the Egalitarian Ethos', in K. Lippert-Rasmussen, (ed.), *The Routledge Handbook of the Ethics of Discrimination* (London: Routledge, 2017).
Fricker, M., *Epistemic Injustice: Power and the Ethics of Knowing* (Oxford: Oxford University Press, 2007).
Frye, M., *The Politics of Reality: Essays in Feminist Theory* (New York: Crossing Press, 1983).
Gailey, J., 'Fat Shame to Fat Pride: Fat Women's Sexual and Dating Experiences', *Fat Studies* 1 (2012): 114–27.
Gendler, T., 'Alief and Belief', *Journal of Philosophy* 105 (2008): 634–63.
Gheaus, A., 'How Much of What Matters Can We Redistribute? Love, Justice, and Luck', *Hypatia* 24 (2009): 63–83.
Gibbard, A., *Wise Choices, Apt Feelings: A Theory of Normative Judgment* (Oxford: Oxford University Press, 1990).
Glasgow, J., 'On the New Biology of Race', *Journal of Philosophy* 100 (2003): 456–74.
Glasgow, J., *A Theory of Race* (London: Routledge, 2010).
Glasgow, J., 'Is Race an Illusion or a (Very) Basic Reality?', in J. Glasgow, S. Haslanger, C. Jeffers, and Q. Spencer (eds), *What Is Race? Four Philosophical Views* (Oxford: Oxford University Press, 2019), 111–49.
Glasgow, J., S. Haslanger, C. Jeffers, and Q. Spencer, *What Is Race? Four Philosophical Views* (Oxford: Oxford University Press, 2019).
Goodin, R. and C. Barry, 'Benefiting from the Wrongdoing of Others', *Journal of Applied Philosophy* 31 (2014): 363–76.
Grealy, L., *In the Mind's Eye. An Autobiography of a Face* (London: Arrow Books, 1995).
Grogan, S., *Body Image: Understanding Body Dissatisfaction in Men, Women and Children* (London: Routledge, 2016).
Hamermesh, D., *Beauty Pays: Why Attractive People Are More Successful* (Princeton, NJ: Princeton University Press, 2011).
Hannaford, I., *Race: The History of an Idea in the West* (Washington, DC: Woodrow Wilson Center Press, 1996).
Hardimon, M., 'The Ordinary Concept of Race', *Journal of Philosophy* 100 (2003): 437–55.
Harper, B., 'Beauty, Stature and the Labour Market: A British Cohort Study', *Oxford Bulletin of Economics and Statistics* 62 (2000): 771–800.
Hart, W., V. Ottati, and N. Krumdick, 'Physical Attractiveness and Candidate Evaluation: A Model of Correction', *Political Psychology* 32 (2011): 181–203.
Haslanger, S., 'Gender and Race: (What) Are They? (What) Do We Want Them To Be?', *Nous* 34 (2000): 31–55.
Hellman, D., *When Is Discrimination Wrong?* (Cambridge, MA: Harvard University Press, 2008).
Hellman, D., 'Discrimination and Social Meaning', in K. Lippert-Rasmussen (ed.), *The Routledge Handbook of the Ethics of Discrimination* (London: Routledge, 2017).
Herman, M. and M. Campbell, 'I Wouldn't, But You Can: Attitudes toward Interracial Relationships', *Social Science Research* 41 (2012): 343–58.

Hervey, T. and P. Rostant, '"All about That Bass"? Is Non-Ideal-Weight Discrimination Unlawful in the UK?', *Modern Law Review* 79 (2016): 248–82.

Hirji, S., 'Oppressive Double Binds', *Ethics* 131 (2021): 643–69.

Hirschmann, N., *The Subject of Liberty: Toward a Feminist Theory of Freedom* (Princeton, NJ: Princeton University Press, 2003).

Holroyd, J., 'The Social Psychology of Discrimination', in K. Lippert-Rasmussen (ed.), *The Routledge Handbook of the Ethics of Discrimination* (London: Routledge, 2017).

Holroyd, J., R. Scaife, and T. Stafford, 'What Is Implicit Bias?', *Philosophy Compass* 12 (2017): e12437.

Huang, W., 'Who Are People Willing to Date? Ethnic and Gender Patterns in Online Dating', *Race and Social Problems* 5 (2013): 28–40.

Irvin, S. (ed.), *Body Aesthetics* (Oxford: Oxford University Press, 2016).

Irvin, S., 'Resisting Body Oppression: An Aesthetic Approach', *Feminist Philosophy Quarterly* 3 (2017): article 3.

Isaacs, T., 'Individual Responsibility for Collective Wrongs', in J. Harrington, M. Milde, and R. Vernon (eds), *Bringing Power to Justice? The Prospects of the International Criminal Court* (Montreal: McGill-Queens University Press, 2006), 167–90.

Jeffers, C., 'The Cultural Theory of Race: Yet Another Look at Du Bois's "The Conservation of Races"', *Ethics* 123 (2013): 403–26.

Kershnar, S., 'The Duty to Hire the Most Qualified Applicant', *Journal of Social Philosophy* 43 (2003): 267–84.

Khaitan, T., *A Theory of Discrimination Law* (Oxford: Oxford University Press, 2015).

Khanna N. (ed.), *Whiter: Asian American Women on Skin Color and Colorism* (New York: New York University Press, 2020).

King, A. and A. Leigh, 'Beautiful Politicians', *Kyklos* 62 (2009): 579–93.

Korsgaard, C., *Creating the Kingdom of Ends* (Cambridge: Cambridge University Press, 1996).

Kutz, C., *Complicity: Ethics and Law for a Collective Age* (Cambridge: Cambridge University Press, 2000).

Langlois, J., L. Kalakanis, A. Rubenstein, A. Larson, M. Hallam, and M. Smoot, 'Maxims or Myths of Beauty? A Meta-Analytic and Theoretical Review', *Psychological Bulletin* 126 (2000): 390–423.

Langton, R., *Sexual Solipsism: Philosophical Essays on Pornography and Objectification* (Oxford: Oxford University Press, 2009).

Lazenby, H. and P. Butterfield, 'Discrimination and the Personal Sphere', in K. Lippert-Rasmussen (ed.), *The Routledge Handbook of the Ethics of Discrimination* (London: Routledge, 2017).

Lee, L., G. Loewenstein, D. Ariely, J. Hong, and J. Young, 'If I'm Not Hot, Are You Hot or Not? Physical-Attractiveness Evaluations and Dating Preferences as a Function of One's Own Attractiveness', *Psychological Science* 19 (2008): 669–77.

Lee, S., M. Pitesa, M. Pillutla, and S. Thau, 'When Beauty Helps and When It Hurts: An Organizational Context Model of Attractiveness Discrimination in Selection Decisions', *Organizational Behavior and Human Decision Processes* 128 (2015): 15–28.

Leslie, S., 'The Original Sin of Cognition: Fear, Prejudice, and Generalization', *Journal of Philosophy* 114 (2017): 393–421.
Lippert-Rasmussen, K., 'The Badness of Discrimination', *Ethical Theory and Moral Practice* 9 (2006): 167–85.
Lippert-Rasmussen, K., *Born Free and Equal? A Philosophical Inquiry into the Nature of Discrimination* (Oxford: Oxford University Press, 2014).
Lippert-Rasmussen, K. (ed.), *The Routledge Handbook of the Ethics of Discrimination* (London: Routledge, 2017).
Lippert-Rasmussen, K., 'Respect and Discrimination', in H. Hurd (ed.), *Moral Puzzles and Legal Perplexities: Essays on the Influence of Larry Alexander* (Cambridge: Cambridge University Press, 2018).
Lippert-Rasmussen, K., *Relational Egalitarianism: Living as Equals* (Cambridge: Cambridge University Press, 2018).
Liu, X., '"No Fats, Femmes, or Asians"', *Moral Philosophy and Politics* 2 (2015): 255–76.
Liu, X., 'Discrimination and Lookism', in K. Lippert-Rasmussen (ed.), *The Routledge Handbook of the Ethics of Discrimination* (London: Routledge, 2017).
Lorimer, J., 'Nonhuman Charisma', *Environment and Planning D: Society and Space* 25 (2007): 911–32.
MacMullen, I., *Faith in Schools? Autonomy, Citizenship, and Religious Education in the Liberal State* (Princeton, NJ: Princeton University Press, 2007).
Mandelbaum, E., 'Attitude, Inference, Association: On the Propositional Structure of Implicit Bias', *Noûs* 50 (2016): 629–58.
Marlowe, C., S. Schneider, and C. Nelson, 'Gender and Attractiveness Biases in Hiring Decisions: Are More Experienced Managers Less Biased?', *Journal of Applied Psychology* 81 (1996): 11–21.
Marmor, A., 'What Is the Right to Privacy?', *Philosophy and Public Affairs* 43 (2015): 3–26.
Mason, A., 'Appearance, Discrimination, and Reaction Qualifications', *Journal of Political Philosophy* 25 (2017): 48–71.
Mason, A., *Levelling the Playing Field: The Idea of Equal Opportunity and Its Place in Egalitarian Thought* (Oxford: Oxford University Press, 2006).
Mason, A., 'What's Wrong with Everyday Lookism?', *Politics, Philosophy and Economics* 20 (2021): 315–35.
Mason, A. and F. Minerva, 'Should the Equality Act 2010 Be Extended to Prohibit Appearance Discrimination?', *Political Studies* 70 (2022): 425–42.
McTernan, E., 'Microaggressions, Equality, and Social Practices', *Journal of Political Philosophy* 26 (2018): 261–81.
Meadows A. and D. Sigrún, 'What's in a Word? On Weight Stigma and Terminology', *Frontiers in Psychology* 7 (2016), https://doi.org/10.3389/fpsyg.2016.01527.
Mendelsohn, G., L. Taylor, A. Fiore, and C. Cheshire, 'Black/White Dating Online: Interracial Courtship in the 21st Century', *Psychology of Popular Media Culture* 3 (2014): 2–18.
Midtgaard, S. F., '"I'm Just Stating a Preference!": Lookism in Online Dating Profiles', *Moral Philosophy and Politics* 10 (2023): 161–83.
Mill, J. S., 'On Liberty', in M. Warnock (ed.), *Utilitarianism* (London: Collins, 1962).

Miller, D., *Principles of Social Justice* (Cambridge, MA: Harvard University Press, 1999).
Mills, C., 'Do Black Men Have a Moral Duty to Marry Black Women?', *Journal of Social Philosophy* 25 (1994): 131–53.
Minerva, F., 'The Invisible Discrimination before Our Eyes: A Bioethical Analysis', *Bioethics* 31 (2017): 180–9.
Mitchell, M. and M. Wells, 'Race, Romantic Attraction, and Dating', *Ethical Theory and Moral Practice* 21 (2018): 945–61.
Mocan, N. and E. Tekin, 'Ugly Criminals', *Review of Economics and Statistics* 92 (2010): 15–30.
Moles, A. and T. Parr, 'Distributions and Relations: A Hybrid Account', *Political Studies* 67 (2019): 132–48.
Moreau, S., 'What Is Discrimination?', *Philosophy & Public Affairs* 38 (2010): 43–179.
Moreau, S., 'Discrimination and Freedom', in K. Lippert-Rasmussen (ed.), *The Routledge Handbook of the Ethics of Discrimination* (London: Routledge, 2017).
Moreau, S., *Faces of Inequality: A Theory of Wrongful Discrimination* (Oxford: Oxford University Press, 2020).
Mulligan, T., *Justice and the Meritocratic State* (New York: Routledge, 2018).
Naumann, L., S. Vazire, P. Rentfrow, and S. Gosling, 'Personality Judgements Based on Personal Appearance', *Personality and Social Psychology Bulletin* 35 (2009): 1661–71.
Note, 'Facial Discrimination: Extending Handicap Law to Employment Discrimination on the Basis of Physical Appearance', *Harvard Law Review* 100 (1987): 2035–52.
Nozick, R., *Anarchy, State, and Utopia* (Oxford: Blackwell, 1974).
Nuffield Council on Bioethics, 'Cosmetic Procedures: Ethical Issues' (2017), available at https://www.nuffieldbioethics.org/publications/cosmetic-procedures.
Nussbaum, M., 'Objectification', *Philosophy & Public Affairs* 24 (1995): 249–91.
O'Shea, T., 'Sexual Desire and Structural Injustice', *Journal of Social Philosophy* 52 (2021): 587–600.
Parfit, D., 'Equality and Priority', in A. Mason (ed.), *Ideals of Equality* (Oxford: Blackwell, 1998).
Parfit, D., *On What Matters*, Vol. 1 (Oxford: Oxford University Press, 2012).
Parr, T., 'How to Identify Disadvantage: Taking the Envy Test Seriously', *Political Studies* 66 (2018): 306–22.
Partridge, J., *Face It. Facial Disfigurement and My Fight for Face Equality* (Pebble Press, 2020).
Phua, V. C. and G. Kaufman, 'The Crossroads of Race and Sexuality: Date Selection among Men in Internet "Personal" Ads', *Journal of Family Issues* 24 (2003): 981–94.
Post, R., *Prejudicial Appearances. The Logic of American Antidiscrimination Law* (Durham, NC: Duke University Press, 2000).
Praino, R., D. Stockemer, and J. Ratis, 'Looking Good or Looking Competent? Physical Appearance and Electoral Success in the 2008 Congressional Elections', *American Politics Research* 42 (2014): 1096–1117.
Puhl, R., T. Andreyeva, and K. Brownell, 'Perceptions of Weight Discrimination: Prevalence and Comparison to Race and Gender Discrimination in America', *International Journal of Obesity* 32 (2008): 992–1000.

Rawls, J., *Political Liberalism* (New York: Columbia University Press, 1996).
Rawls, J., *A Theory of Justice*, revised edition (Oxford: Oxford University Press, 1999).
Rawls, J., *The Law of Peoples* (Cambridge, MA: Harvard University Press, 1999).
Rawls, J., *Justice as Fairness: A Restatement* (Cambridge, MA: Harvard University Press, 2001).
Review of the Regulation of Cosmetic Interventions, chaired by Bruce Keogh, available at https://www.gov.uk/government/publications/review-of-the-regulation-of-cosmetic-interventions.
Rhode, D., 'The Injustice of Appearance', *Stanford Law Review* 61 (2009): 1033–1101.
Rhode, D., *The Beauty Bias: The Injustice of Appearance in Life and Law* (Oxford: Oxford University Press, 2010).
Rhodes, G., L. Simmons, and M. Peters, 'Attractiveness and Sexual Behaviour: Does Attractiveness Enhance Mating Success?', *Evolution and Human Behaviour* 26 (2005): 186–201.
Ritts, V., M. Patterson, and M. Tubbs, 'Expectations, Impressions, and Judgments of Physically Attractive Students: A Review', *Review of Educational Research* 62 (1992): 413–26.
Robinson, R., 'Structural Dimensions of Romantic Preferences', *Fordham Law Review* 76 (2008): 2787–819.
Robnett B. and C. Feliciano, 'Patterns of Racial-Ethnic Exclusion by Internet Daters', *Social Forces* 89 (2011): 807–28.
Rudder, C., *Dataclysm: Who We Are (When We Think No One's Looking)* (London: Fourth Estate, 2014).
Ruffle, B. and Z. Shtudiner, 'Are Good-Looking People More Employable?', *Management Science* 61 (2015): 1760–76.
Sangiovanni, A., *Humanity without Dignity: Moral Equality, Respect, and Human Rights* (Cambridge, MA: Harvard University Press, 2017).
Sangrador, J. and C. Yela, '"What Is Beautiful Is Loved": Physical Attractiveness in Love Relationships in a Representative Sample', *Social Behavior and Personality: An International Journal* 28 (2000): 207–18.
Saunders, H., 'The Invisible Law of Visible Difference: Disfigurement in the Workplace', *Industrial Law Journal* 48 (2019): 487–514.
Scanlon, T., *Moral Dimensions: Permissibility, Meaning, Blame* (Cambridge, MA: Harvard University Press, 2008).
Scanlon, T., *Why Does Inequality Matter?* (Oxford: Oxford University Press, 2018).
Schemmel, C., *Justice and Egalitarian Relations* (New York: Oxford University Press, 2021).
Segall, S., 'Should the Best Qualified Be Appointed?', *Journal of Moral Philosophy* 9 (2012): 31–54.
Sher, G., 'Qualifications, Fairness, and Desert', in N. Bowie (ed.), *Equal Opportunity* (Boulder, CO: Westview Press, 1988).
Shields, L., *Just Enough: Sufficiency as a Demand of Justice* (Edinburgh: Edinburgh University Press, 2016).
Singer, P., 'Is Racial Discrimination Arbitrary?', *Philosophia* 8 (1978): 185–203.
Slavny, A. and T. Parr, 'Harmless Discrimination', *Legal Theory* 21 (2015): 100–14.

Smith, R., D. Veríssimo, N. Isaac, and K. Jones, 'Identifying Cinderella Species: Uncovering Mammals with Conservation Flagship Appeal', *Conservation Letters* 5 (2012): 205–12.
Sorell, T., 'The Ethics of Saving a Face: The Case of Lucy Grealy' (unpublished paper).
Spencer, Q., 'How to Be a Biological Racial Realist', in J. Glasgow, S. Haslanger, C. Jeffers, and Q. Spencer, *What Is Race? Four Philosophical Views* (Oxford: Oxford University Press, 2019), 73–110.
Sprecher, S., Q. Sullivan, and E. Hatfield, 'Mate Selection Preferences: Gender Differences Examined in a National Sample', *Journal of Personality and Social Psychology* 66 (1994): 1074–80.
Srinivasan, A., 'Does Anyone Have the Right to Sex', *London Review of Books* 40 (2018): 5–10.
Srinivasan, A. *The Right to Sex* (London: Bloomsbury, 2021).
Stewart, J., 'Appearance and Punishment: The Attraction-Leniency Effect in the Courtroom', *Journal of Social Psychology* 125 (1985): 373–8.
Stewart, J., 'Defendant's Attractiveness as a Factor in the Outcome of Criminal Trials: An Observational Study', *Journal of Applied Social Psychology* 10 (1980): 348–61.
Stockemer, D. and R. Praino, 'Blinded by Beauty? Physical Attractiveness and Candidate Selection in the US House of Representatives', *Social Science Quarterly* 96 (2015): 430–43.
Taylor, P., 'Appiah's Uncompleted Argument: W. E. B. Du Bois and the Reality of Race', *Social Theory and Practice* 26 (2000): 103–28.
Taylor, P., *Black Is Beautiful: A Philosophy of Black Aesthetics* (Malden, MA: Wiley-Blackwell, 2016).
Thomas, L., 'Split-Level Equality: Mixing Love and Equality', in S. Babbitt and S. Campbell (eds), *Racism and Philosophy* (Ithaca, NY: Cornell University Press, 1999).
Tietje, L. and S. Cresap, 'Is Lookism Unjust? The Ethics of Aesthetics and Public Policy Implications', *Journal of Libertarian Studies* 19 (2005): 31–50.
Todorov, A., A. Mandisodza, A. Goren, and C. Hall, 'Inferences of Competence from Faces Predict Election Outcomes', *Science* 308 (2005): 1623–6.
Tomlin, P., 'What Is the Point of Egalitarian Social Relationships?', in A. Kaufman (ed.), *Distributive Justice and Access to Advantage: G. A. Cohen's Egalitarianism* (Cambridge: Cambridge University Press, 2014).
Tovar, V., 'What It's Really Like to Date as a Fat Woman', https://www.goodhousekeeping.com/life/relationships/a35730257/plus-size-dating/.
Tuvel, R., 'In Defense of Transracialism', *Hypatia* 32 (2017): 263–78.
UK Government Equalities Office, 'Body Confidence: Findings from the British Social Attitudes Survey', 2014, available at https://www.gov.uk/government/publications/body-confidence-a-rapid-evidence-assessment-of-the-literature.
Umberson, D. and M. Hughes, 'The Impact of Physical Attractiveness on Achievement and Psychological Well-Being', *Social Psychology Quarterly* 50 (1987): 227–36.
Waldron, J., *One Another's Equals. The Basis of Human Equality* (Cambridge, MA: Harvard University Press, 2017).

Walton, A., 'Resources In-Kind, Considering the Case of Housing' (unpublished paper).
Wang, L., 'Weight Discrimination: One Size Fits All Remedy', *Yale Law Journal* 117 (2007): 1900–45.
Wertheimer, A., 'Jobs, Qualifications, and Preferences', *Ethics* 94 (1983): 99–112.
White, G., 'Physical Attractiveness and Courtship Progress', *Journal of Personality and Social Psychology* 39 (1980): 660–8.
White, J., S. Reisner, E. Dunham, and M. Mimiaga, 'Race-Based Sexual Preferences in a Sample of Online Profiles of Urban Men Seeking Sex with Men', *Journal of Urban Health* 91 (2014): 1–8.
Widdows, H., *Perfect Me: Beauty as an Ethical Ideal* (Princeton, NJ: Princeton University Press, 2018).
Widdows, H., 'Structural Injustice and the Requirements of Beauty', *Journal of Social Philosophy* 52 (2021): 251–69.
Williams, A., 'Incentives, Inequality, and Publicity', *Philosophy & Public Affairs* 27 (1998): 225–47.
Williams, A. and M. Merten, 'Romantic Relationships among Women Experiencing Obesity: Self-Perception and Weight as Barriers to Intimacy', *Family and Consumer Sciences Research Journal* 41 (2021): 284–98.
Willis, E., 'Lustful Horizons: Is the Women's Movement Pro-Sex?', in E. Willis and N. Willis Aronowitz (eds), *The Essential Ellen Willis* (Minneapolis, MN: University of Minnesota Press, 2014), 200–8.
Wolf, N., *The Beauty Myth. How Images of Beauty Are Used against Women* (London: Chatto and Windus, 1990).
Wolff, J., 'Fairness, Respect, and the Egalitarian Ethos', *Philosophy & Public Affairs* 27 (1998): 97–122.
Wolff, J., 'Fairness, Respect and the Egalitarian Ethos Revisited', *Journal of Ethics* 14 (2010): 335–50.
Young, I., *Justice and the Politics of Difference* (Princeton, NJ: Princeton University Press, 1990).
Young, I., *Responsibility for Justice* (Oxford: Oxford University Press, 2011).
Zack, N., 'Life after Race', in N. Zack (ed.), *American Mixed Race: The Culture of Microdiversity* (Lanham, MD: Rowman and Littlefield, 1995), 297–307.
Zheng, R., 'Why Yellow Fever Isn't Flattering: A Case against Racial Fetishes', *Journal of the American Philosophical Association* 2 (2016): 400–19.

Index

For the benefit of digital users, indexed terms that span two pages (e.g., 52–53) may, on occasion, appear on only one of those pages.

aesthetic judgements
  and appearance norms 11, 92, 94–6, 214–15
  and employment 69, 74–5, 92–6, 98–9, 110, 127, 190–1
  and prevention measures 190–1
  and racial discrimination 74–5, 92–6, 110
  and reaction qualifications 110, 127, 190–1
  and romantic relationships 144–5
  as source of appearance discrimination 10–11, 74–5
affirmative action 47, 49; *see also* positive discrimination
age 5, 84–5, 216
agency *see* autonomous agency
agent relative reasons 64
aggressiveness 2, 88
Alexander, Larry 39–40
ancestry 76–81
Anderson, Elizabeth 207–8
Andreyeva, Tatiana 83–4
animals 3–4, 39–40
appearance
  importance attached to 198–9, 212–17, 220–1
  reduction to 137–43, 158
appearance codes 2, 9, 55–6, 99–100, 107–9, 120–1, 186, 214–15
appearance discrimination, defining 6–12, 34–6
appearance norms
  and aesthetic judgements 11, 92, 94–6, 214–15
  and age 5, 216
  and body shape 2, 5, 94–5, 161–2, 214–15
  and clothing 5, 161–3, 169–70, 214
  compliance with 5, 94–5, 161–77, 215–20
  and disability 5, 95, 161–2, 216
  and disadvantaged groups 5, 27, 94–5, 144–5, 161–3, 176–7, 216
  and employment 82–3, 94–6, 100, 171–2, 216
  endorsement of 5, 8–9, 92–4, 160, 164–76, 216–19
  and everyday lookism 2, 27–8, 160–77
  and gender 5, 94–5, 120–1, 160, 168–70, 216
  harm caused by 161–2, 172–6
  and height 2, 143–4
  internalization of 10–12, 92, 100, 130, 143–4, 164–6, 176–7
  naturally biased norms 95–6, 161–2
  and racial discrimination 5, 11–12, 94, 120, 161–2, 216
  reforming inclusivity of 24, 29, 198–9, 212–21
  and romantic relationships 130, 144–5, 172
  and socio-economic status 95, 169–70
  and weight 2, 94–5, 130, 143–4, 169, 214–15
Arneson, Richard 66
attractiveness
  association with competence 3–4, 10, 86–7, 118–20
  criteria for classifying attractiveness 193–4
  and earnings 3–4, 82–4, 95–6
  and education 3–4
  and election success 3–4
  and employment 15–17, 81–4, 89–90, 105, 107–9, 118–20, 189, 193–4, 204–5, 208
  and gender 81–2, 120
  and height 2, 88
  and hypothetical insurance 204–5, 207–9, 220–1

234   INDEX

attractiveness (*cont.*)
  and the justice system 3–4
  and reaction qualifications 15–17, 105, 107, 118–20
  and romantic relationships 3–4, 27, 129–30, 141–4, 154, 200, 209, 211
attractiveness thresholds 141–4, 154
autonomous agency
  and employment 60–1, 91, 93, 99, 109–11, 114–15, 118–23, 191
  and everyday lookism 27–8, 162–8, 170–2, 176–7
  importance of 21–2, 58–63
  and prevention measures 183–4, 191
  and romantic relationships 134–5, 138–40, 142, 144

beards *see* facial hair
beauty ideals 160, 168, 171
beauty industry 11–12, 217, 219–20
beauty premium 3–4, 82
beneficiaries (of unjust distribution) 204
Bicchieri, Cristina 217–18
biological significance 76–9
birthmarks 112–13, 185–6, 188, 209
blameworthiness 18, 23–5, 50–4, 90, 202–3
Blum, Lawrence 66
body anxiety 27–8, 159, 169–71, 176–7, 200
body dysmorphia 206
body hair 161, 169
body shaming 88–9, 159, 169–71, 173, 188–9, 219–20
body shape
  and appearance norms 2, 5, 94–5, 161–2, 214–15
  and bullying 2
  and control 85–6
  and employment 2, 7, 93–4, 185–6
  and everyday lookism 1–2, 160
  and gender 94–5
  and romantic relationships 2, 130
  and stigmatization 13, 88, 130
  see also weight
Brownwell, Kelly 83–4
bullying 1–2, 219–20

capabilities 21–2, 56–7
causal consequences 19, 25–6, 33, 36–7, 49, 63, 87
Chambers, Clare 174–6, 212–13

choice 96–102, 113–14, 119, 138–9, 150–1, 174, 200
client preferences *see* customer preferences
clothing 5, 7–8, 75, 99–100, 107–9, 119–21, 161–3, 169–70, 186, 214
Cohen, G. A. 101
collective responses 23–4, 29, 202, 218
colourism 80; *see also* racial discrimination; skin tone
comparative disrespect 41–2
compensation 20–1, 28–9, 57, 168, 181–4, 195, 200–13, 216–17, 219–21
competence 3–4, 10, 86–7, 118–20
compliance 5, 94–5, 161–77, 215–20
conditional wrongness 65, 182–3, 200–1
consequentialist theories 56, 66–8
contingent wrongness 19, 25–6, 33–4, 36–7, 50–70, 176–7
contributory actions 25, 50–4
control 13, 26–7, 74–5, 84–102, 119, 121–2, 162, 200
core cases 106–7, 116–18
cosmetic surgery 10–11, 28–9, 119, 168–9, 172–7, 209–10, 212–13, 219–21
crime 3–4, 20
curricula vitae (CVs) 81–2, 184
customer preferences 12, 14–17, 26–7, 75, 103–28, 190–3

dating websites 129, 134–5
deliberative freedom 61–3, 91, 135
deliberative unfairness
  and compensation 200–1, 216
  and employment 26, 46–9, 90, 92–4, 97–9, 102, 111–15, 119–20, 122–3, 128, 190–1, 216
  and legitimate expectation 49
  and prevention measures 182–3, 190–1
  and racial discrimination 26, 60–1, 73–4, 80–1, 97–9
  and reaction qualifications 111–15, 119–20, 122–3, 128
  as source of wrongness 19–20, 25–6, 33–4, 45–9, 63–5, 69
demeaning
  and compensation 200–1, 216
  and disadvantaged groups 43–4, 89, 123
  and employment 43–5, 88–90, 190
  and everyday lookism 27–8, 161–3, 176–7, 198–9

INDEX 235

and facial difference 90
as non-contingent wrong 36–7, 44–5
and power relations 43–4, 88–9, 132–4
and romantic relationships 132–4, 137–8, 145–7, 151–3, 197
desert 48–9, 66, 69
dieting 85–6, 168–9
direct discrimination 5, 7–11, 54–6, 92, 94–5, 186–7, 190, 192–3
disability 5, 55–6, 95, 137–8, 161–2, 186–90, 216
disadvantaged groups
  demeaning of 43–4, 89, 123
  discrimination in favour of 36
  and appearance norms 5, 27, 94–5, 144–5, 161–3, 176–7, 216
  and reaction qualifications 109–11, 115, 117–23, 127–8, 156–8
discrimination against 34–6
discrimination on basis of 34–6
disfigurement 2, 10, 90, 107, 112–13, 121–2, 187–90, 209
disparate impact 54–5
disrespect
  comparative disrespect 41–2
  and compensation 182–3
  and employment 73–4, 80–1, 87–90, 109, 111–12, 117, 120–3, 126–7
  and prevention measures 182–3, 197–8
  and racial discrimination 20, 26, 39, 42–3, 73–4, 80–1, 87–8, 102, 109, 122–3, 126–7, 132, 151
  and reaction qualifications 109, 111–12, 117, 120–3, 126–7, 156–7
  and romantic relationships 27, 137–44, 151–2, 156–8, 197–8
  as source of wrongness 19–20, 25–6, 33–4, 39–45, 63–9, 102
distributive justice 20–2, 47–8, 56–8, 60, 95–6, 100–2, 135–7, 144–5, 200–2, 211–12
dreadlocks 8–9, 105, 107, 122–3, 186
dress *see* clothing
dress codes *see* appearance codes; religious dress codes
duty 10–11, 52–3, 151, 153–5, 164–5
Dworkin, Ronald 28–9, 101–2, 204–5, 220–1

earnings 3–4, 54, 60, 82–4, 93–6
education 3–4, 136–7, 183–4, 210–11, 214, 217, 219–20

egalitarianism 20–1, 56–7, 95–6, 144–5, 201–2, 211–12; *see also* equality
Eidelson, Benjamin 20
elections 3–4
employment
  and aesthetic judgements 69, 74–5, 92–6, 98–9, 110, 127, 190–1
  appearance codes 2, 9, 55–6, 99–100, 107–9, 120–1, 186
  and appearance norms 82–3, 94–6, 100, 172, 216
  application assessment 81–2, 184–5
  and attractiveness 15–17, 81–4, 89–90, 105, 107–9, 118–20, 189, 193–4, 204–5
  and autonomous agency 60–1, 91, 93, 99, 109–11, 114–15, 118–23, 191
  and body shape 2, 7, 93–4, 185–6
  candidate rejection 7–9, 12, 41, 46–7, 60–1, 69, 92
  and clothing 75, 99–100, 107–9, 119–21, 186
  and customer preferences 12, 14–17, 26–7, 75, 103–28, 190–3
  and deliberative fairness 26, 46–9, 90, 92–3, 97–9, 102, 111–15, 119–20, 122–3, 128, 190–1, 216
  and demeaning 43–5, 88–90, 190
  and disability 55–6, 186–90
  discrimination prevention measures 28, 181, 184–96, 199
  and disfigurement 90, 107, 112–13, 121–2, 187–90
  and disrespect 73–4, 80–1, 87–90, 109, 111–12, 117, 120–3, 126–7
  earnings 3–4, 54, 60, 82–4, 93–6
  essential purpose of a job 15–16
  and facial difference 2, 90, 105, 107, 112–13, 115, 121–2
  and gender 54, 81–4, 99–100, 106–7, 118, 120–1, 186
  and hairstyles 1–2, 8–9, 105, 107, 115, 122–3, 185–6
  and height 2, 7, 82–4, 88, 113, 185–6
  and hypothetical insurance 208, 220–1
  legislation 28, 184–96
  libertarian moral approaches 12–13
  and moral judgements 69, 74–5, 98–100, 110, 127, 190–1

employment (*cont.*)
  and non-rational responses 69, 74–5, 89–92, 97–8, 102, 109–10, 114–15, 118–20, 122–3, 127, 191–2
  and prejudice 12, 46–7, 69, 74–5, 85–91, 106–7, 116–20, 124, 191–3
  and racial discrimination 1, 8–9, 13, 26, 54, 60–1, 65–8, 73–5, 83–4, 92, 104–7, 109–10, 116–18, 124–7
  and reaction qualifications 14–17, 26–7, 75, 103–28, 190–3, 199
  and religious dress codes 107, 121, 123, 186
  and tattoos 1–2, 98–102, 105, 107, 110, 114–15, 122, 189
  and unjust consequences 26, 73–4, 80–1, 91, 93–4, 97, 99–102, 110, 112, 216
  utilitarian moral approaches 13–17
  and weight 2, 7, 82–4, 88, 108–9, 119, 185–6
envy test 101–2, 205–6
equality 19–20, 56, 66, 205; *see also* egalitarianism
everyday lookism
  and appearance norms 2, 27–8, 160–77
  and autonomy 27–8, 162–8, 170–2, 176–7
  body shaming 88–9, 159, 169–71, 173, 188–9, 219–20
  and body shape 1–2, 160
  and clothing 161–3, 169–70
  and demeaning 27–8, 161–3, 176–7, 198–9
  discrimination prevention measures 181, 198–9
  and disfigurement 2
  and facial difference 2
  and gender 160–1, 168–70
  harm caused by 27–8, 161–2, 172–7
  legislation 198–9
  libertarian moral approaches 12
  and moral judgements 160
  oppressiveness of 27–8, 162–72, 176–7, 198–9, 213–14
  and social media 2, 12, 27–8, 159, 171, 198–9, 219–20
  and unjust consequences 161–3, 176–7
  and weight 1–2, 160
evolutionary theory 11–12, 194–5, 218–19
extrinsic wrongness 36–7, 44–5

facial difference
  and bullying 2
  and control 85–6, 121–2
  and employment 2, 90, 105, 107, 112–13, 115, 121–2
  and everyday lookism 2
  facial tattoos 101–2, 105, 122
  and hypothetical insurance 209–10, 212–13
  and romantic relationships 2, 143–4, 157–8
  and stigmatization 91, 121–2, 143–4, 212–13
facial features 22–3, 80, 112, 188–9, 209–10
facial hair 85–6, 97, 114
false beliefs 39–41, 113
family 131–2, 155–8, 166–8
fat shaming 88–9, 171, 188–9; *see also* body shaming
female patients 106, 118
fetishism 130
flourishing 21–2, 58–60, 62–3, 136–7, 143–4, 153, 201–2, 205, 207
Fourie, Carina 132–3, 146
free association 152, 197
Fricker, Miranda 37
friendships *see* personal relationships

gender
  and appearance norms 5, 94–5, 120–1, 160, 168–70, 216
  and attractiveness 81–2, 120
  and body shape 94–5
  and clothing 7–8, 99–100, 107–9, 120–1, 186
  and employment 54, 81–4, 99–100, 106–7, 118, 120–1, 186
  and everyday lookism 160–1, 168–70
  and makeup 94–5, 99–100, 169, 186
  and medicine 106, 118
  non-binary gender identities 7–8, 145–6
  and romantic relationships 129, 145–50, 154–5
  and weight 94–5, 169
generalizations 20, 66, 86–7; *see also* stereotypes
genetics 75–6, 87, 95
geographical origin 76–81
Gibbard, Alan 18, 24, 42–3, 202–3
guilt 162–7, 172–3, 175, 219

hair
    Black/mixed-race hair types 1-2, 5, 9, 80,
        94, 115, 122-3, 161-2, 186
    and employment 1-2, 8-9, 105, 107, 115,
        122-3, 185-6
    hair colour 87-8, 189
    hairstyles 1-2, 8-9, 85-6, 105, 107, 115,
        122-3, 185-6
Hamermesh, Daniel 3-4, 13-16, 82-4, 195-6
Hardimon, Michael 77-8
headscarves *see* hijab
health 136-7, 168-9, 172-7, 186, 210-11;
    see also medicine; mental health;
    well-being
height
    and appearance norms 2, 143-4
    and attractiveness 2, 88
    and control 13, 84-6, 88
    and earnings 82-4
    and employment 2, 7, 82-4, 88,
        113, 185-6
    and romantic relationships 1-2, 137-8,
        143-4, 157-8
    and stigmatization 88, 137-8, 143-4
Hellman, Deborah 43-4, 66, 89, 132-3, 161
hijab 7-8, 107, 123, 186
homophobia 59-60, 147, 154-5, 169
homosexuality 7-8, 59-60, 99, 145-50,
    154-5
hypothetical insurance 20-1, 28-9, 202-13,
    216-21

illegitimate reaction qualifications 105-28,
    156, 191
implants 98-9, 174-6, 219-20
inclusivity 24, 29, 198-9, 212-21
income *see* earnings
indirect discrimination 5, 7, 9, 54, 94-5,
    186, 192-3
individual wrong-doing 14-27, 50-4
indoctrination 58-60
inequalities 20-1, 56-7, 91, 94-6,
    200, 211-12
inferiority complexes 2, 86-8
interests
    balancing of 112-13, 191
    giving due weight to 19-20, 45-7, 49, 90,
        93, 97-9, 102, 111-23, 127-8
    principle of equal consideration
        of 16-17

internalization 10-12, 92, 100, 130, 143-4,
    164-6, 176-7
intrinsic wrongness 36-7, 44-5, 65
Islam 7-8, 107, 123, 186
Islamophobia 7-8, 123

just inequality 20-1, 56-7
justice 20-2, 47-8, 55-8, 60, 69, 95-6,
    100-2, 135-7, 168-9, 200, 211-12

key cases 107-8, 118-23

Langton, Rae 140-2
least-unjust outcomes 24-5
legal system 3-4, 193
legislation 24, 28, 131, 181-200
legitimate expectation 48-9, 69, 90
legitimate reaction qualifications 105-11,
    118, 121-3, 125, 127-8, 156, 191
libertarian theories 12-13, 17-18
Lippert-Rasmussen, Kasper 35-6,
    39-41, 123-6
Liu, Xiaofei 147-8
luck egalitarianism 20-1, 56-7, 95-6, 211-12

makeup 11-12, 94-5, 98-100, 119, 138-9,
    169-70, 186
marketable talents 183-4, 204-5, 208, 220-1
media 169
medicine 42, 45, 55, 106, 118;
    see also health
mental health 2, 176-7, 187-9
meritocratic approaches 48-9, 69, 123-4
Mill, John Stuart 20-1, 58-9
Mills, Charles 133-4
Mitchell, Megan 151
monist theories 33, 63, 66-8
moral ethos 98-9
moral judgements
    and employment 69, 74-5, 98-100, 110,
        127, 190-1
    and prevention measures 190-1
    and racial discrimination 26-7,
        74-5, 98, 110
    and reaction qualifications 110, 127, 190-1
    as source of appearance discrimination
        10-11, 26-7, 74-5
moral norms 165-6
moral prerogatives 53, 131-2, 151-8, 196-7,
    200, 203

moral significance 25, 50–2
moral standing
   failure to take account of 27, 41–3, 45, 68, 87–8, 90, 109, 120, 132, 138–42, 156
   false beliefs about 39–44
   lowering of 19–20, 27, 50, 70, 91, 93–4, 102, 109–10, 121–2, 134–5, 137–8, 161–2, 183, 200–1
   moral equality 26–7, 38–43, 63, 88, 98, 201–2
   moral inferiority 38–43, 50, 65–6, 69, 109–10, 117–18, 132–3, 161
morally objectionable preferences 16–17, 157
Moreau, Sophia 61–3, 66, 135

non-contingent wrongness 19, 33–49, 63, 65–8, 176–7, 182–3
non-individualized attitudes 123–6
non-rational responses
   and employment 69, 74–5, 89–92, 97–8, 102, 109–10, 114–15, 118–20, 122–3, 127, 191–2
   and prevention measures 191–2
   and racial discrimination 25–6, 38–9, 42, 74–5, 89–91
   and reaction qualifications 109–10, 114–15, 118–20, 122–3, 127, 191–2
   as source of appearance discrimination 10, 74–5
normal customers 106–7, 116, 125–6
normative extraneity 61–2
Nozick, Robert 215
Nussbaum, Martha 140

obesity 88–9, 144, 155–8, 187;
   see also weight
objectification 118, 120, 140–2, 158, 161
objective list theory 205–6
objective wrongness 18, 24, 42–3, 51–2, 202–3
oppression 11–12, 22, 27–8, 126, 162–72, 176–7, 213–14, 216
ownership relations 46–8

Parr, Tom 205–6
Partridge, James 214–15
personal relationships
   access to 143–5
   and aesthetic judgements 144–5

and appearance norms 130, 144–5, 172
and attractiveness 3–4, 27, 129–30, 141–4, 154, 200, 209, 211
and autonomous agency 134–5, 138–40, 142, 144
and body shape 2, 130
and demeaning 132–4, 137–8, 145–7, 151–3, 197
discrimination prevention measures 131, 181, 196–8, 203
and disrespect 27, 137–44, 151–2, 156–8, 197–8
and distributive justice 135–7
and facial difference 143–4, 157–8, 209–10
and gender 129, 145–50, 154–5
and height 1–2, 137–8, 143–4, 157–8
and hypothetical insurance 209–12, 220–1
legislation 131, 196–8
libertarian moral approaches 12–13
opinions of family and friends 131–2, 155–8
and prejudice 149–50, 156–7
and racial discrimination 53, 131–8, 145–51, 154–7
and reaction qualifications 155–8
and reduction to appearance 137–43, 158
rejection of partners 1, 27, 132–5, 137–8, 140–2, 144, 200
and unjust consequences 134–5, 144, 150–1, 197
and weight 2, 130, 137–8, 143–4, 157–8
piercings 1, 98–9, 189
pluralist theories 18–22, 25–6, 33–4, 49, 63–70, 73, 109
policing 66, 113, 126
politeness 106–7, 112, 116, 125–6
positive discrimination 36; see also affirmative action
power
   and ability to demean 43–4, 88–9, 132–4
   power relations 22–3, 43–4, 88–9
   reinforcement of power structures 20, 22–3, 50–1, 161–2
   and sexual assault 139–40
prejudice
   and employment 12, 46–7, 69, 74–5, 85–91, 106–7, 116–20, 124, 191–3
   and prevention measures 191–3

and racial discrimination 8-9, 25-6, 37-9, 74-5, 85-91, 106-7, 116-18, 122-4, 149-50, 156
and reaction qualifications 106-7, 116-20, 122-4, 191-3
and romantic relationships 149-50, 156-7
as source of appearance discrimination 2, 10, 37-9, 74-5
prejudiced customers 106-7, 116-18, 124
prevention measures 28, 131, 181-202, 212, 219-20
prioritarianism 20-1, 56-7, 66
privacy 28, 131, 198
private productivity 13-15
Puhl, Rebecca 83-4

quasi-egalitarianism 20-1, 56-7

racial discrimination
and aesthetic judgements 74-5, 92-6, 110
and appearance norms 5, 11-12, 94, 120, 161-2, 216
conceptualizations of race 75-80
and deliberative unfairness 26, 60-1, 73-4, 80-1, 97-9
and disrespect 20, 26, 39, 42-3, 73-4, 80-1, 87-8, 102, 109, 122-3, 126-7, 132, 151
and earnings 83-4
and employment 1, 8-9, 13, 26, 54, 60-1, 65-8, 73-5, 83-4, 92, 104-7, 109-10, 116-18, 124-7
and friendships 154
libertarian moral approaches 13
and medicine 55
and moral judgements 26-7, 74-5, 98, 110
and non-rational responses 25-6, 38-9, 42, 74-5, 89-91
and oppression 11-12, 126
origins of 80
and policing 126
and prejudice 8-9, 25-6, 37-9, 74-5, 85-91, 106-7, 116-18, 122-4, 149-50, 156
racial profiling 20, 66, 68
and reaction preferences 104-5, 109-10, 116-18, 124-7
relation to appearance discrimination 8-9, 13, 17-18, 26-7, 33-4, 73-103, 105, 110
and romantic relationships 53, 131-8, 145-51, 154-7

and stigmatization 60, 65-6, 73, 109-10, 137-8, 145-6, 149-50
and unjust consequences 26, 55, 66, 80-1, 110, 134-5, 150-1
racial profiling 20, 66, 68
Rawls, John 136, 160
reaction qualifications 14-17, 26-7, 75, 103-28, 155-8, 185-6, 190-2
regulation 28, 131, 198-9, 219-20
rejection
of job candidates 7-9, 12, 41, 46-7, 60-1, 69, 92
of romantic partners 1, 27, 132-5, 137-8, 140-2, 144, 200
relational egalitarianism 201-2
religious discrimination 7-8, 99
religious doctrines 118, 121-2, 219
religious dress codes 7-8, 107, 121, 123, 161-2, 186
resentment 46-7
resistance 24
resources 101-2, 135, 205
responsibility 20-1, 56-7, 114-15, 202
Rhode, Deborah 195
romantic relationships see personal relationships

salaries see earnings
Saunders, hannah 188
scars 6-7, 10, 90, 107, 112-13, 121-2, 188, 209; see also disfigurement
segregated customers 117-18, 124-5
segregation 38-9, 84, 117-18, 124-5, 149-50, 156
self-confidence 27-8, 60, 65-6, 134-5, 143-4, 159, 169-73, 188-9
self-discipline 2, 10, 86-7, 157, 169
self-esteem 27-8, 60, 65-6, 134-5, 143-4, 159, 169-70, 172-3, 188-9, 215
self-expression 99, 101-2, 107, 122, 163-4, 166, 171-2, 193
sexual assault 139-40
sexuality 7-8, 59-60, 99, 107-9, 120-1, 145-50, 152-5, 161, 218-19
shameful revelation 208, 210
Singer, Peter 16
skin tone 7-8, 11-12, 16-17, 75-6, 79-80, 84-5, 92, 94, 124-5, 137-8, 148, 150-1; see also racial discrimination
skin tags 84-5

slut shaming 169–70
social construction 76–9, 206–7
social esteem 54, 60
social hierarchies 132–3, 147, 155–7
social media 2, 12, 27–8, 159, 171, 198–9, 217–20
social model of disability 187–90
socio-economic status 5, 95, 169–70
social productivity 13–16
social structures, reproduction of 22–3
socialization 89–90, 164–7, 175–7
Srinivasan, Amia 153
stereotypes 10, 37, 69, 87, 89–90, 120, 133–4; *see also* generalizations
stigmatization
　and body shape 13, 88, 130
　and disability 137–8
　and disfigurement 187–8
　and facial difference 91, 121–2, 143–4, 212–13
　of groups 22, 53, 109–10, 115, 137–8
　and height 88, 137–8, 143–4
　and racial discrimination 60, 65–6, 73, 109–10, 137–8, 145–6, 149–50
　and sexual orientation 145–6
　and weight 1–2, 88–9, 130, 137–8, 143–4
structural injustice 22–5, 217
subjective wrongness 18, 42–3
sufficientarianism 20–1, 56–7, 144–5, 211–12
symmetric theory 108–11

tattoos 1–2, 10–11, 26–7, 84–6, 97–102, 105, 107, 110, 114–15, 122, 189
taxation 57, 183, 200–1, 208
Thomas, Lawrence 148–50
transgender people 145–6, 216
turbans 186

unconditional wrongness 65, 182–3
unfairness *see* deliberative unfairness
unjust consequences
　and employment 26, 73–4, 80–1, 91, 93–4, 97, 99–102, 110, 112, 216
　and everyday lookism 161–3, 176–7
　and hypothetical insurance 202–3

　and racial discrimination 26, 55, 66, 80–1, 110, 134–5, 150–1
　and reaction qualifications 110, 112
　and romantic relationships 134–5, 144, 150–1, 197
　as source of wrongness 20, 25–6, 33–4, 50–7, 63–6, 69–70
unjust institutions 52–3
utilitarian theories 12, 15–18

value pluralism 59
visible physical features 76–80

weight
　and appearance norms 2, 130, 143–4, 169, 214–15
　associated with lack of self-discipline 2, 10, 86–7, 157, 169
　and bullying 1–2
　and control 85–6
　and earnings 82–4
　and employment 2, 7, 82–4, 88, 107, 119, 185–6
　and everyday lookism 1–2, 160, 169
　and gender 94–5, 169
　and moral judgements 2, 10
　obesity 88–9, 144, 155–8, 187
　and romantic relationships 2, 130, 137–8, 143–4, 157–8
　and stigmatization 1–2, 88–9, 130, 137–8, 143–4
　see also body shape
well-being 21–2, 56–9, 66–8, 100–1, 135–6, 143–4, 162, 168–70, 188–9, 205, 211
Wells, Mark 151
Wertheimer, Alan 104
Widdows, Heather 160, 168–9, 177
Wolff, Jonathan 208
work ethic 164, 172–3, 175–6
wrinkles 84–5, 214–15

Young, Iris Marion 22–3

Zack, Naomi 78
Zheng, Robin 133–4, 147